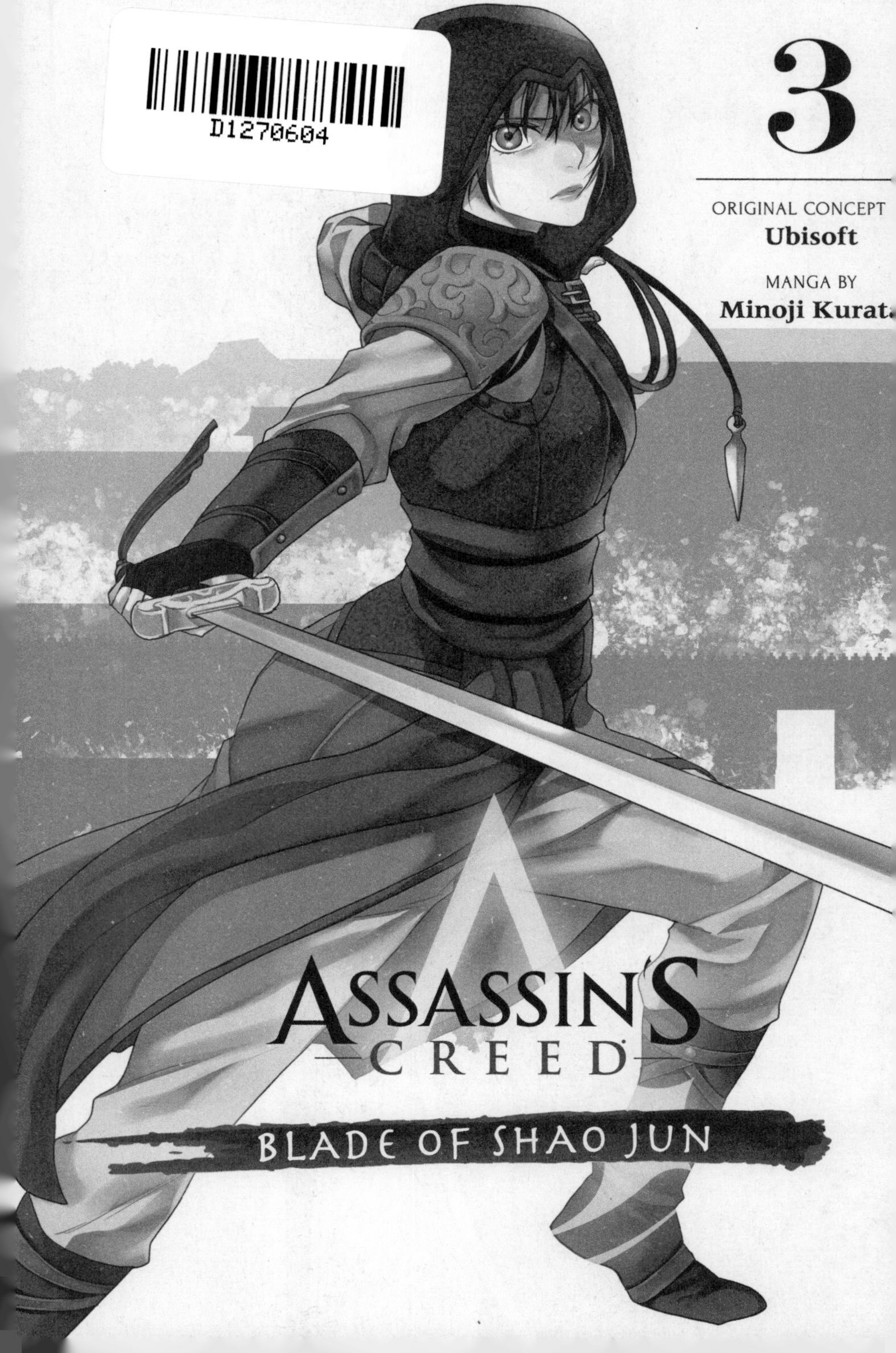

D1270604
3
ORIGINAL CONCEPT
Ubisoft
MANGA BY
Minoji Kurat.
ASSASSIN'S
CREED
BLADE OF SHAO JUN

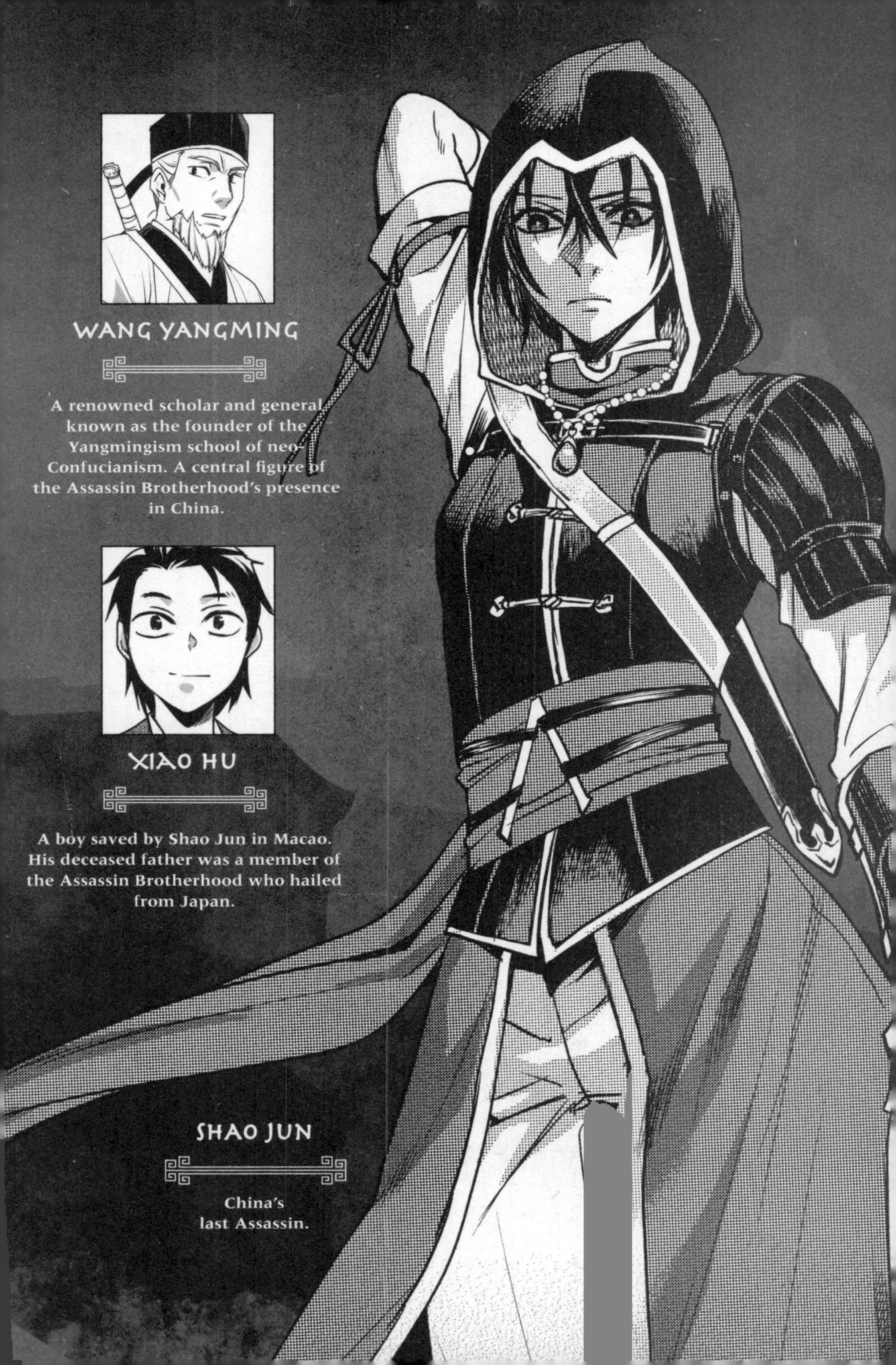
WANG YANGMING
A renowned scholar and general known as the founder of the Yangmingism school of neo-Confucianism. A central figure of the Assassin Brotherhood's presence in China.
XIAO HU
A boy saved by Shao Jun in Macao. His deceased father was a member of the Assassin Brotherhood who hailed from Japan.
SHAO JUN
China's last Assassin.

BACKGROUND

The Ming Dynasty ruled in 16th-century China.

During the chaos created by the emperor's political purge, eunuchs aligned with the Templar Order known as the Eight Tigers took the opportunity to slay the allies of Shao Jun, leaving her China's last remaining assassin.

During her quest for revenge, Shao Jun's master, Wang Yangming, has fallen into the enemy's trap, and she must hurry to his aid lest he meet his end.

These memories are all carved into the very DNA of Lisa—a girl in modern-day Yokohama and Shao Jun's descendant! Little by little, Lisa is being influenced by her connection with Shao Jun and is drawn into the ongoing war between the Templar Order and the Assassin Brotherhood. As she witnesses more of Shao Jun's life, Lisa will explore the depths of her own resolve!

MODERN DAY

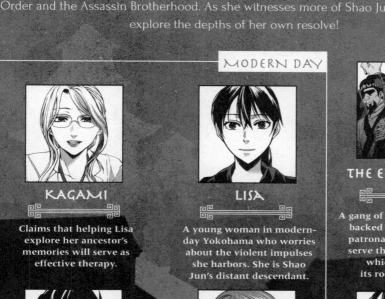

KAGAMI

Claims that helping Lisa explore her ancestor's memories will serve as effective therapy.

LISA

A young woman in modern-day Yokohama who worries about the violent impulses she harbors. She is Shao Jun's distant descendant.

KIYOSHI TAKAKURA

A mystery man who acts like yakuza. On behalf of the Assassin Brotherhood, he tells Lisa that the war against the Templar Order still continues.

MARI

Lisa's close friend, who was once saved by Lisa's actions.

THE EIGHT TIGERS

A gang of tyrannical eunuchs backed by the emperor's patronage. In truth, they serve the Templar Order, which has spread its roots into China.

QIXIE

Shao Jun's dear friend from the inner court. She eventually became empress, but is there more to her story?

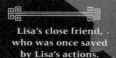

CONTENTS

Chapter 9: Trap

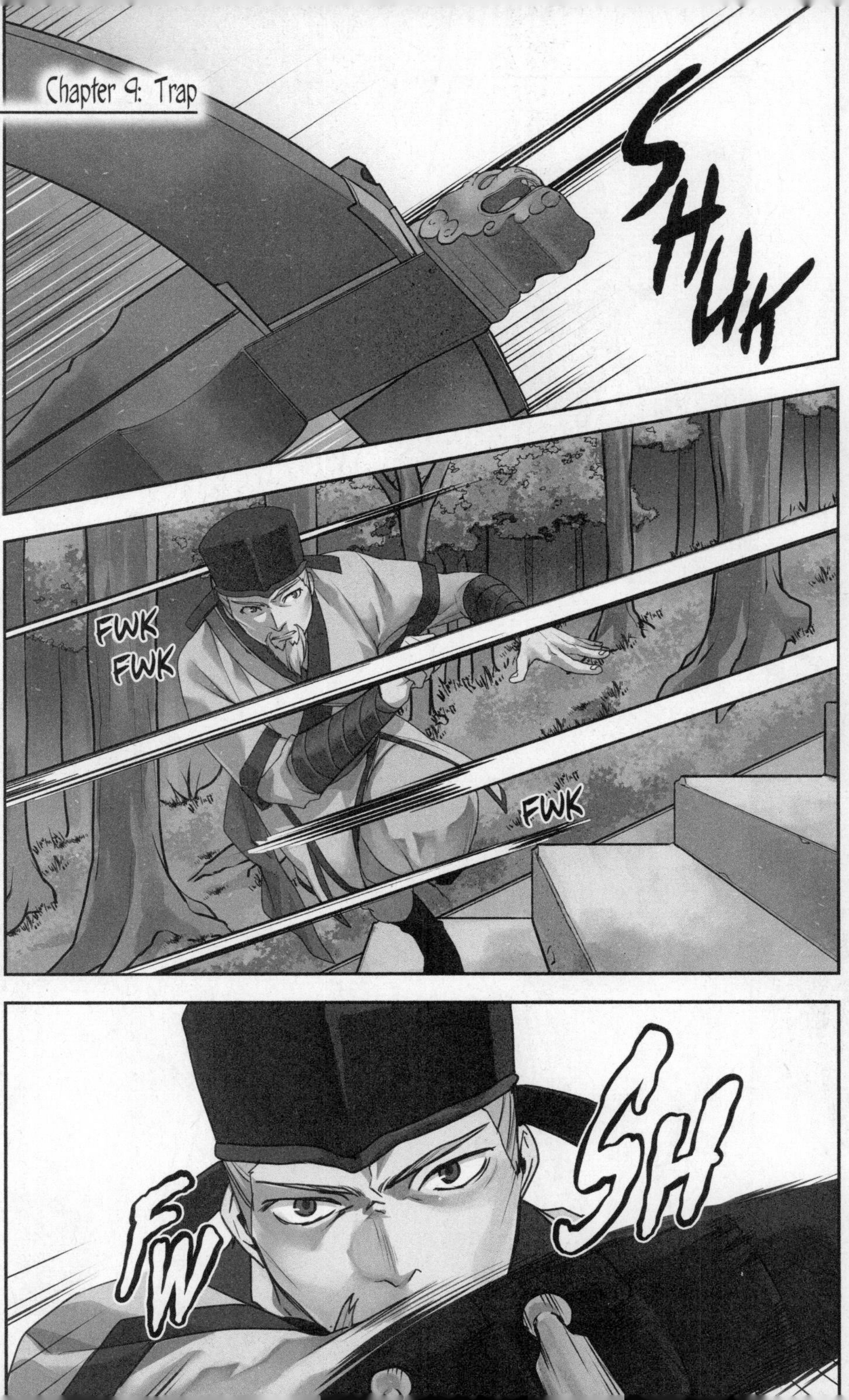
SHUK
FWK
FWK
FWK
SH
FW

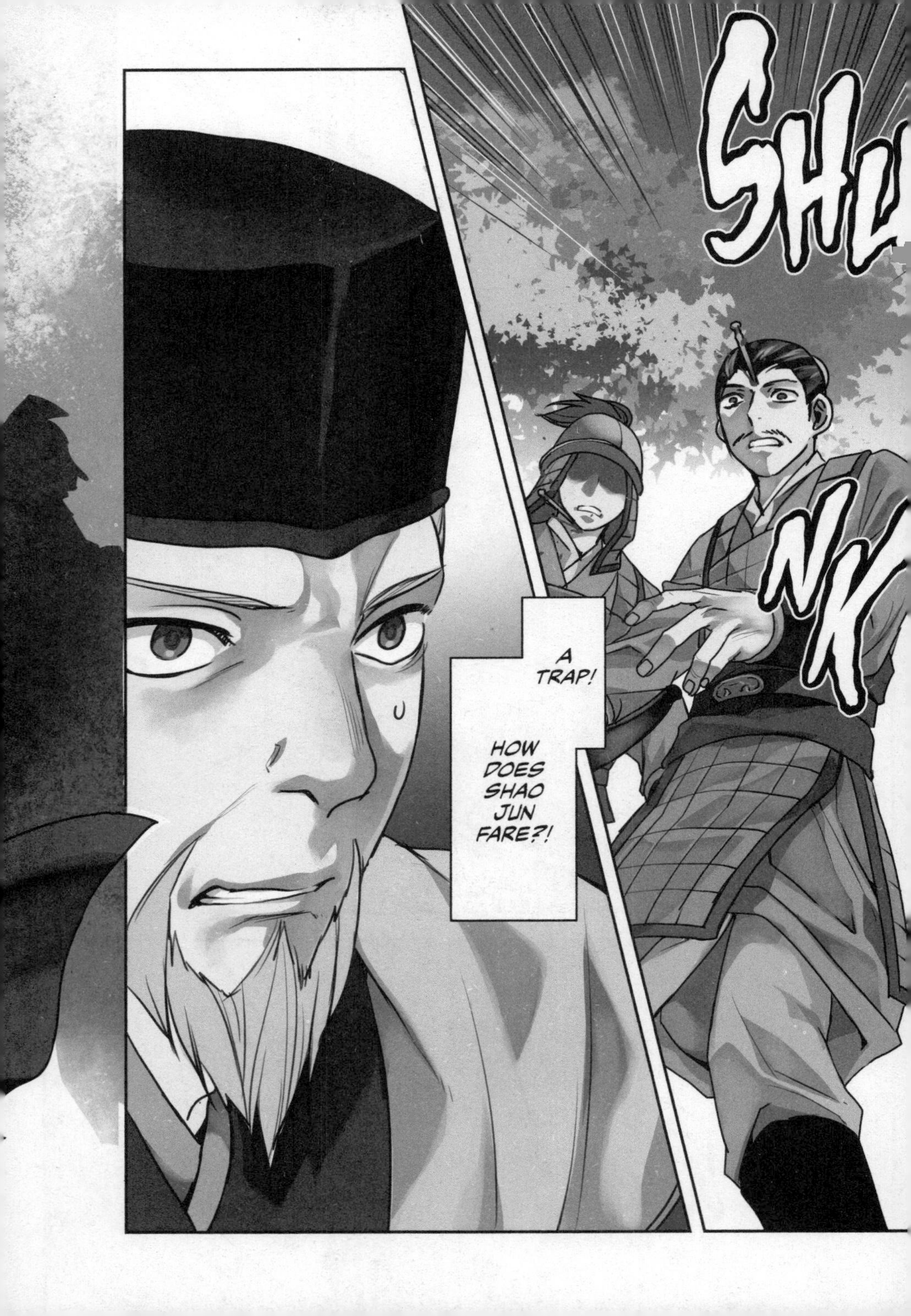
SHUNK
A TRAP!
HOW DOES SHAO JUN FARE?!

Chapter 9: Trap

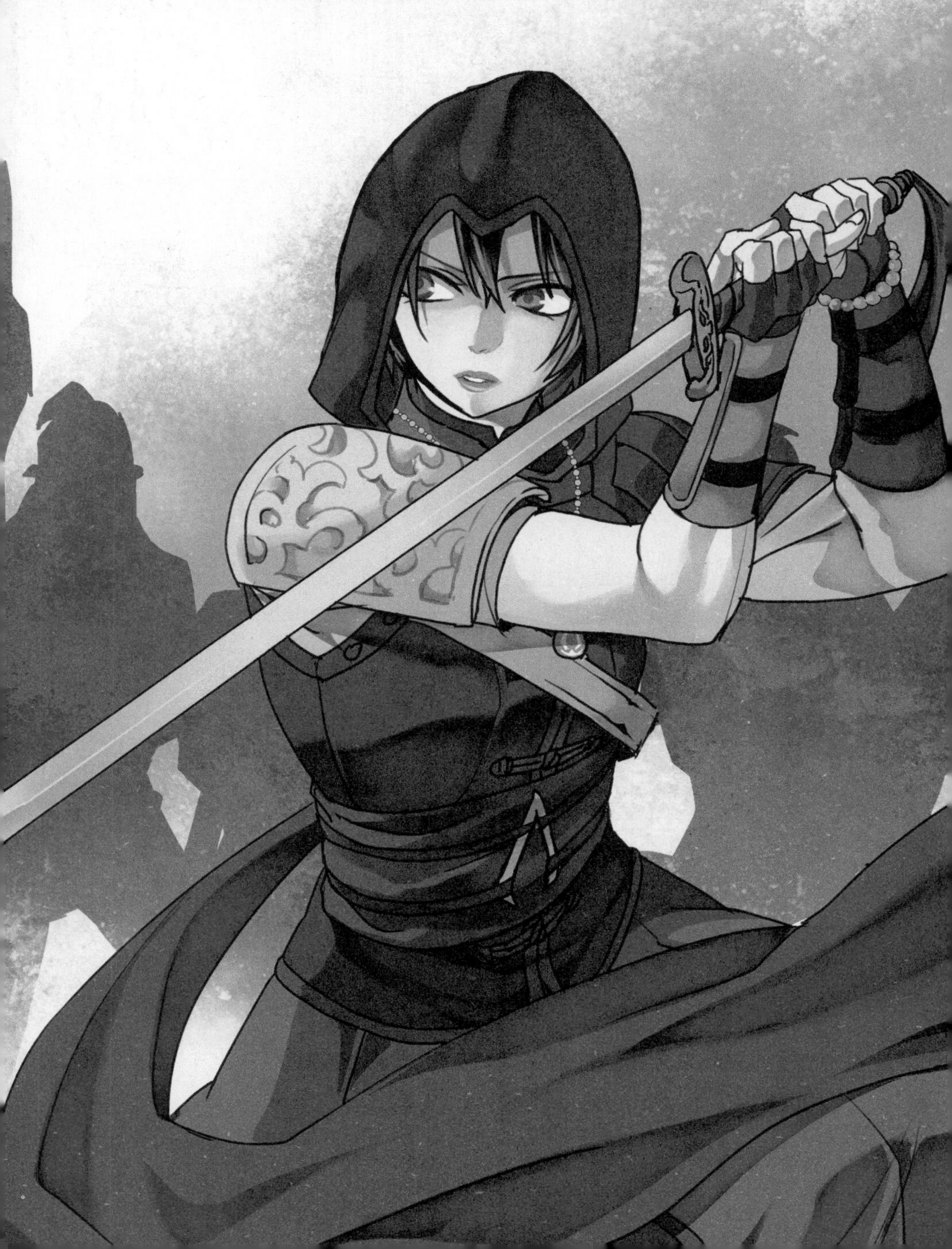

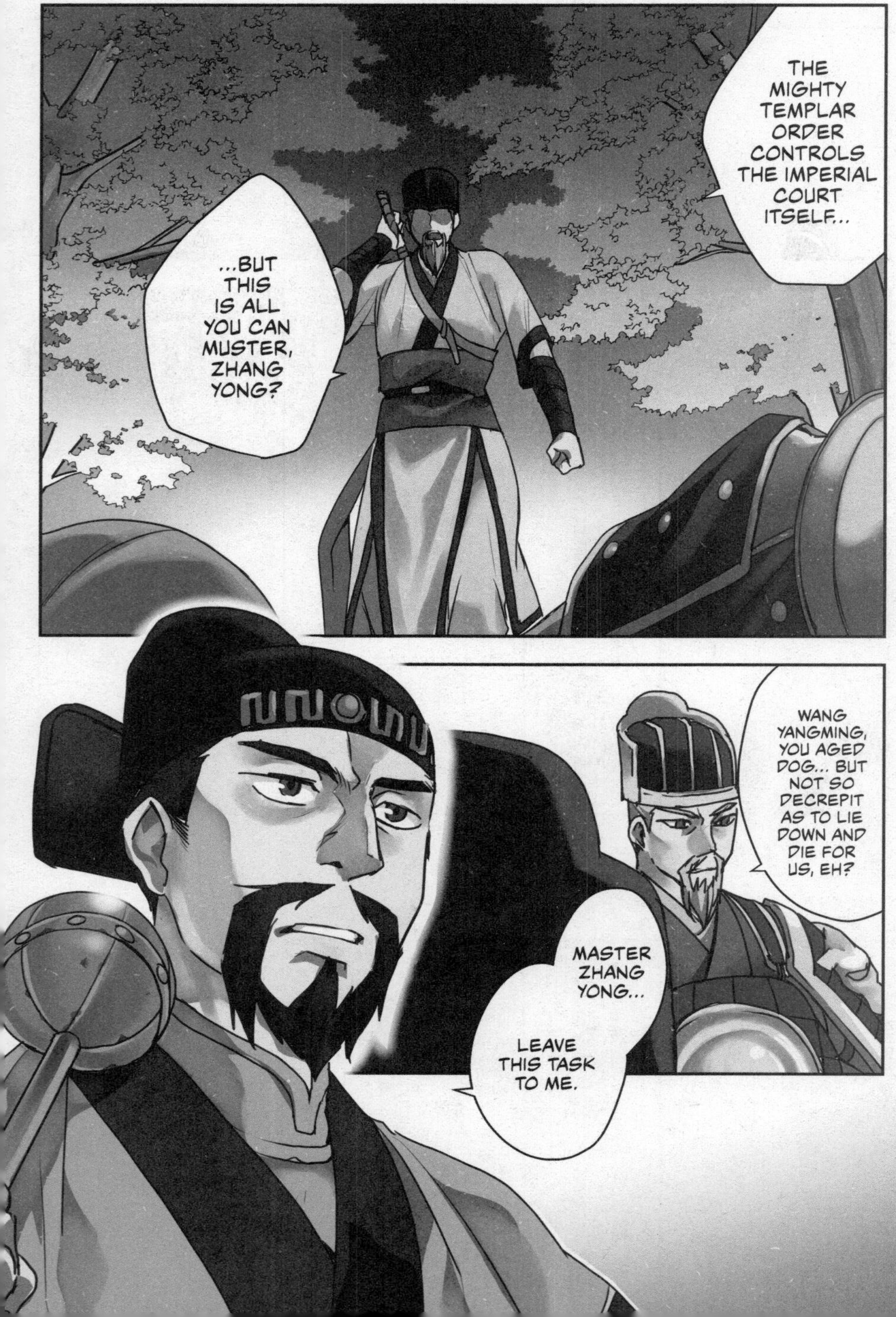
THE MIGHTY TEMPLAR ORDER CONTROLS THE IMPERIAL COURT ITSELF...
...BUT THIS IS ALL YOU CAN MUSTER, ZHANG YONG?
WANG YANGMING, YOU AGED DOG... BUT NOT SO DECREPIT AS TO LIE DOWN AND DIE FOR US, EH?
MASTER ZHANG YONG...
LEAVE THIS TASK TO ME.

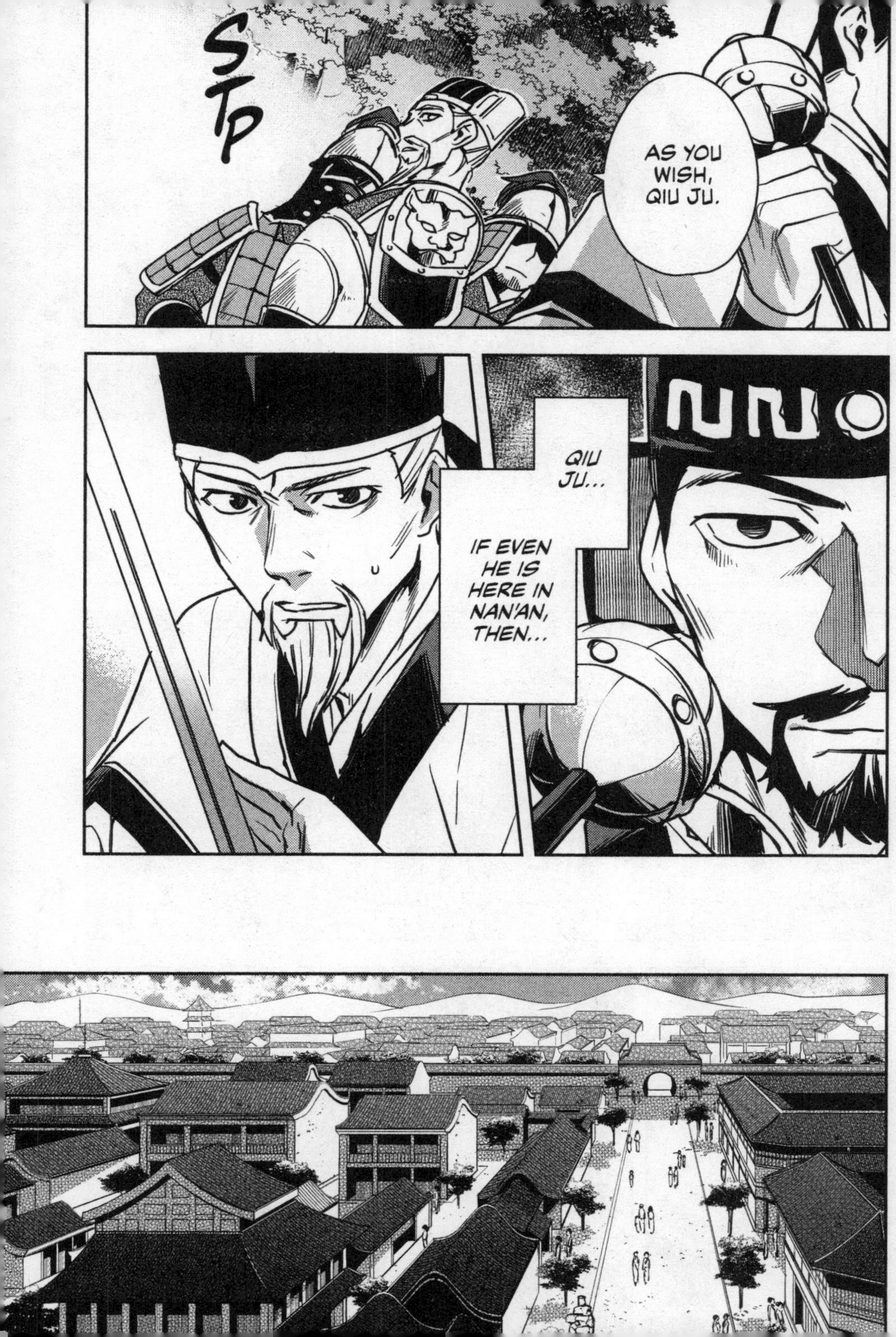
AS YOU WISH, QIU JU.
STP
QIU JU...
IF EVEN HE IS HERE IN NAN'AN, THEN...

STP

STP

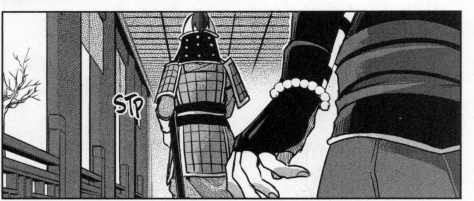

STP

SHH...

SHP

?!

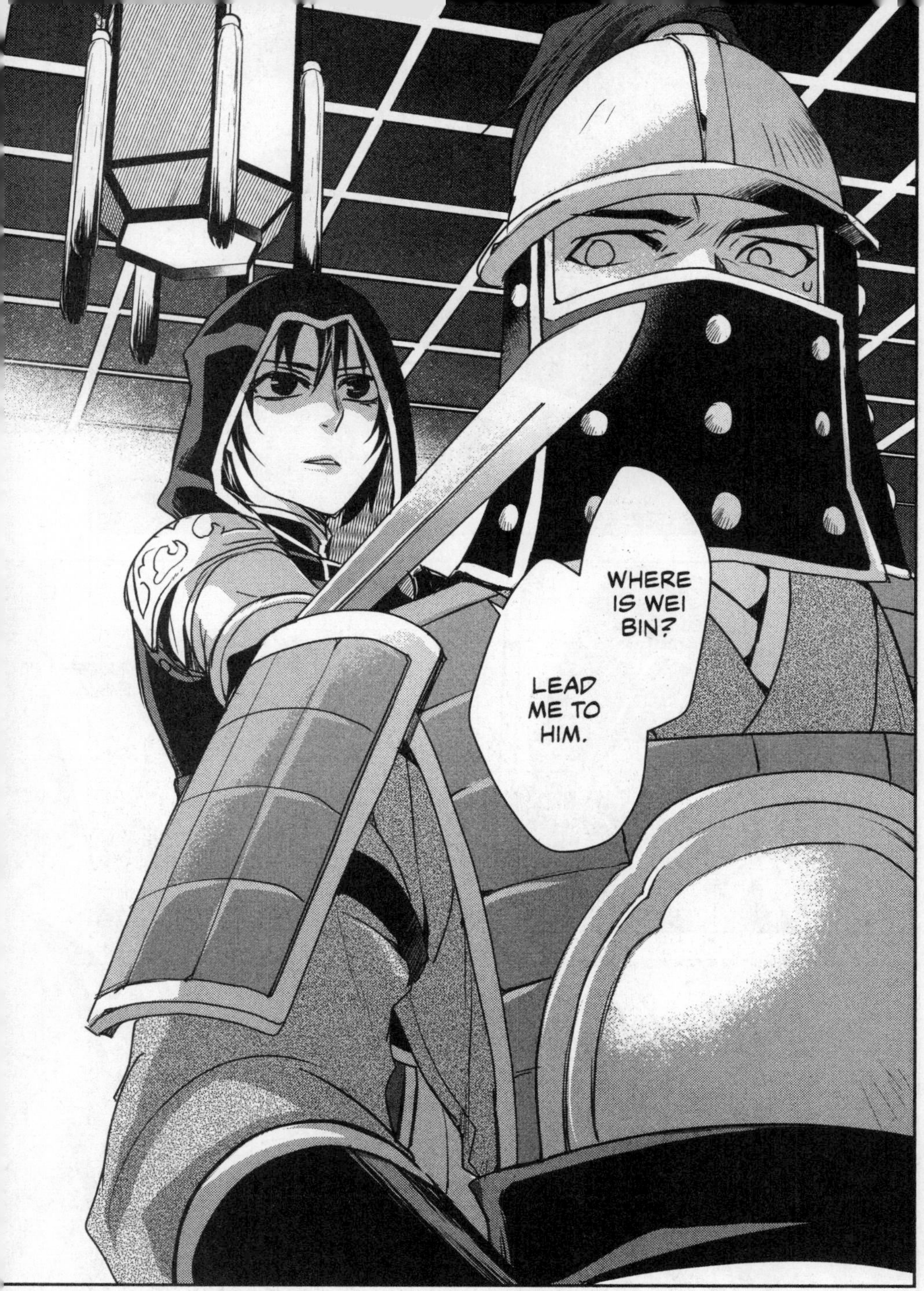
WHERE IS WEI BIN?
LEAD ME TO HIM.

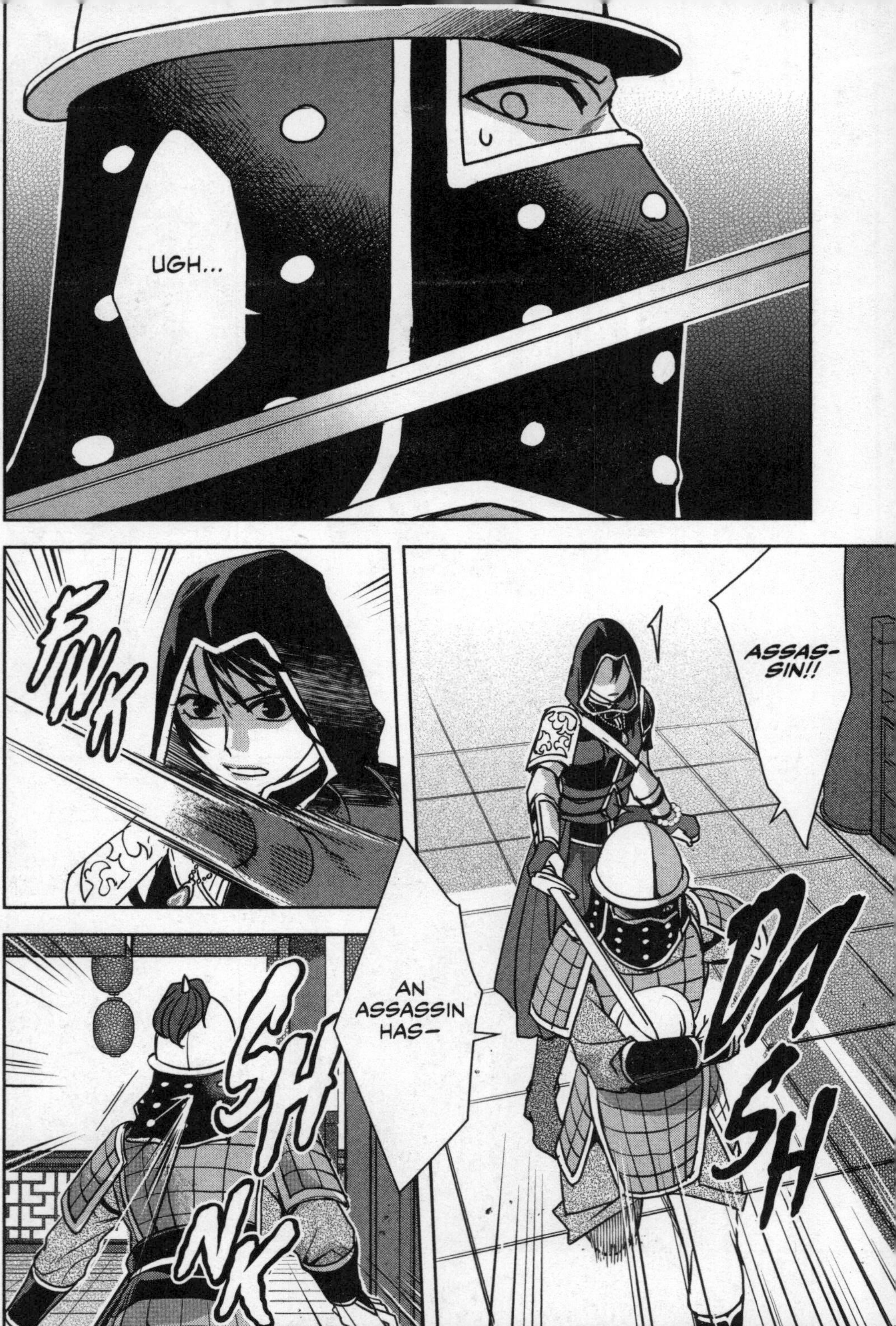
UGH...
ASSAS-SIN!!
DASH
FWNK
AN ASSASSIN HAS—
SHNK

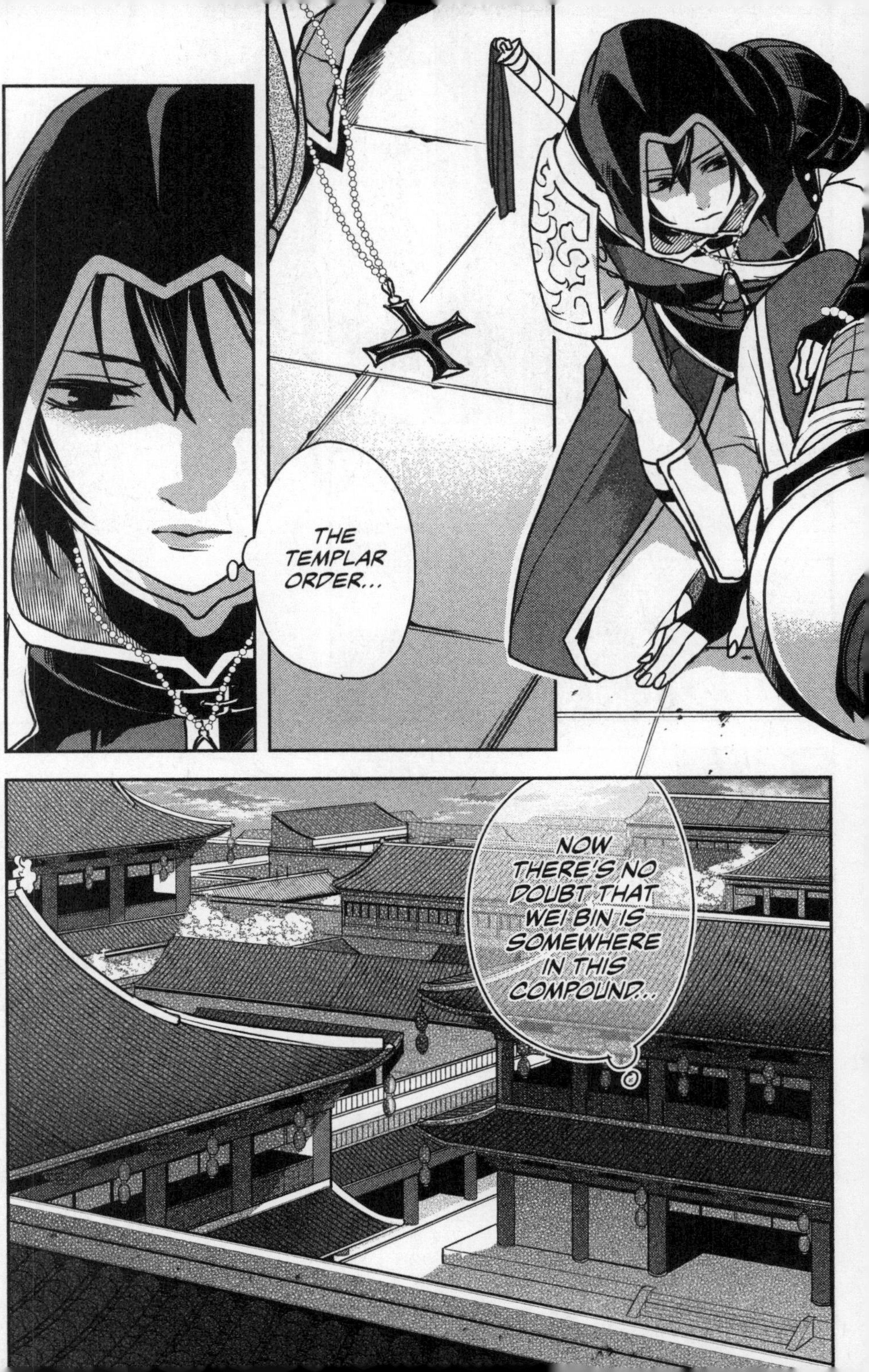
THE TEMPLAR ORDER...
NOW THERE'S NO DOUBT THAT WEI BIN IS SOMEWHERE IN THIS COMPOUND...

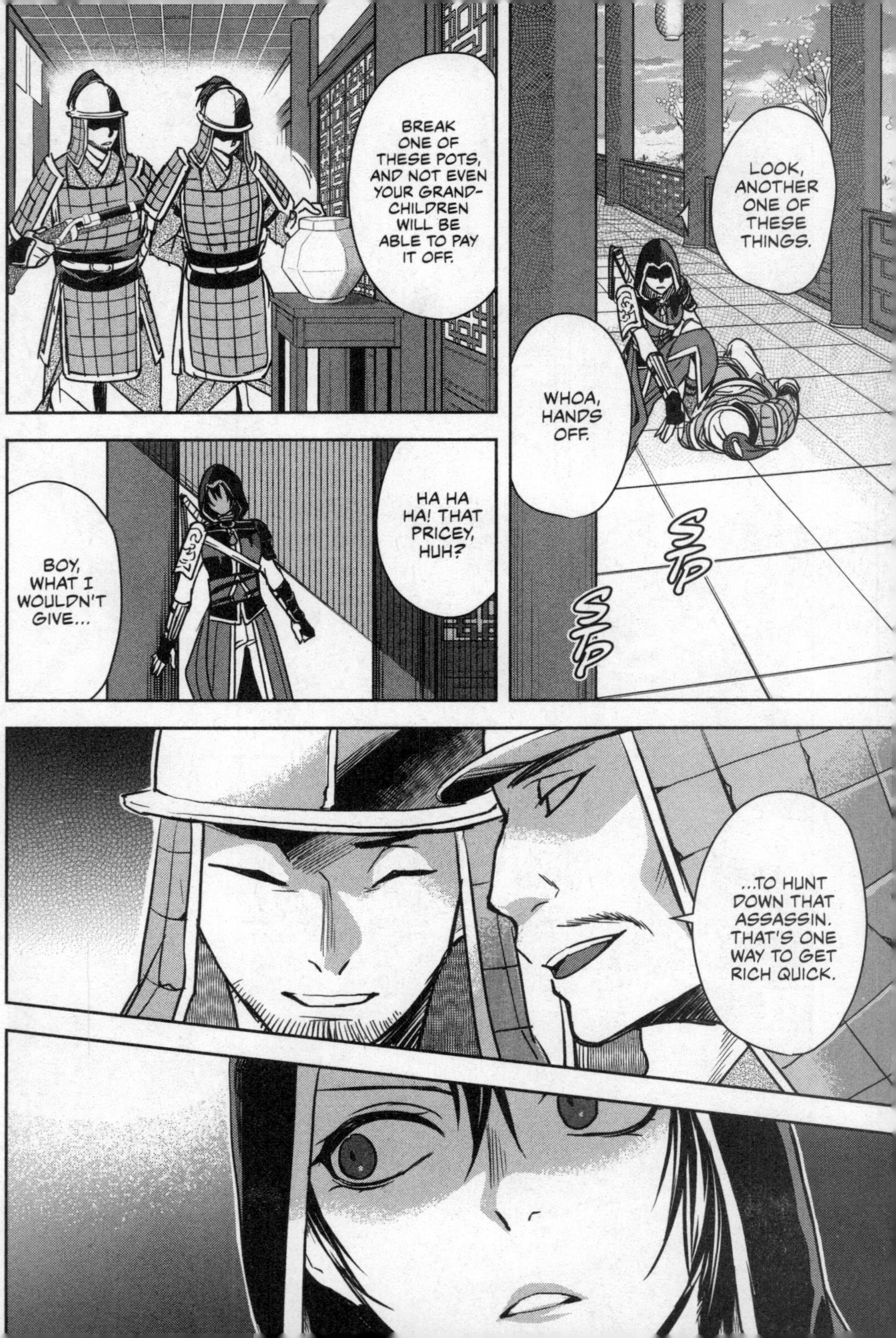
LOOK, ANOTHER ONE OF THESE THINGS.
WHOA, HANDS OFF.
STP
STP
BREAK ONE OF THESE POTS, AND NOT EVEN YOUR GRAND-CHILDREN WILL BE ABLE TO PAY IT OFF.
HA HA HA! THAT PRICEY, HUH?
BOY, WHAT I WOULDN'T GIVE...
...TO HUNT DOWN THAT ASSASSIN. THAT'S ONE WAY TO GET RICH QUICK.

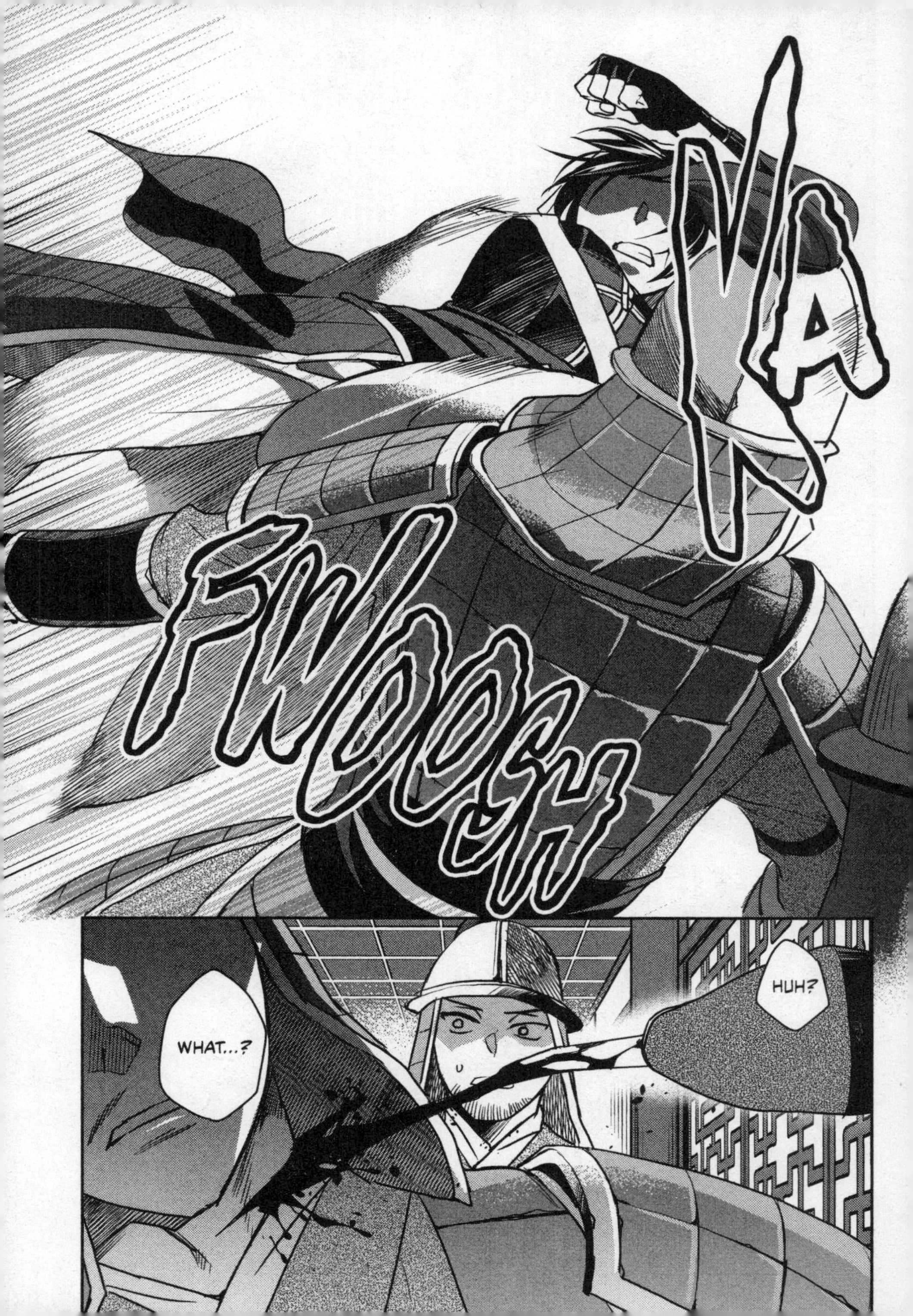
YA
FWOOSH
HUH?
WHAT...?

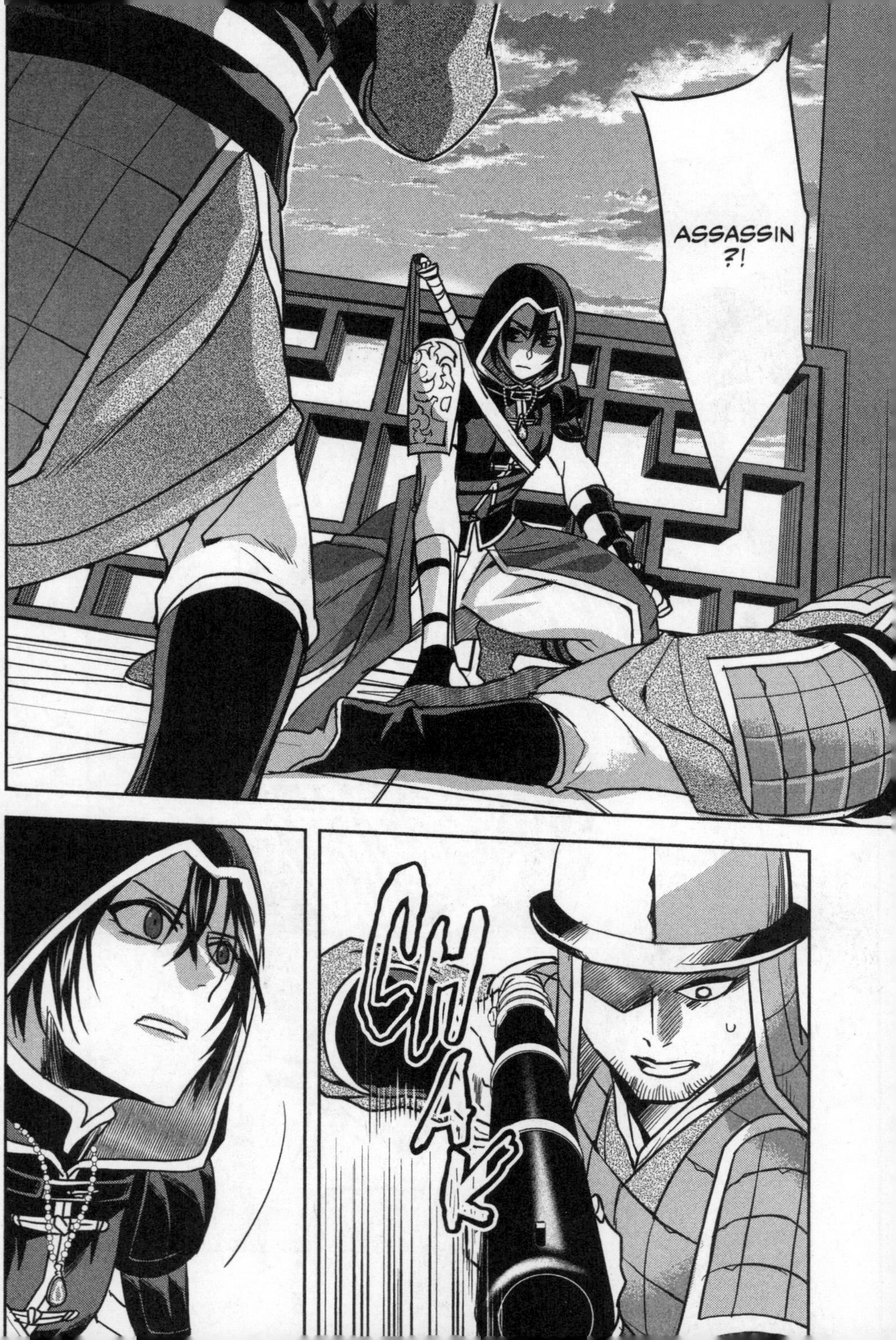
ASSASSIN ?!
CHAK

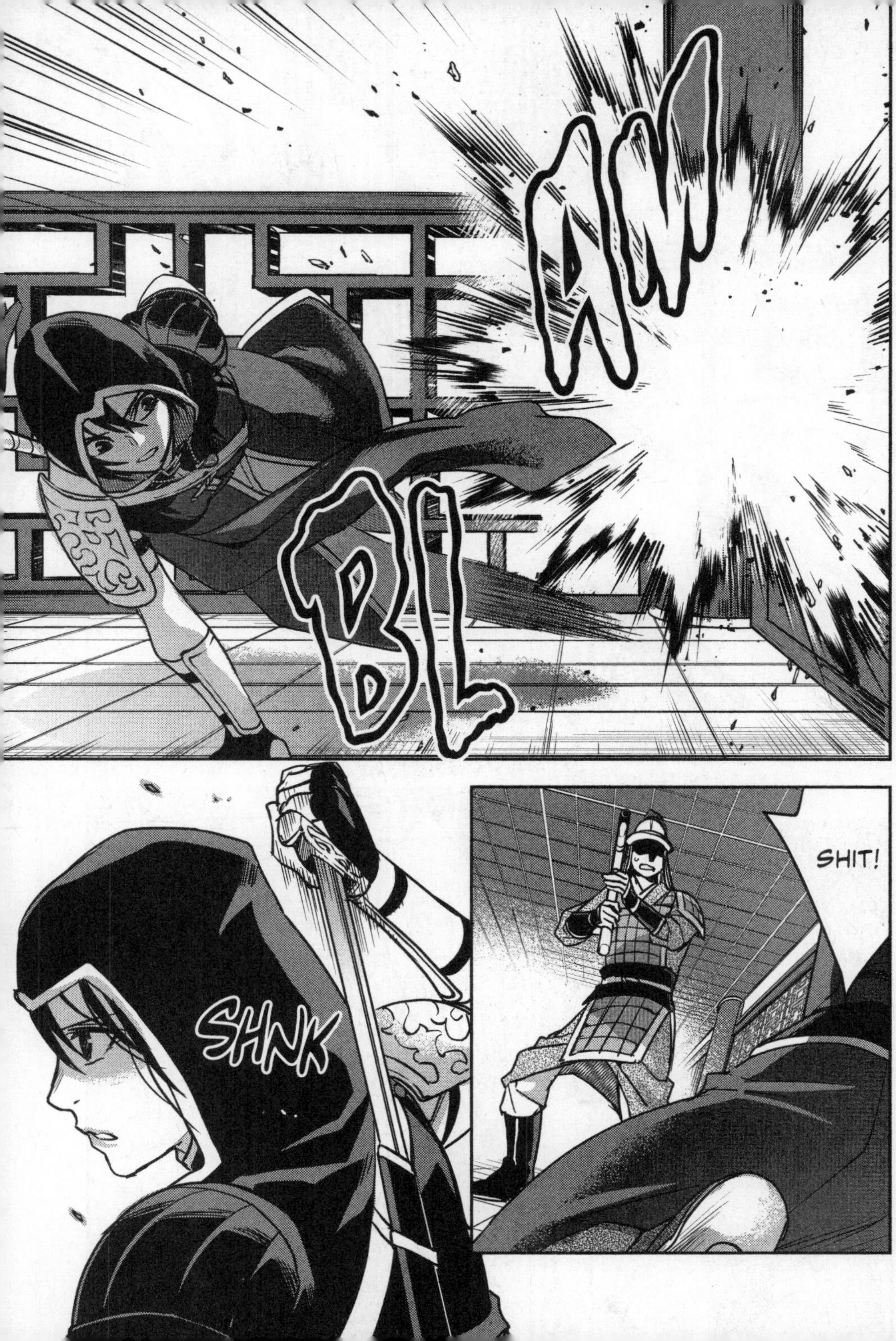
BLAM
SHIT!
SHNK

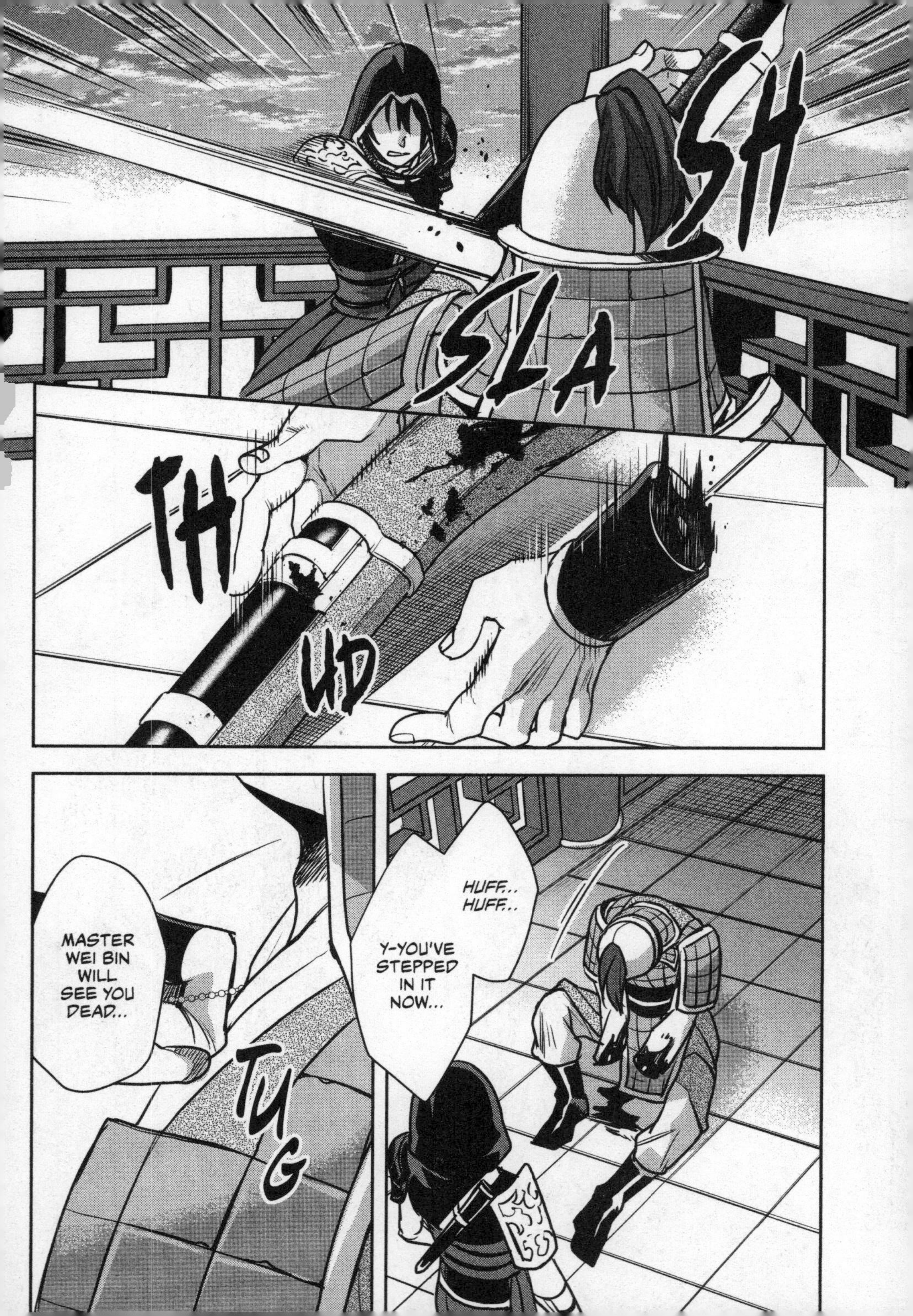
SLASH
THUD
HUFF... HUFF...
Y-YOU'VE STEPPED IN IT NOW...
MASTER WEI BIN WILL SEE YOU DEAD...
TUG

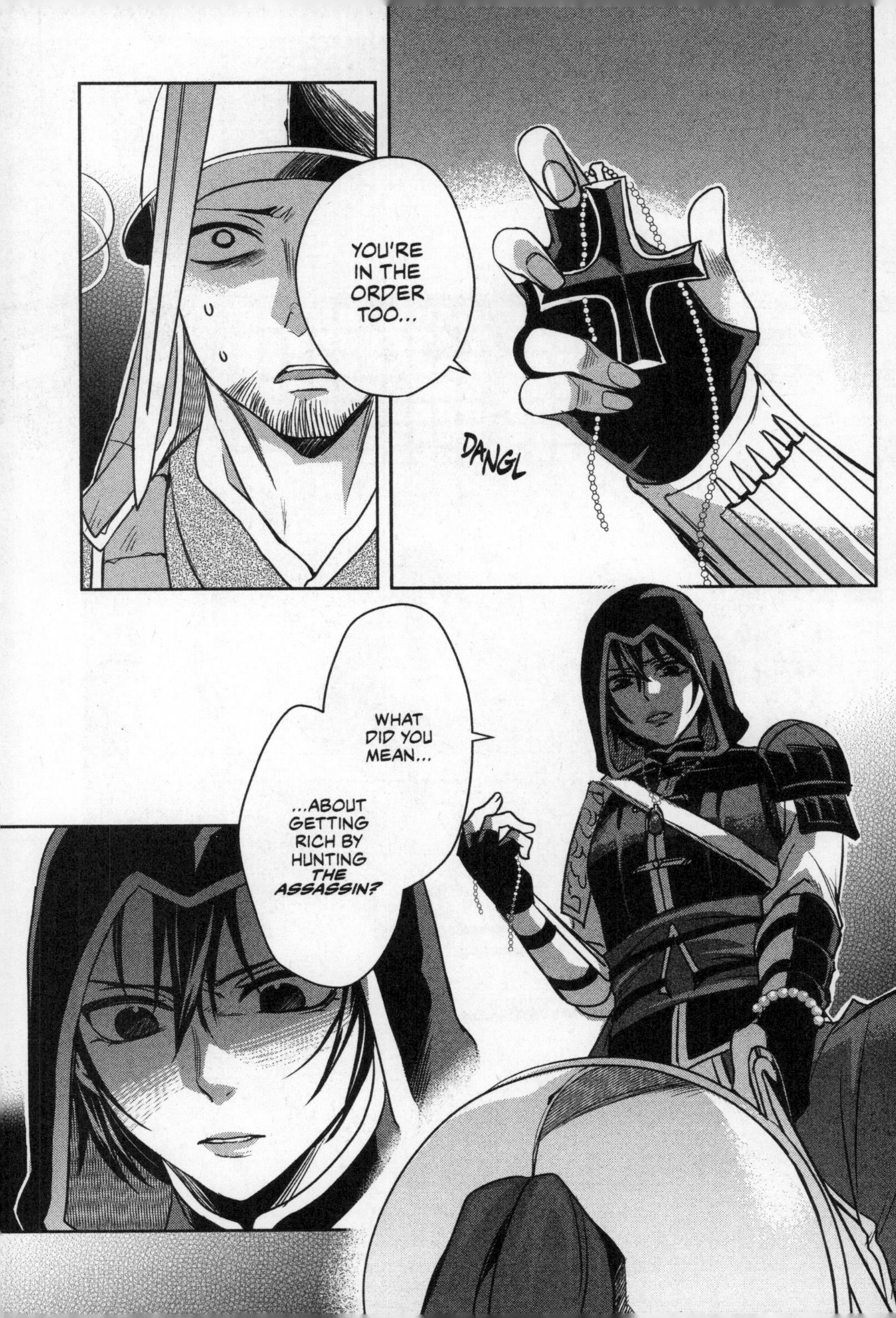
DANGL
YOU'RE IN THE ORDER TOO...
WHAT DID YOU MEAN...
...ABOUT GETTING RICH BY HUNTING *THE ASSASSIN?*

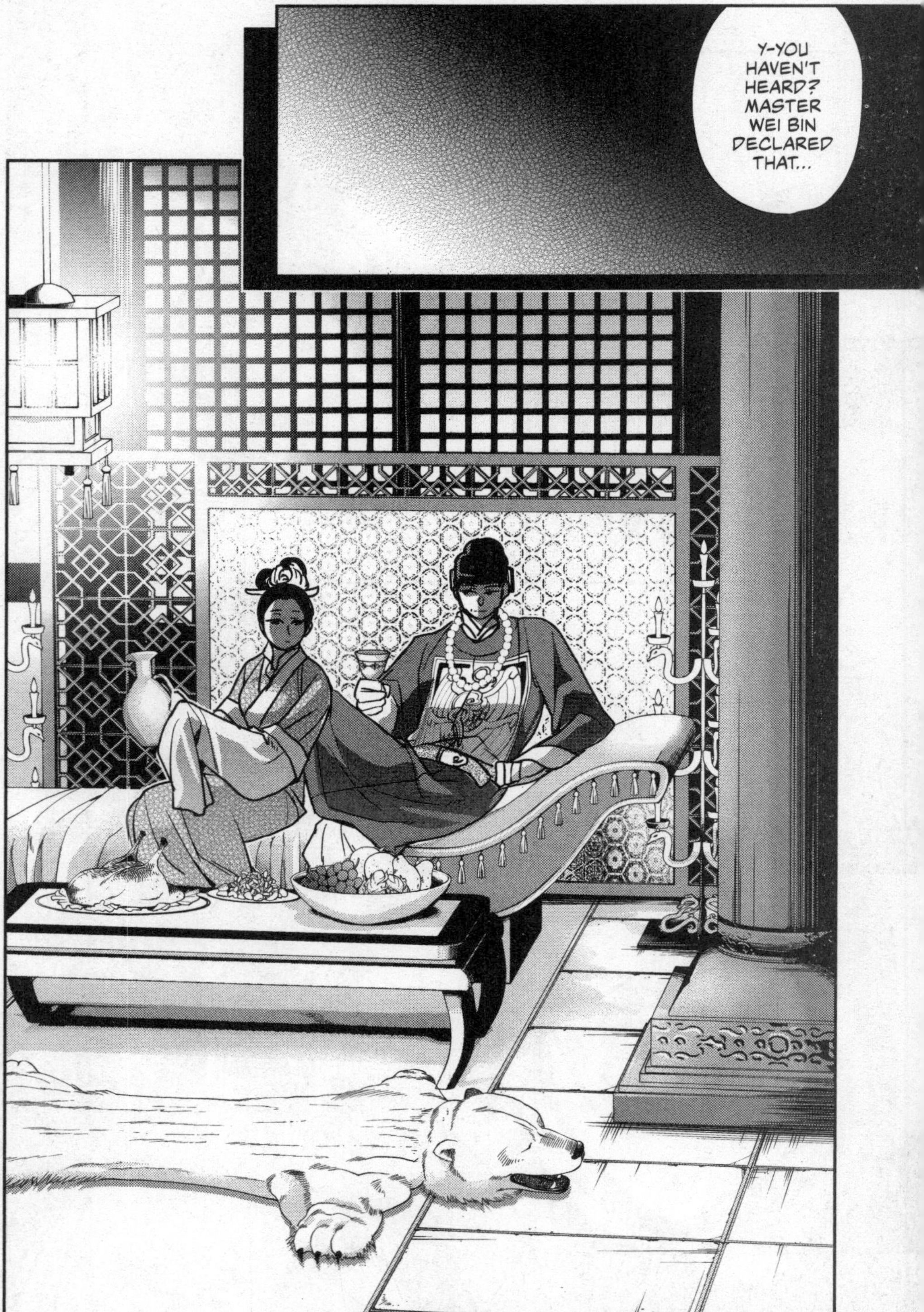
Y-YOU HAVEN'T HEARD? MASTER WEI BIN DECLARED THAT...

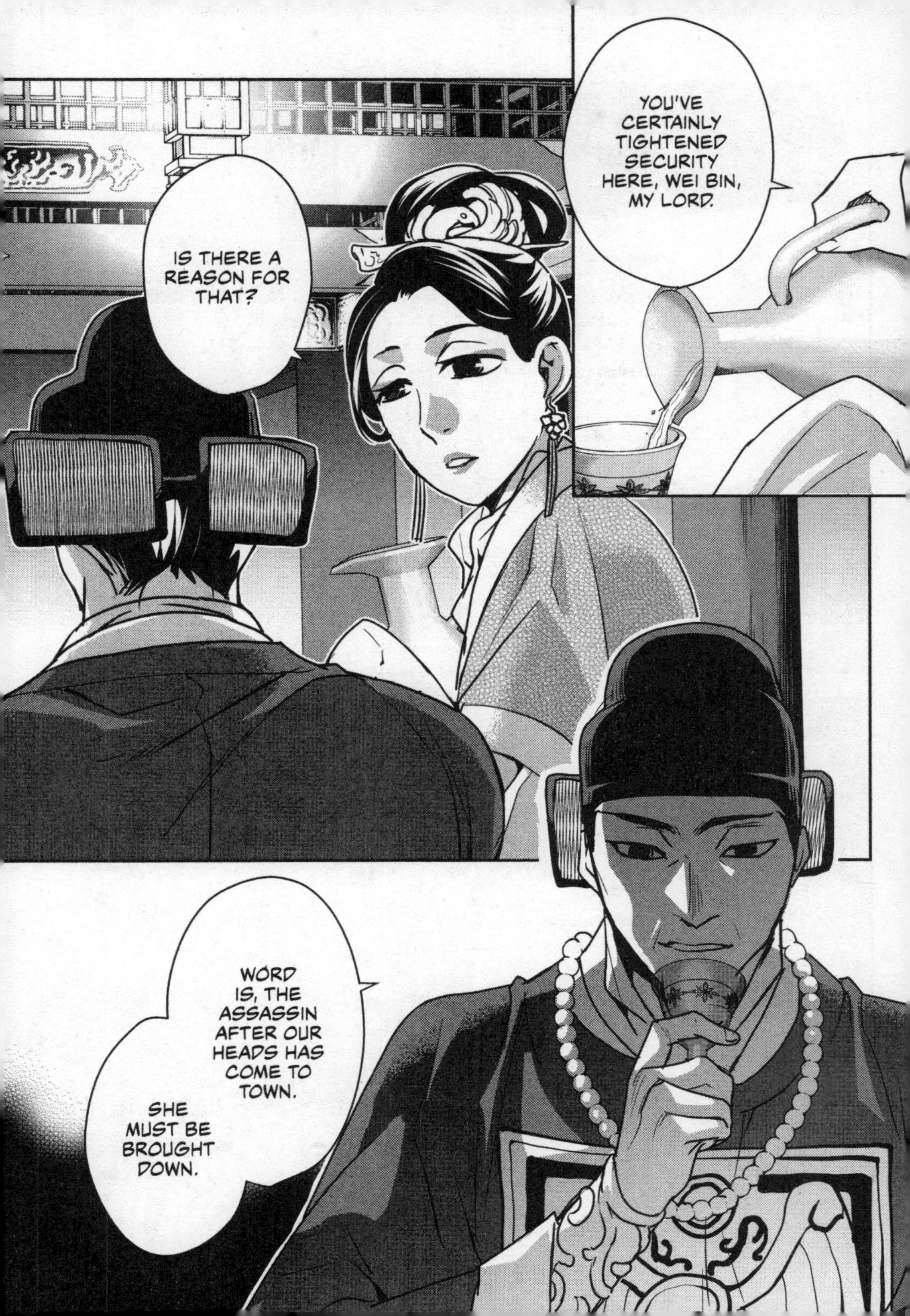
YOU'VE CERTAINLY TIGHTENED SECURITY HERE, WEI BIN, MY LORD.
IS THERE A REASON FOR THAT?
WORD IS, THE ASSASSIN AFTER OUR HEADS HAS COME TO TOWN.
SHE MUST BE BROUGHT DOWN.

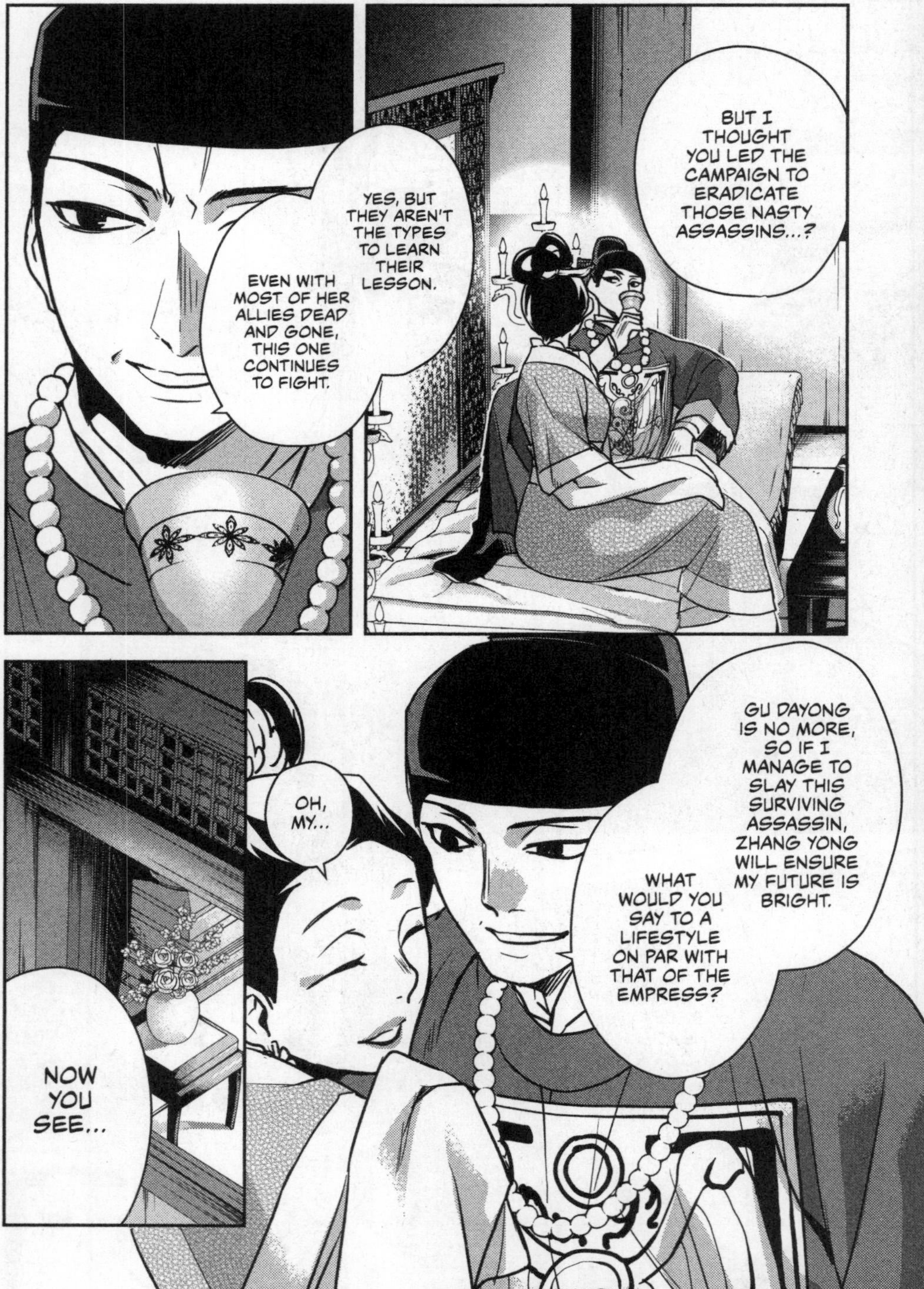
BUT I THOUGHT YOU LED THE CAMPAIGN TO ERADICATE THOSE NASTY ASSASSINS...?
YES, BUT THEY AREN'T THE TYPES TO LEARN THEIR LESSON.
EVEN WITH MOST OF HER ALLIES DEAD AND GONE, THIS ONE CONTINUES TO FIGHT.
GU DAYONG IS NO MORE, SO IF I MANAGE TO SLAY THIS SURVIVING ASSASSIN, ZHANG YONG WILL ENSURE MY FUTURE IS BRIGHT.
WHAT WOULD YOU SAY TO A LIFESTYLE ON PAR WITH THAT OF THE EMPRESS?
OH, MY...
NOW YOU SEE...

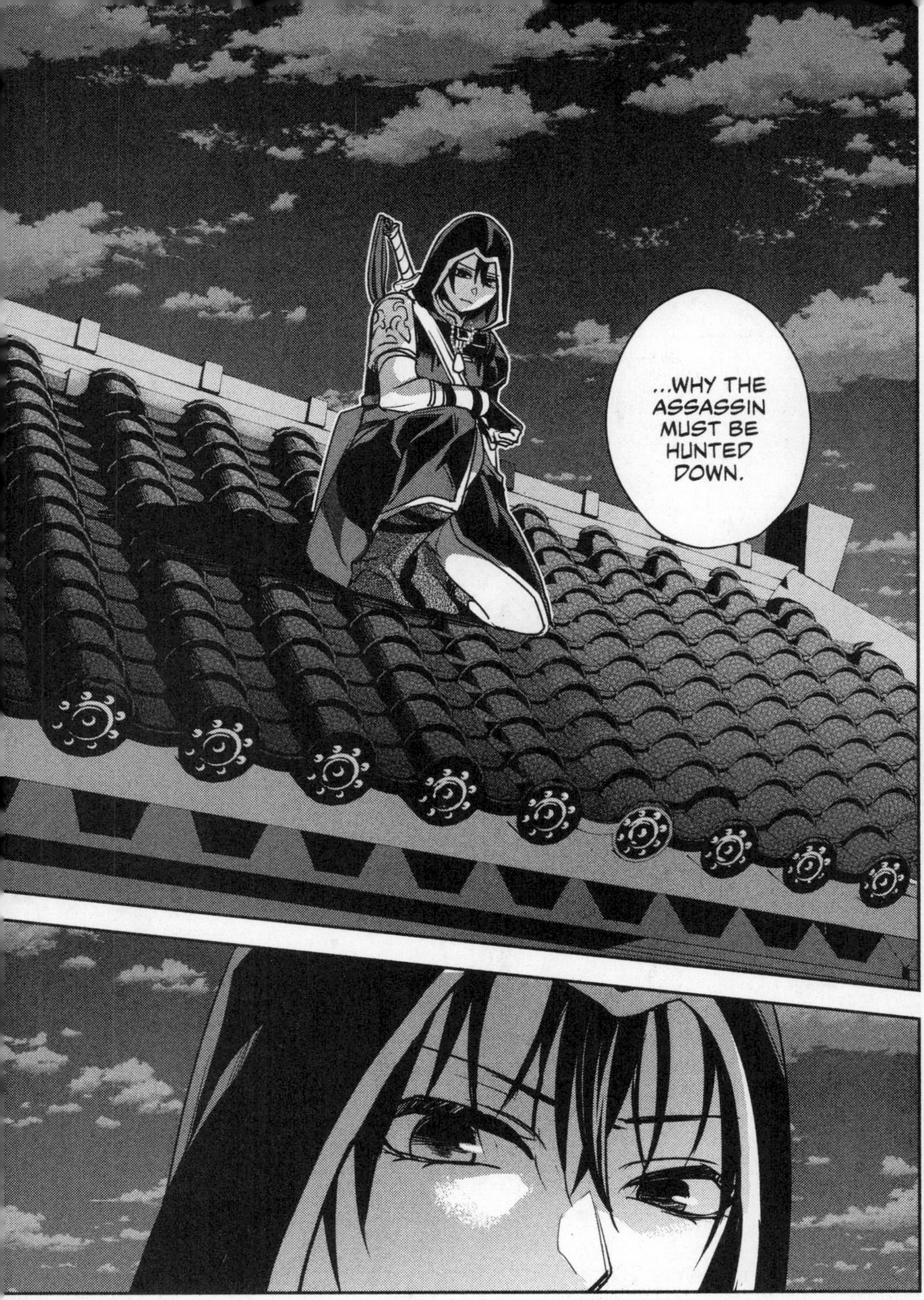
...WHY THE ASSASSIN MUST BE HUNTED DOWN.

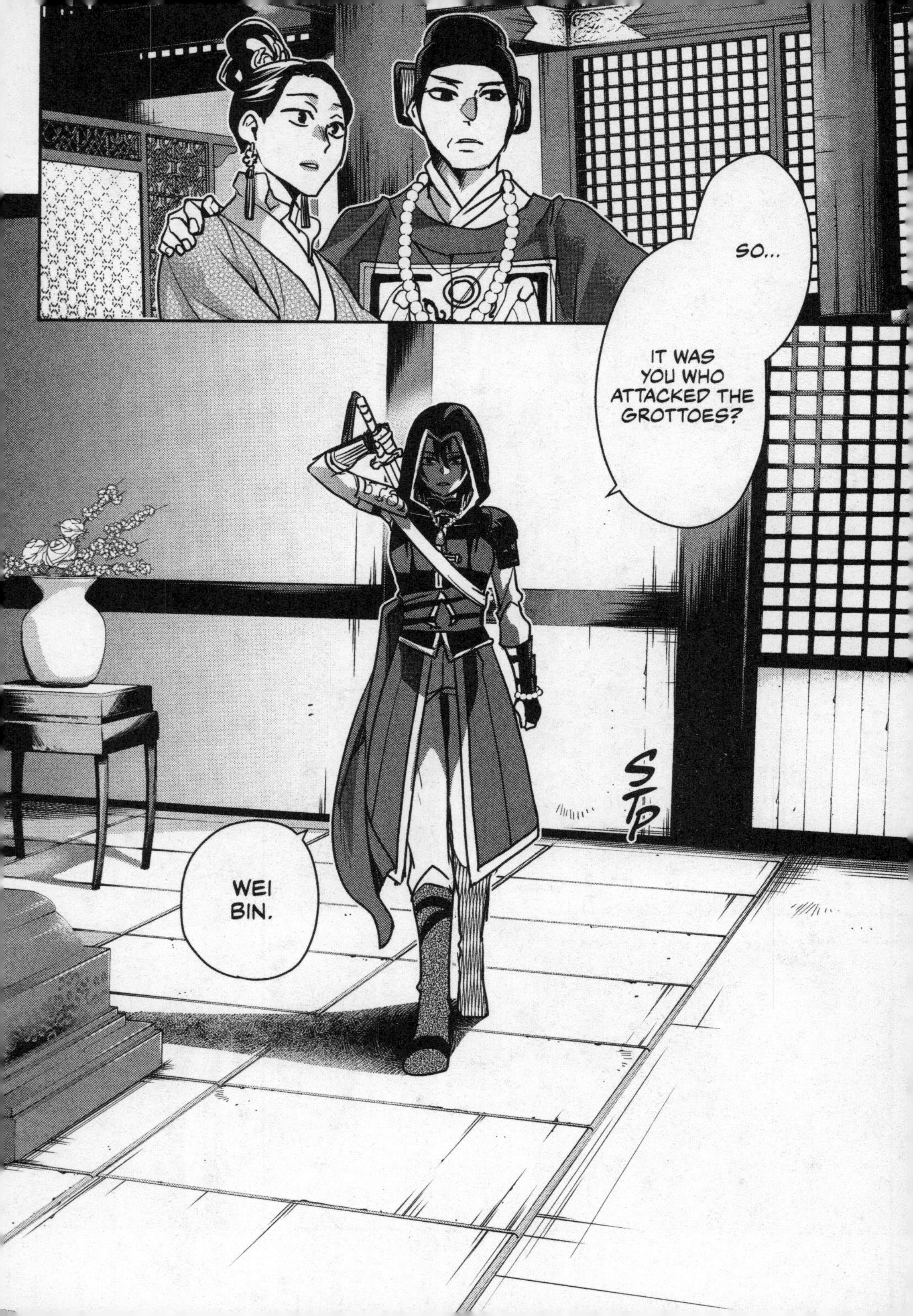
SO...
IT WAS YOU WHO ATTACKED THE GROTTOES?
STP
WEI BIN.

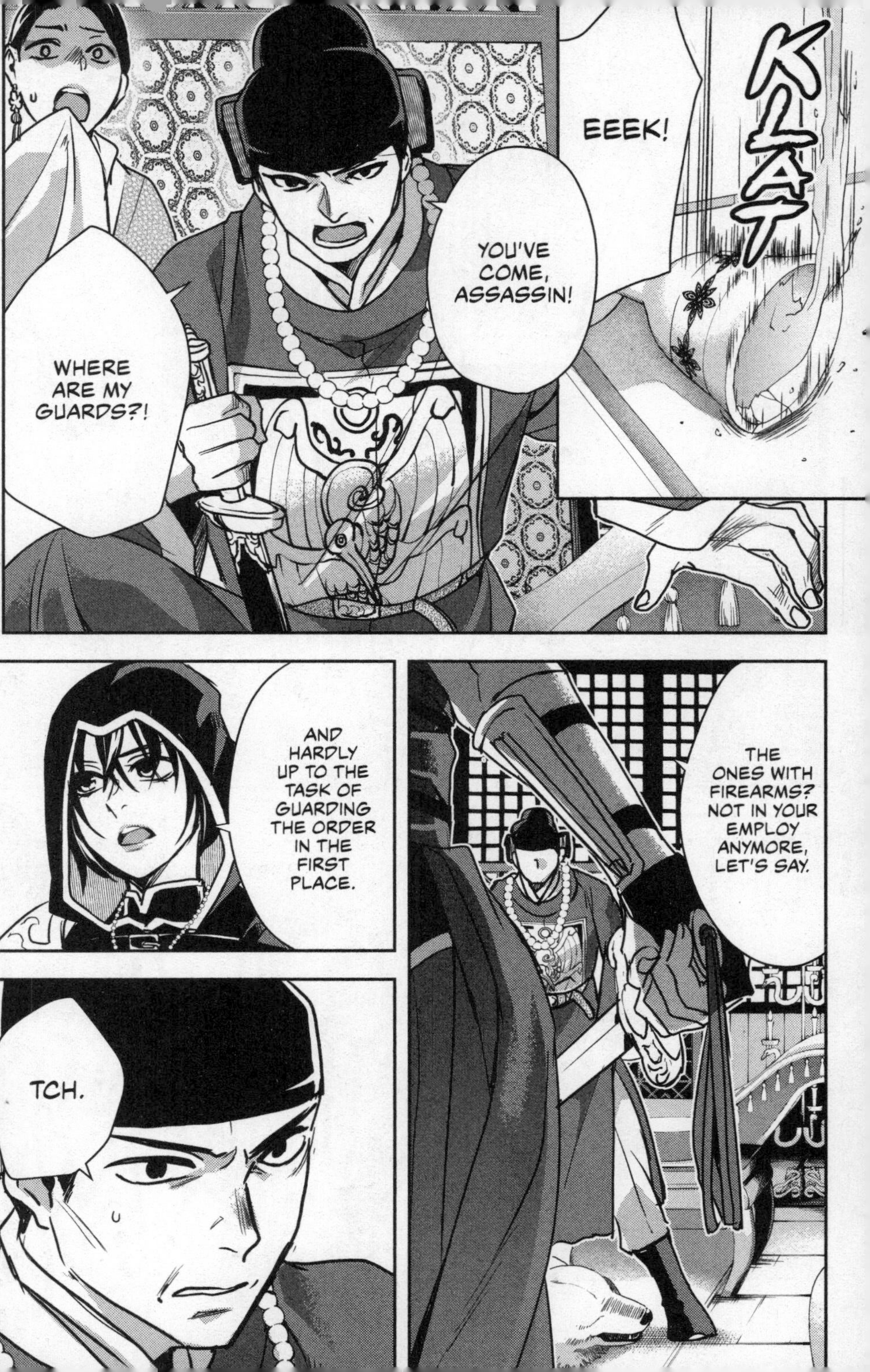
KLAT
EEEK!
YOU'VE COME, ASSASSIN!
WHERE ARE MY GUARDS?!
THE ONES WITH FIREARMS? NOT IN YOUR EMPLOY ANYMORE, LET'S SAY.
AND HARDLY UP TO THE TASK OF GUARDING THE ORDER IN THE FIRST PLACE.
TCH.

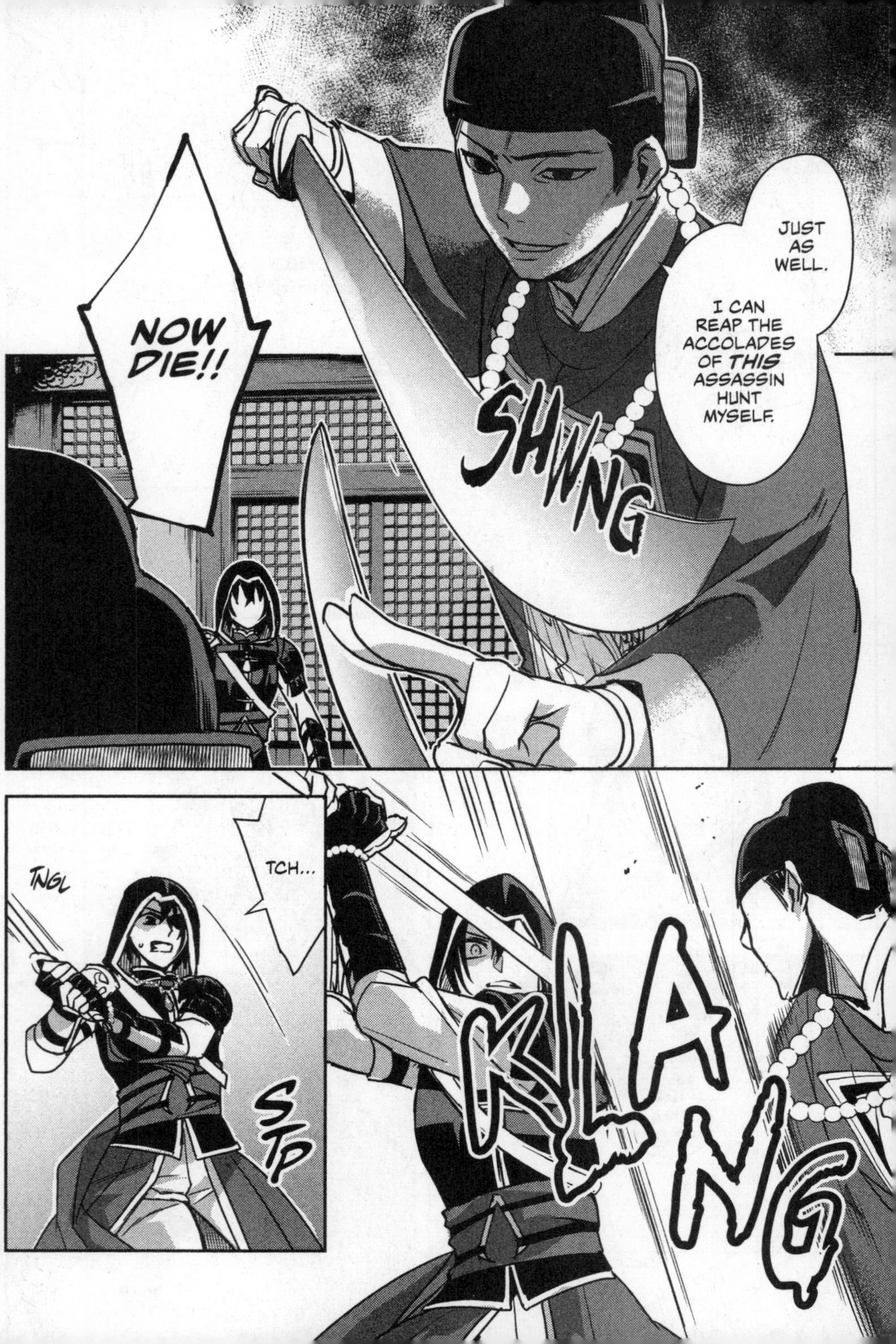
JUST AS WELL.
I CAN REAP THE ACCOLADES OF THIS ASSASSIN HUNT MYSELF.
SHWNG
NOW DIE!!
KLANG
TCH...
TNGL
STP

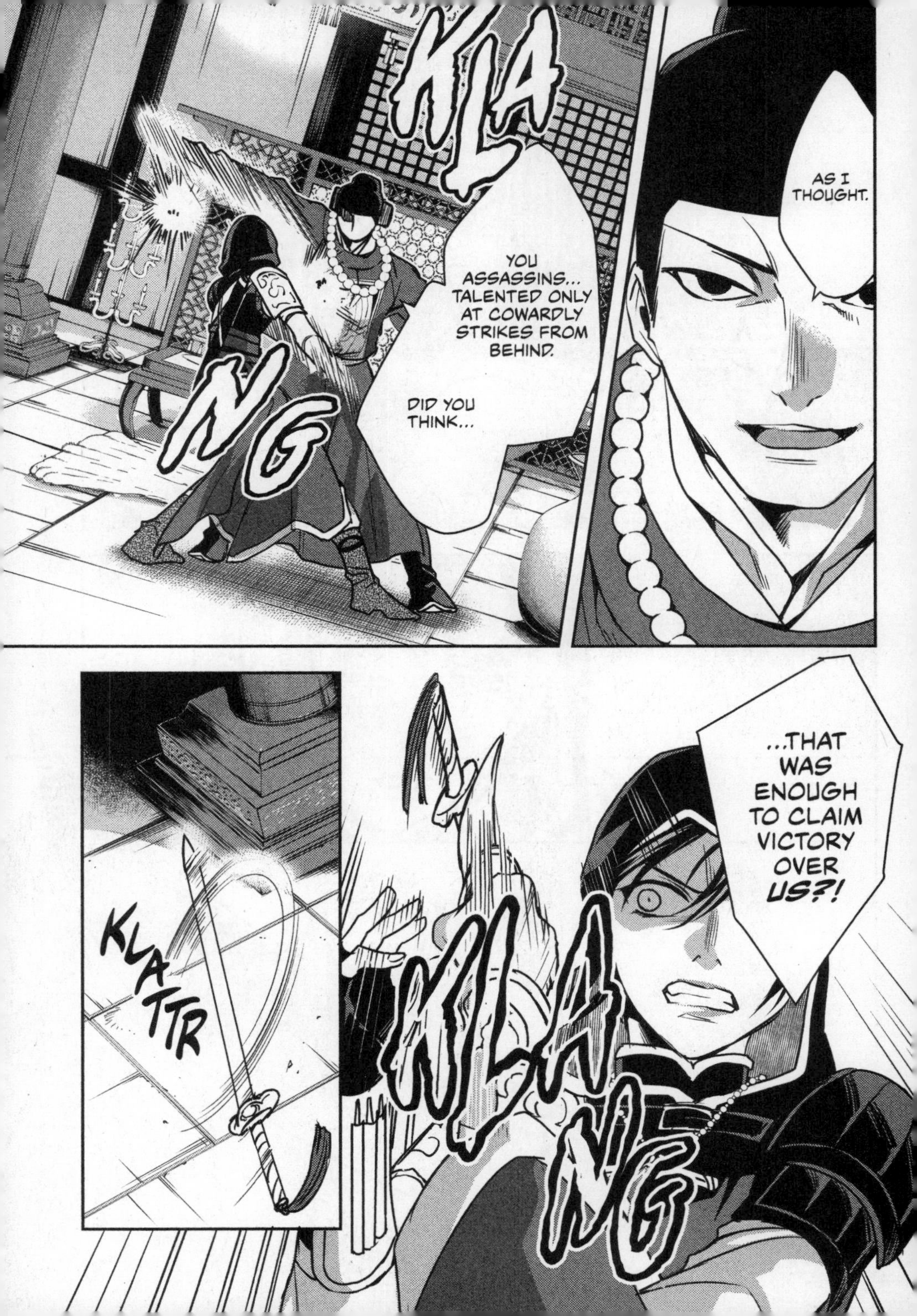
AS I THOUGHT.
KLANG
YOU ASSASSINS... TALENTED ONLY AT COWARDLY STRIKES FROM BEHIND.
DID YOU THINK...
...THAT WAS ENOUGH TO CLAIM VICTORY OVER US?!
KLANG
KLATTR

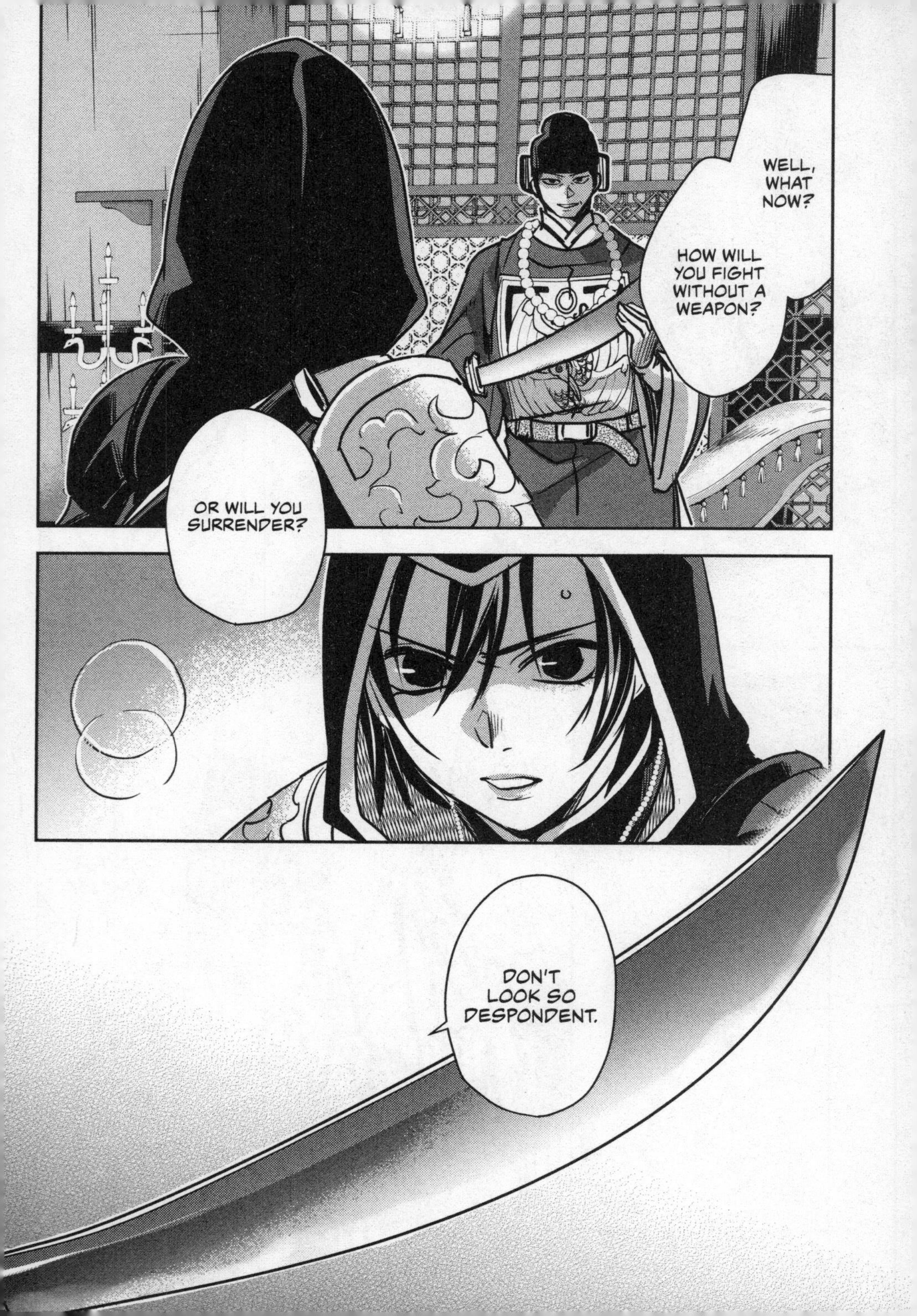
WELL, WHAT NOW?
HOW WILL YOU FIGHT WITHOUT A WEAPON?
OR WILL YOU SURRENDER?
DON'T LOOK SO DESPONDENT.

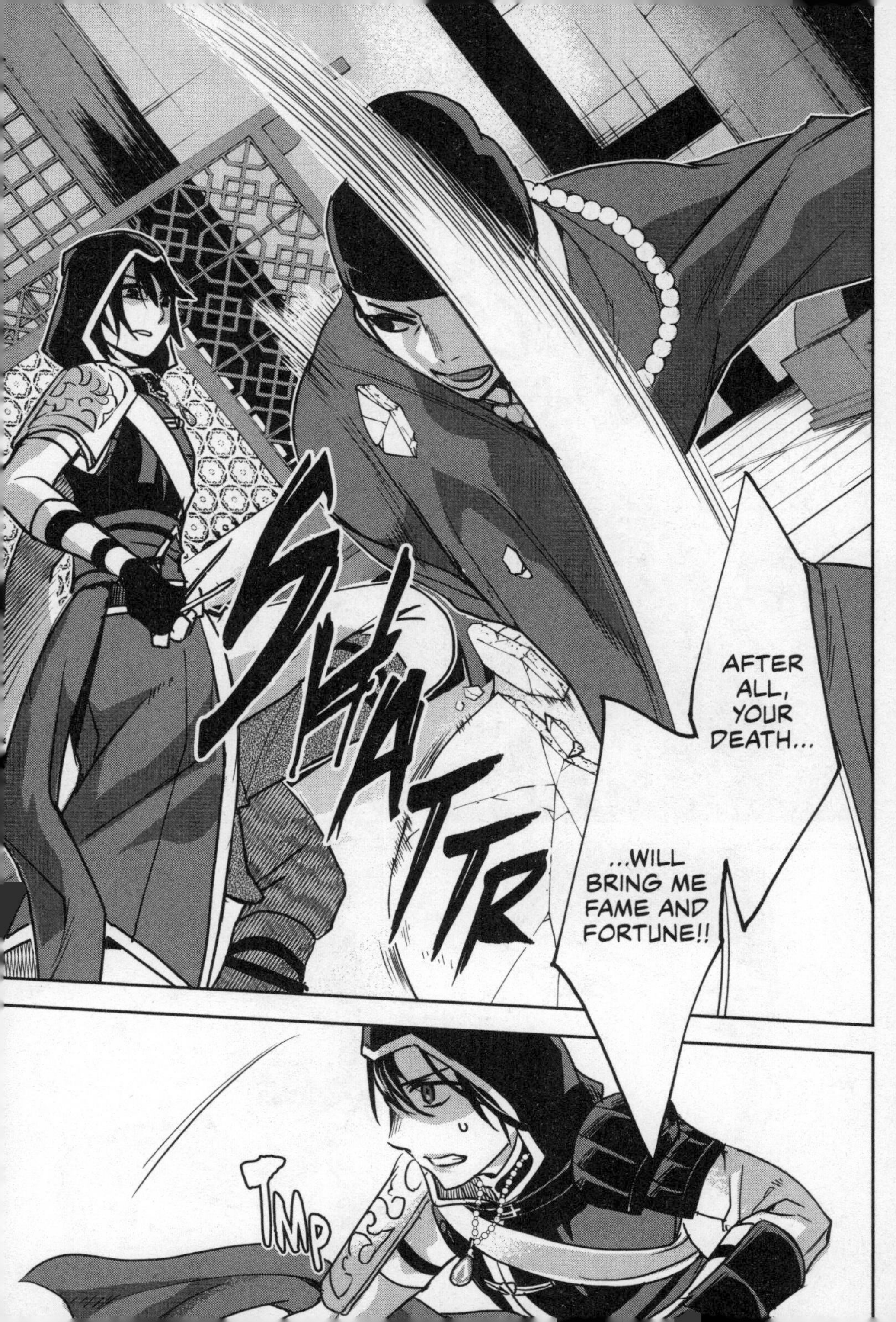
AFTER ALL, YOUR DEATH...
...WILL BRING ME FAME AND FORTUNE!!
SHATTR
TMP

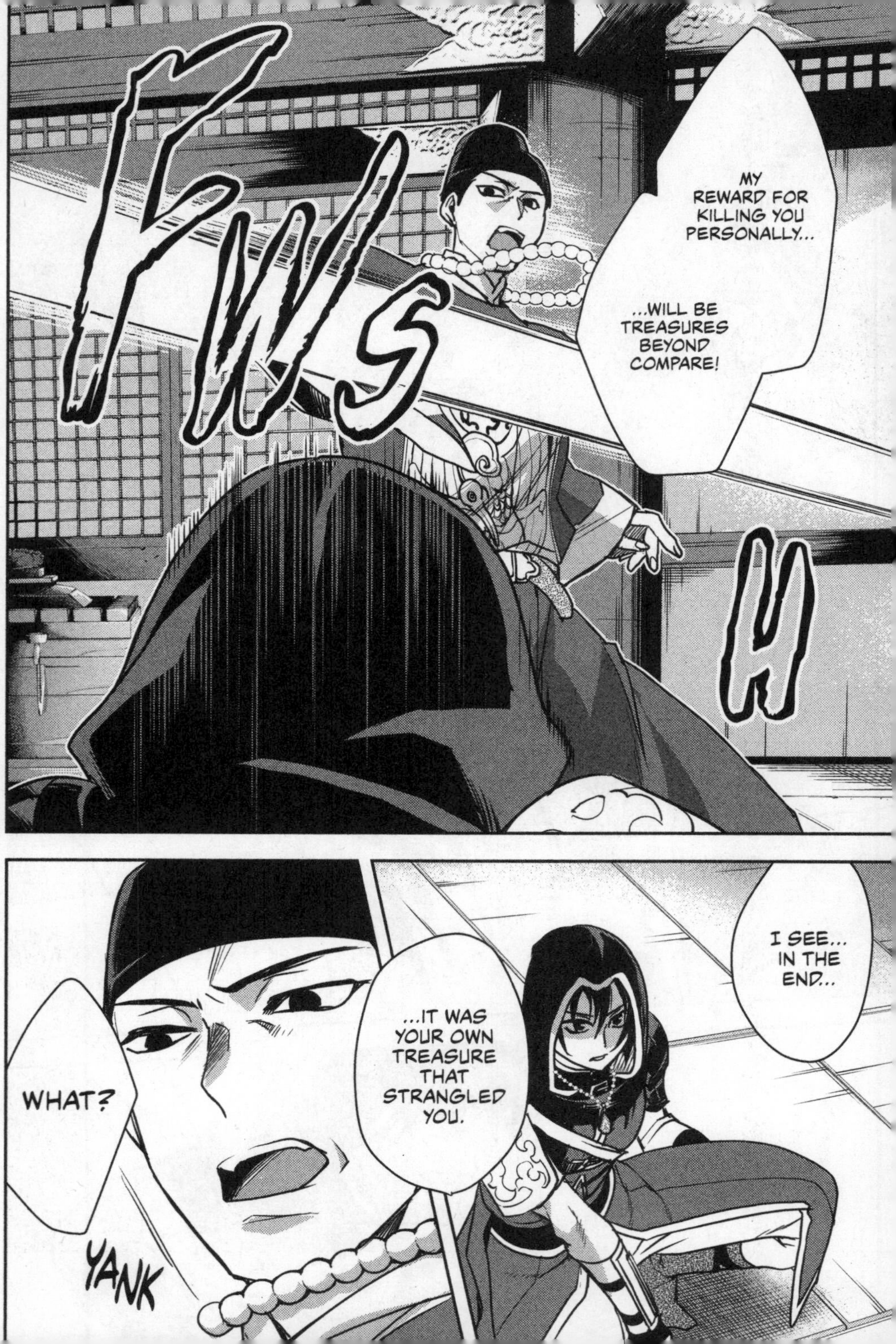
MY REWARD FOR KILLING YOU PERSONALLY...
...WILL BE TREASURES BEYOND COMPARE!
FWSH
I SEE... IN THE END...
...IT WAS YOUR OWN TREASURE THAT STRANGLED YOU.
WHAT?
YANK

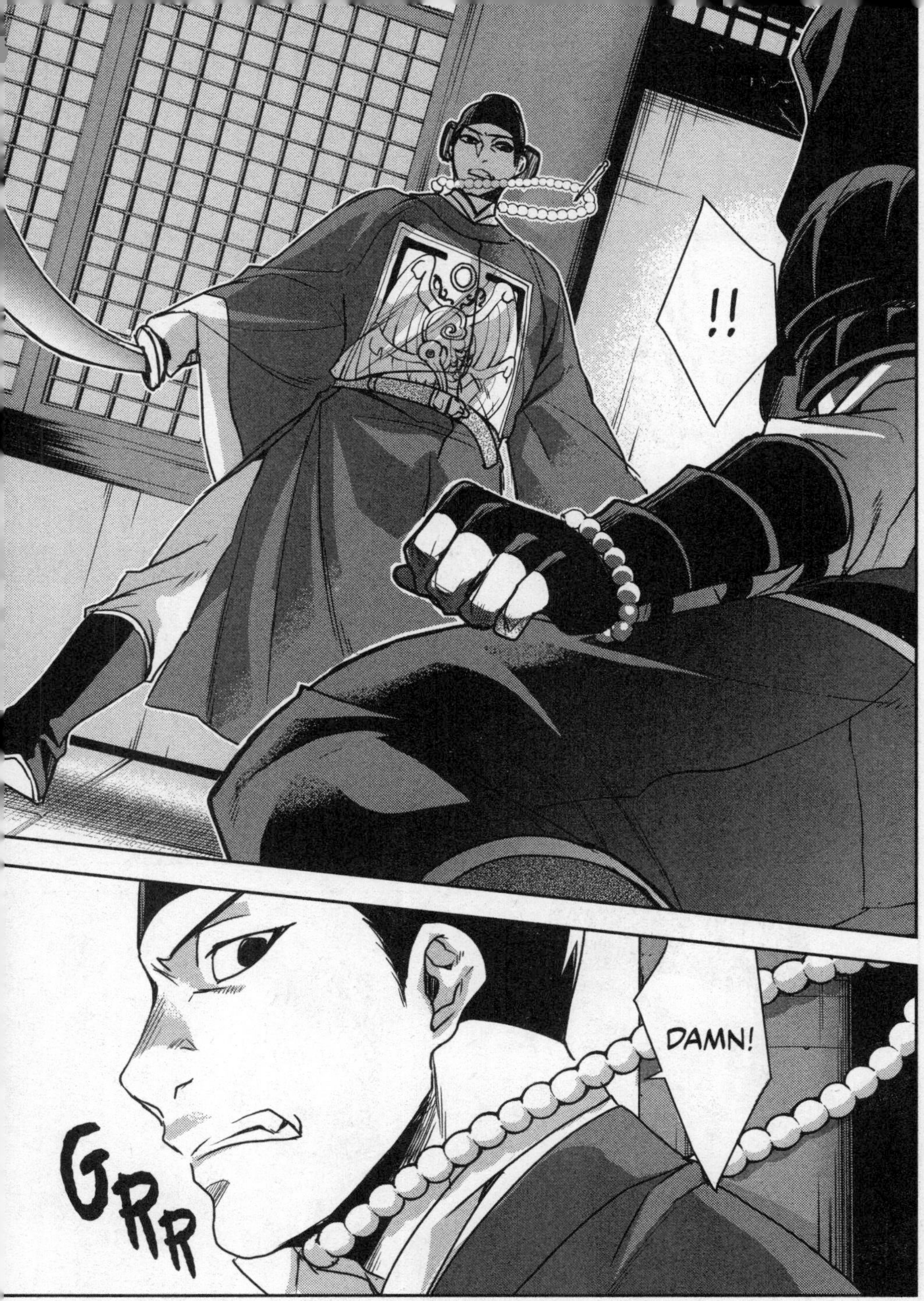
!!
DAMN!
GRR

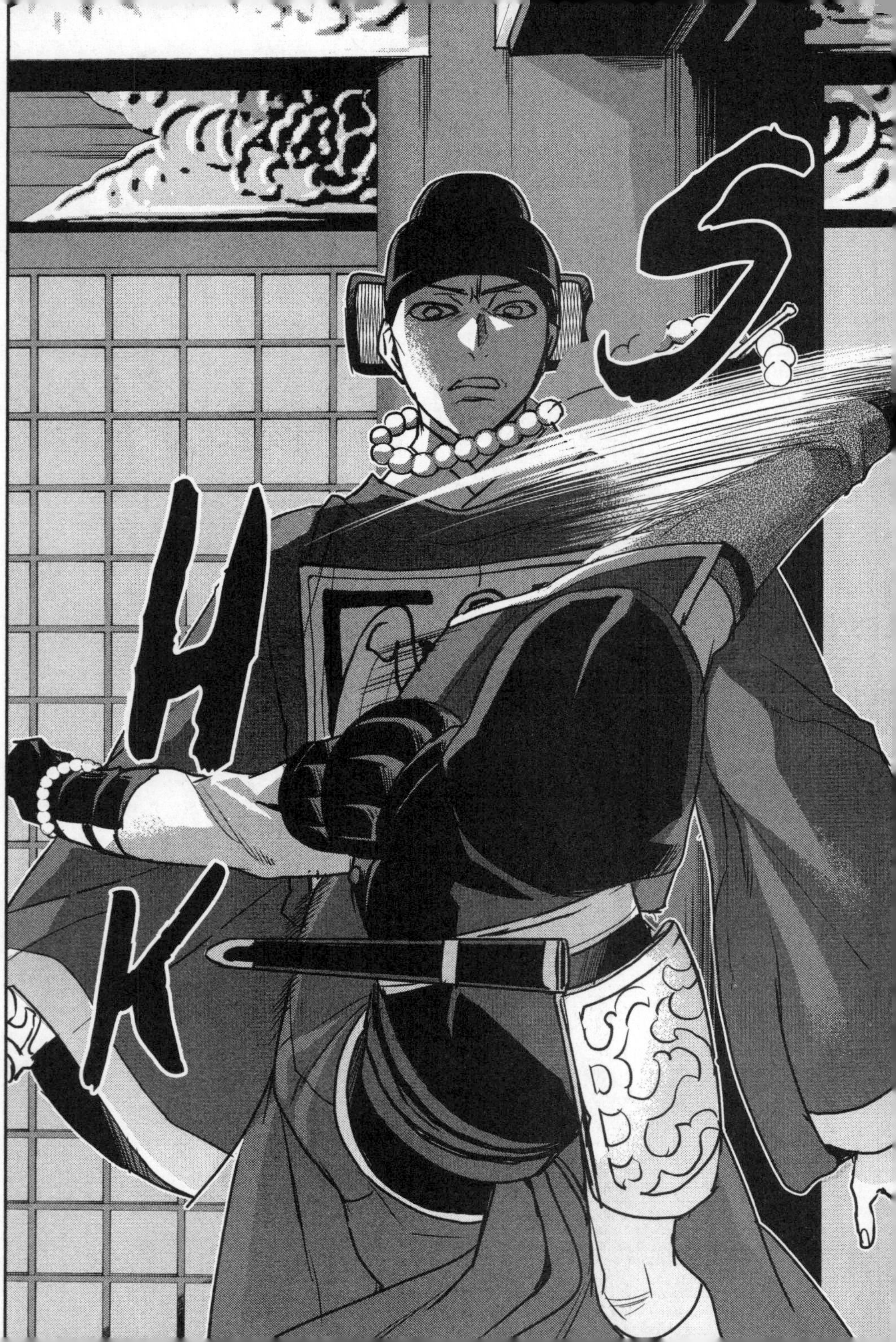
SHK

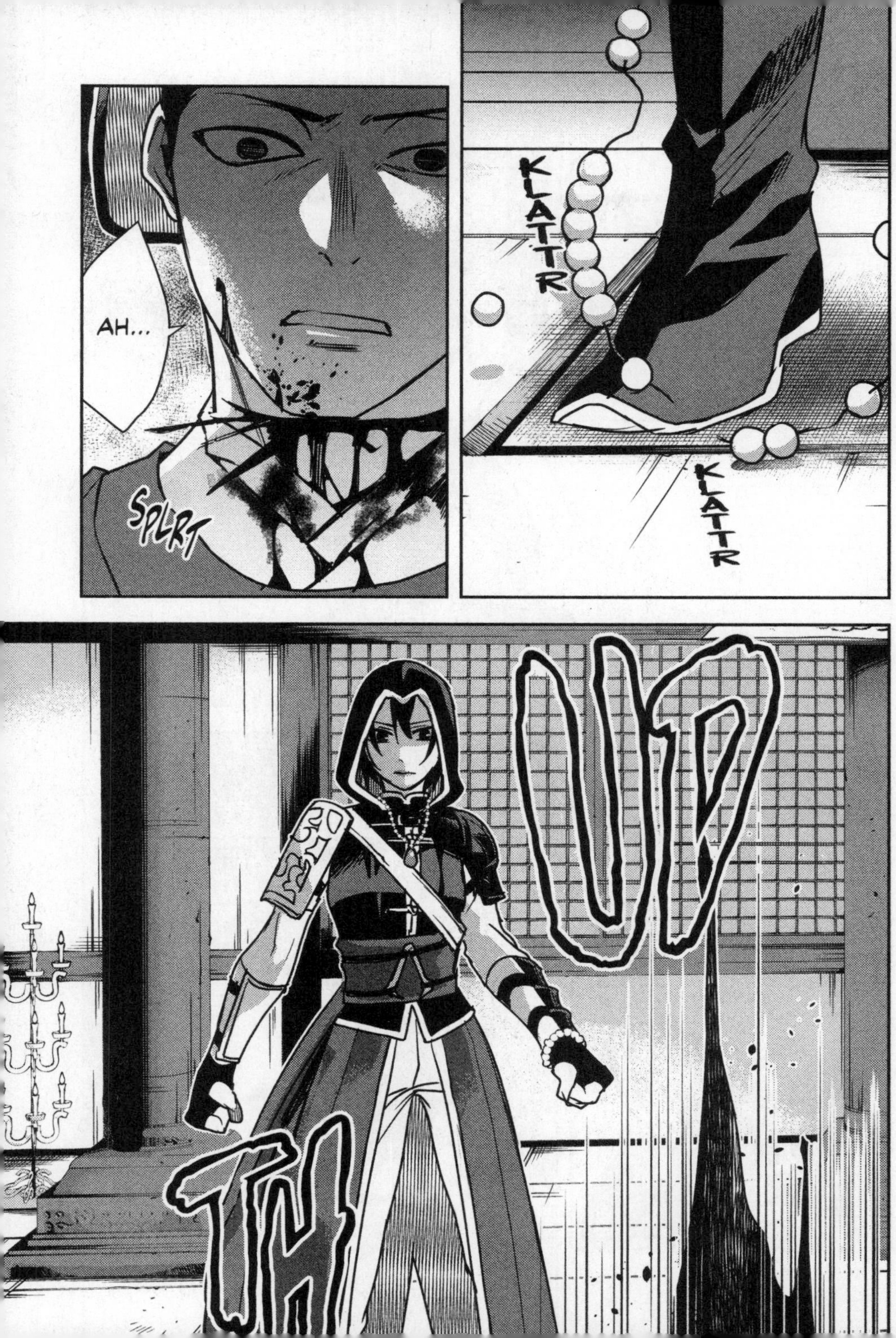
KLATTR
KLATTR
AH...
SPLRT
THUD

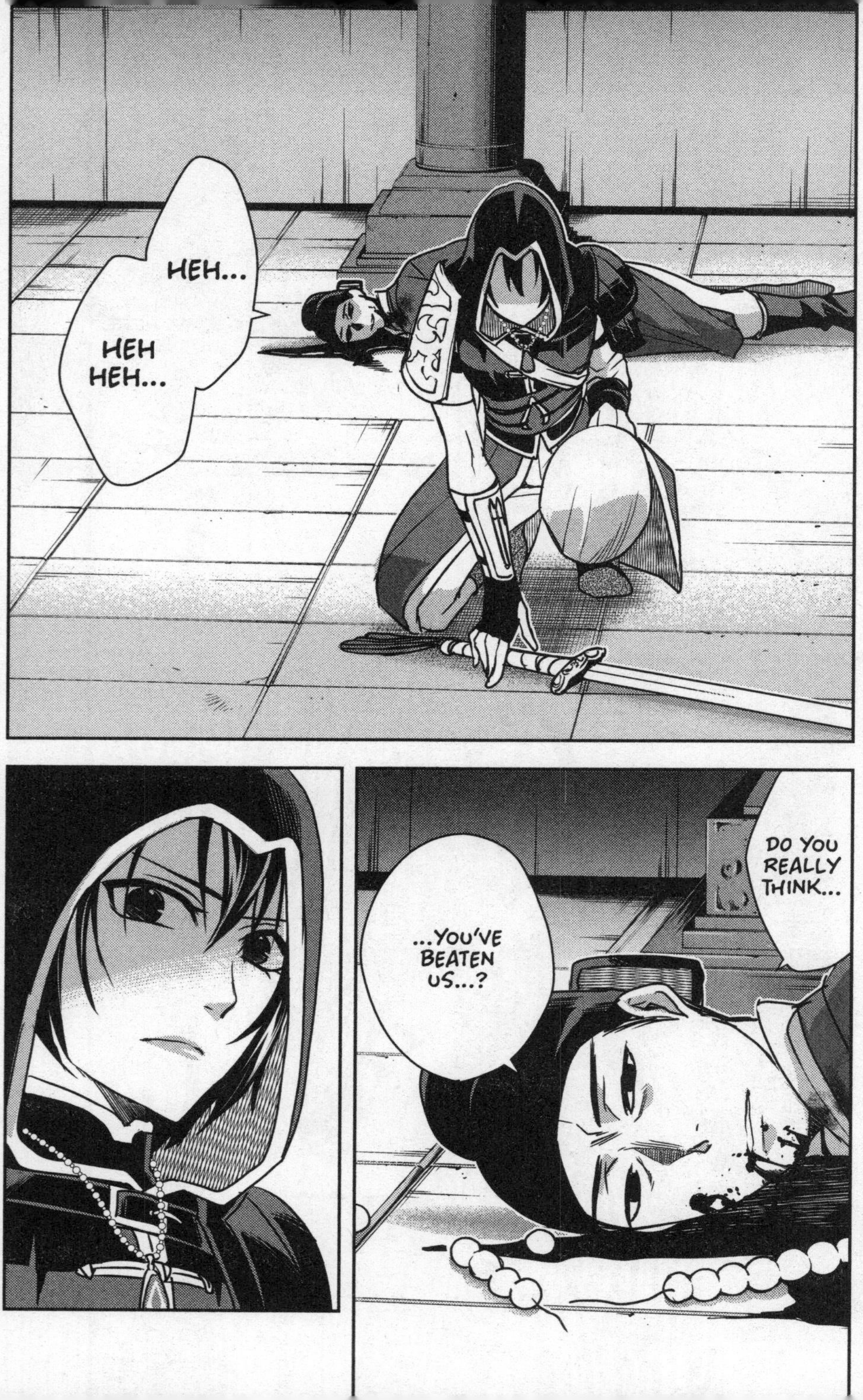
HEH...
HEH HEH...
DO YOU REALLY THINK...
...YOU'VE BEATEN US...?

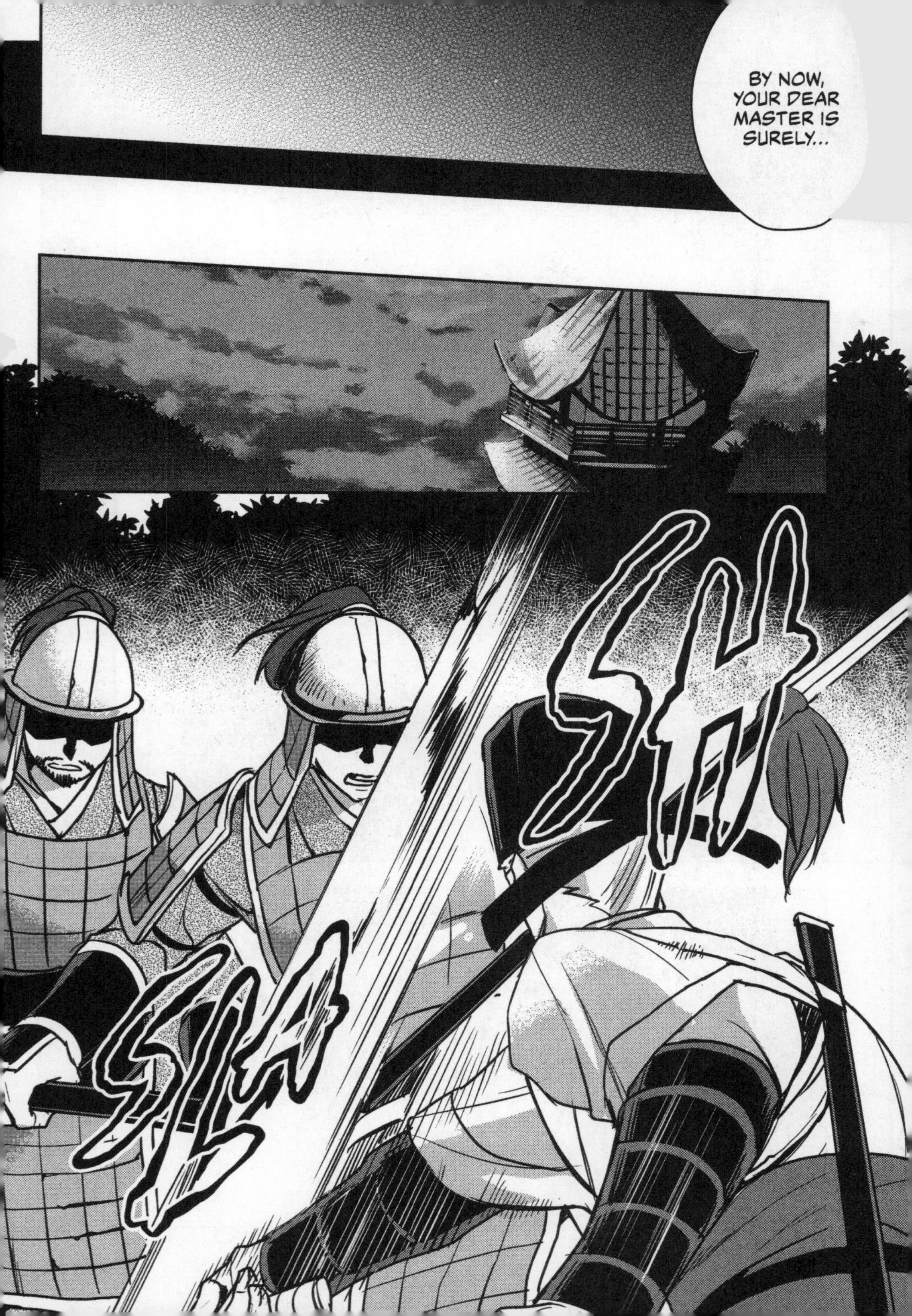
BY NOW, YOUR DEAR MASTER IS SURELY...
SHH
SHA

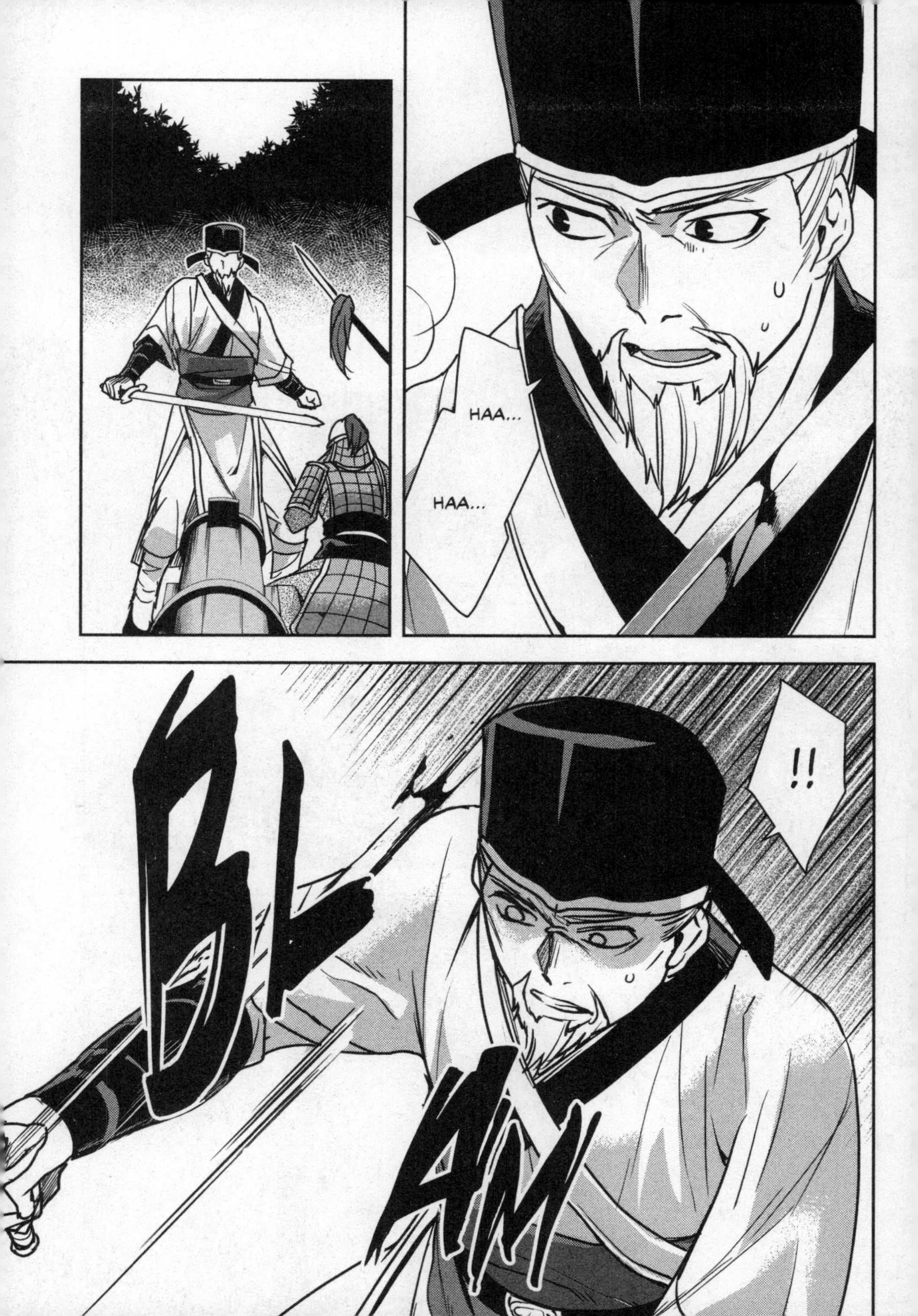
HAA...
HAA...
!!
BLAM

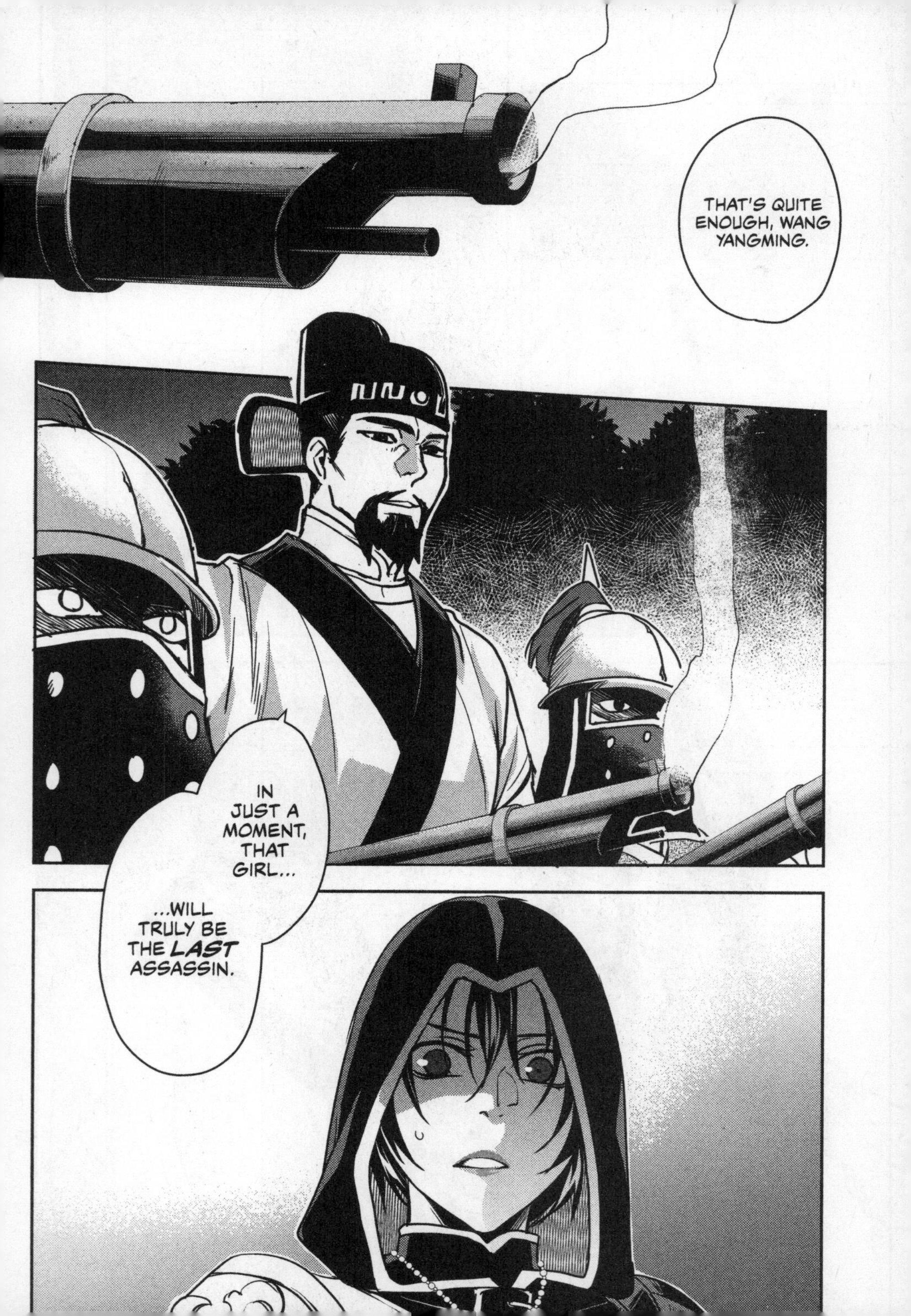
THAT'S QUITE ENOUGH, WANG YANGMING.
IN JUST A MOMENT, THAT GIRL...
...WILL TRULY BE THE LAST ASSASSIN.

Chapter 10: Funeral Pyre

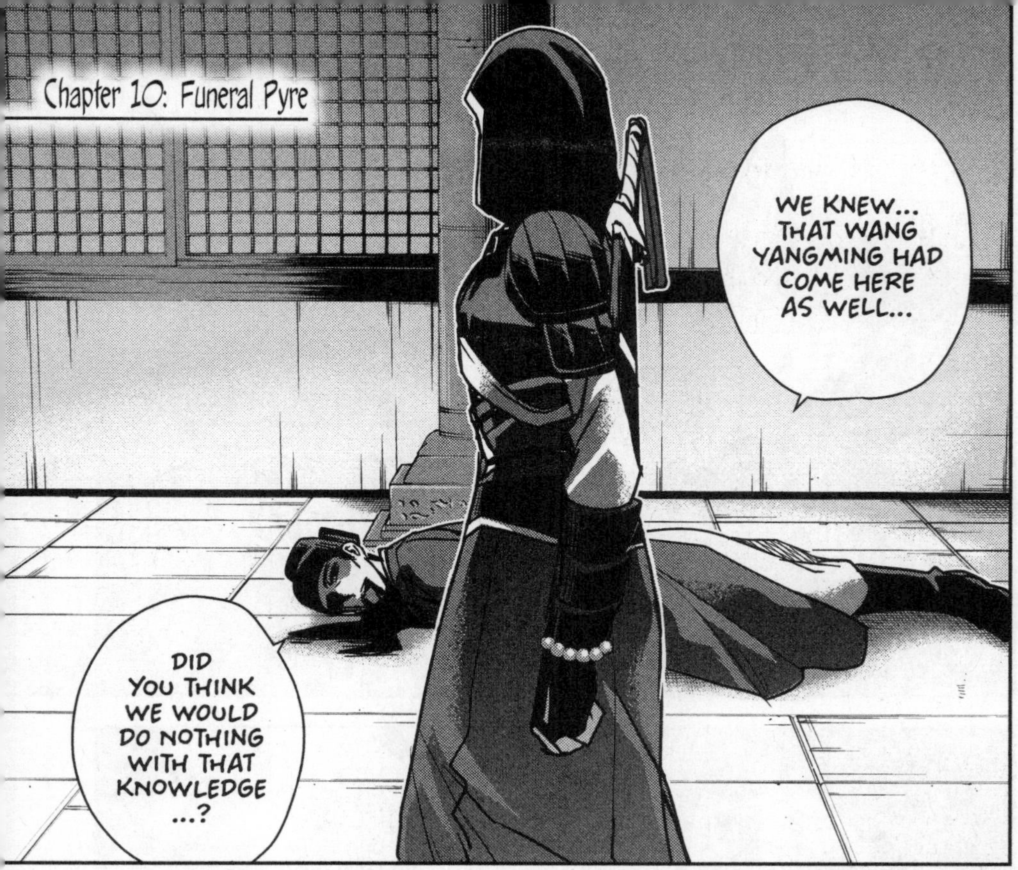
WE KNEW... THAT WANG YANGMING HAD COME HERE AS WELL...
DID YOU THINK WE WOULD DO NOTHING WITH THAT KNOWLEDGE ...?

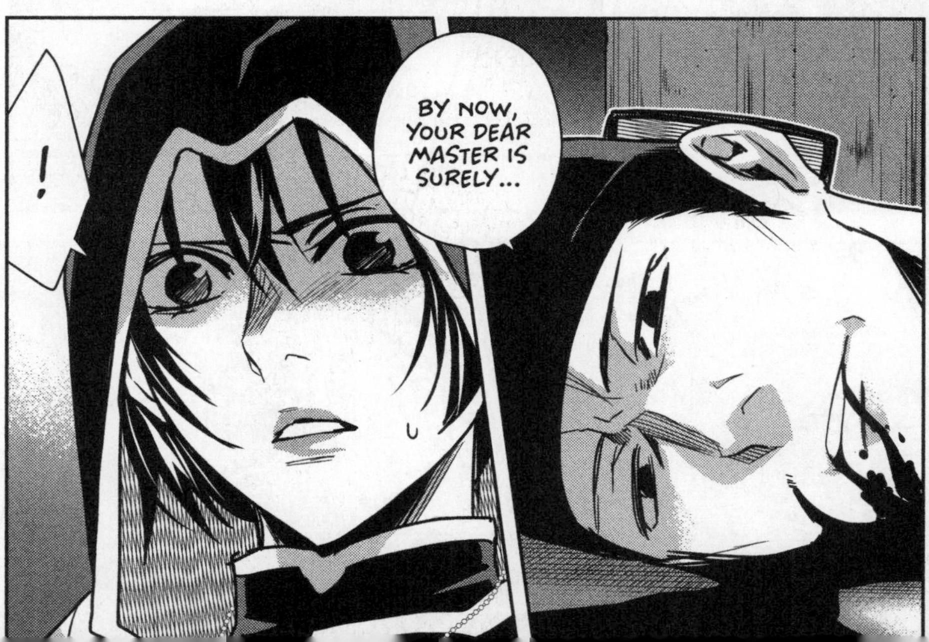
BY NOW, YOUR DEAR MASTER IS SURELY...
!

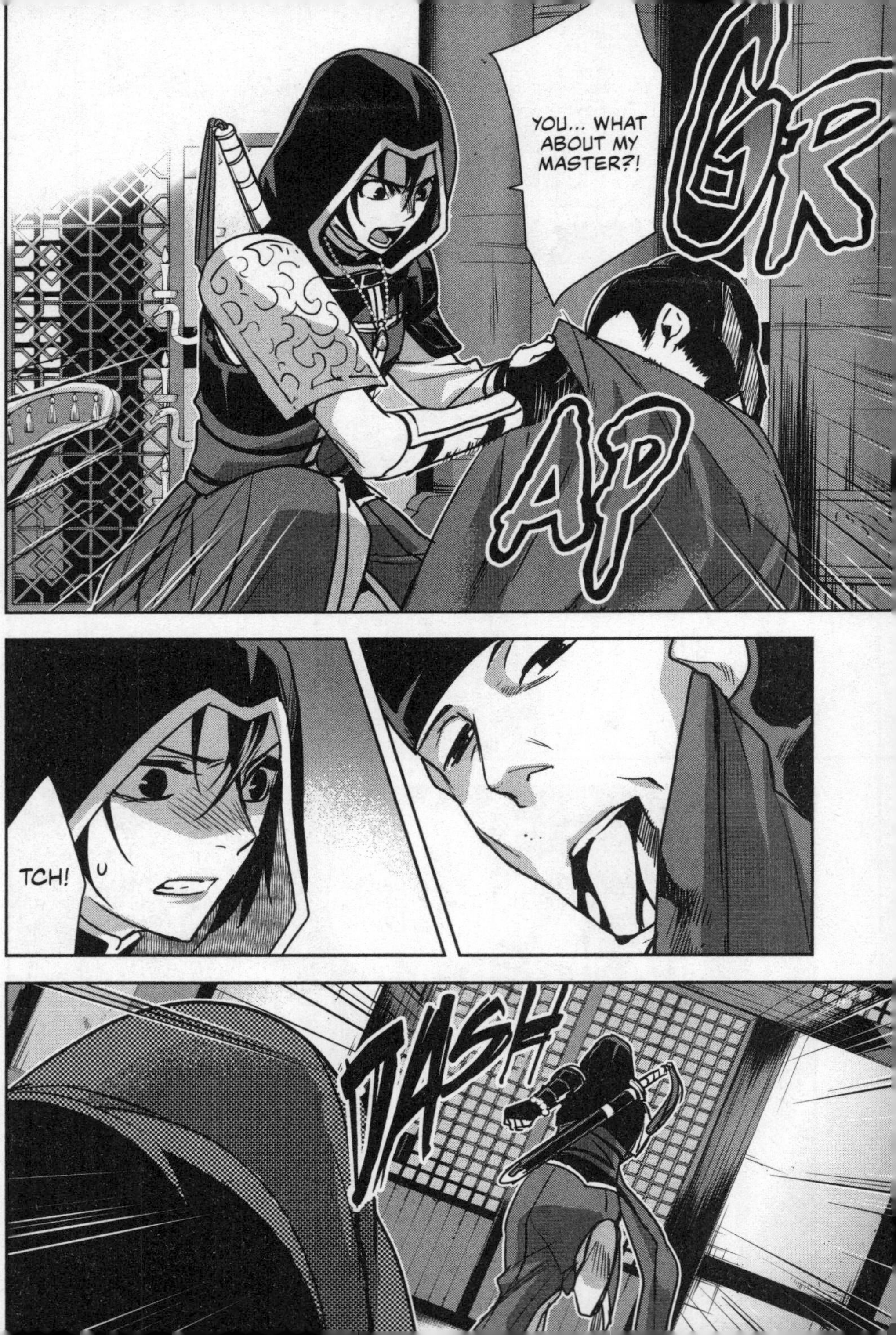
GR
YOU... WHAT ABOUT MY MASTER?!
AP
TCH!
DASH

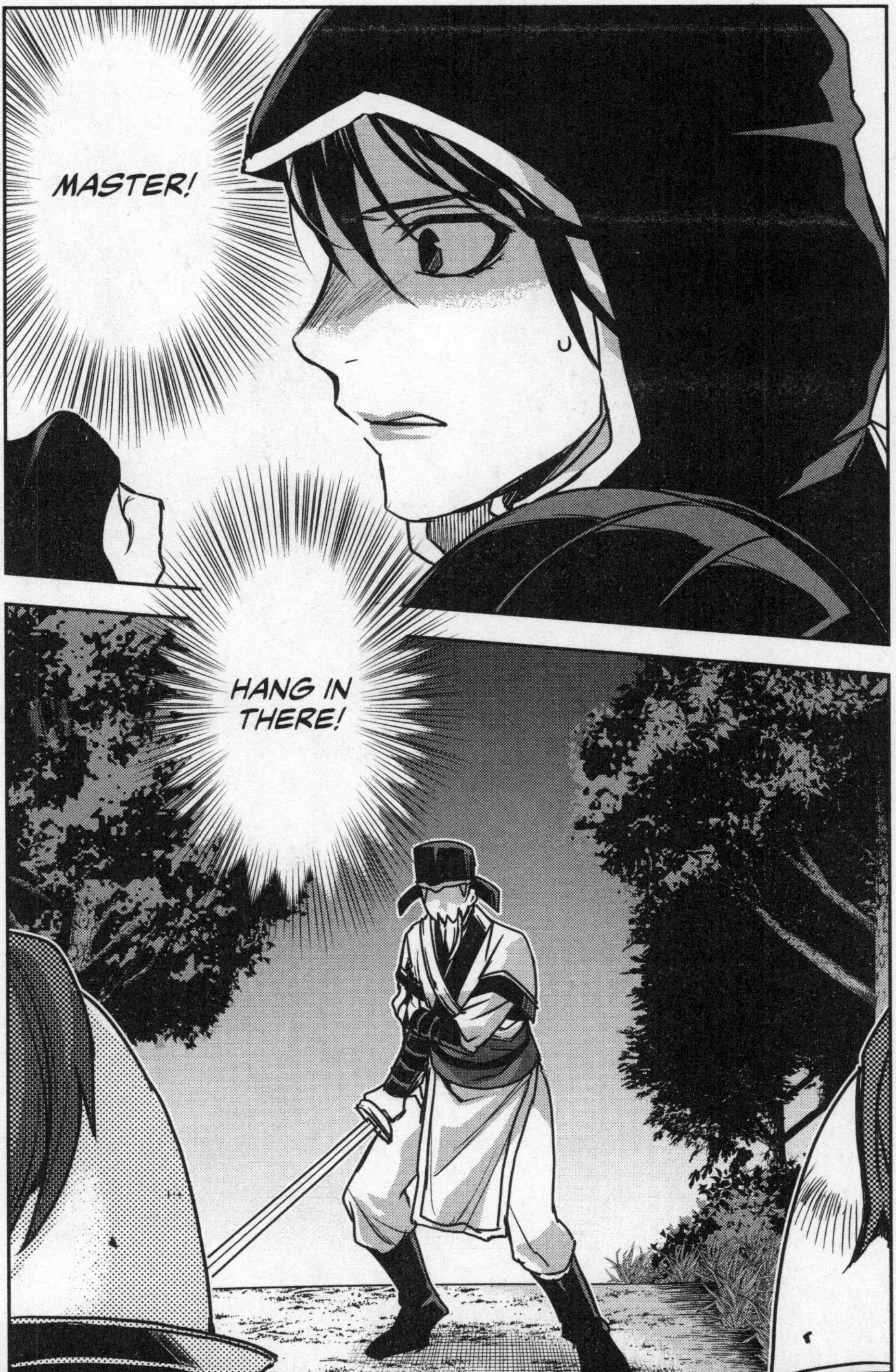
MASTER!
HANG IN
THERE!

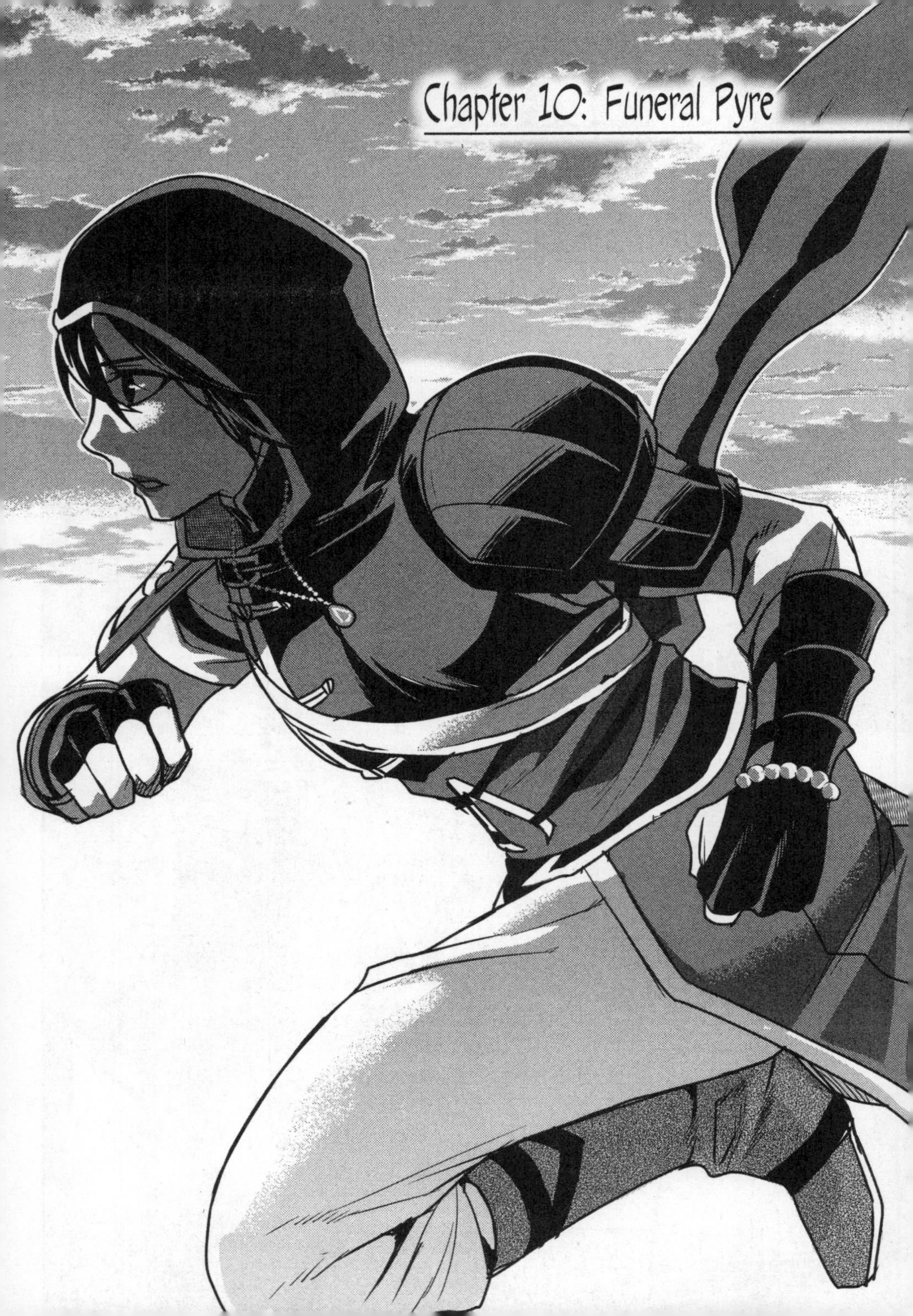
Chapter 10: Funeral Pyre

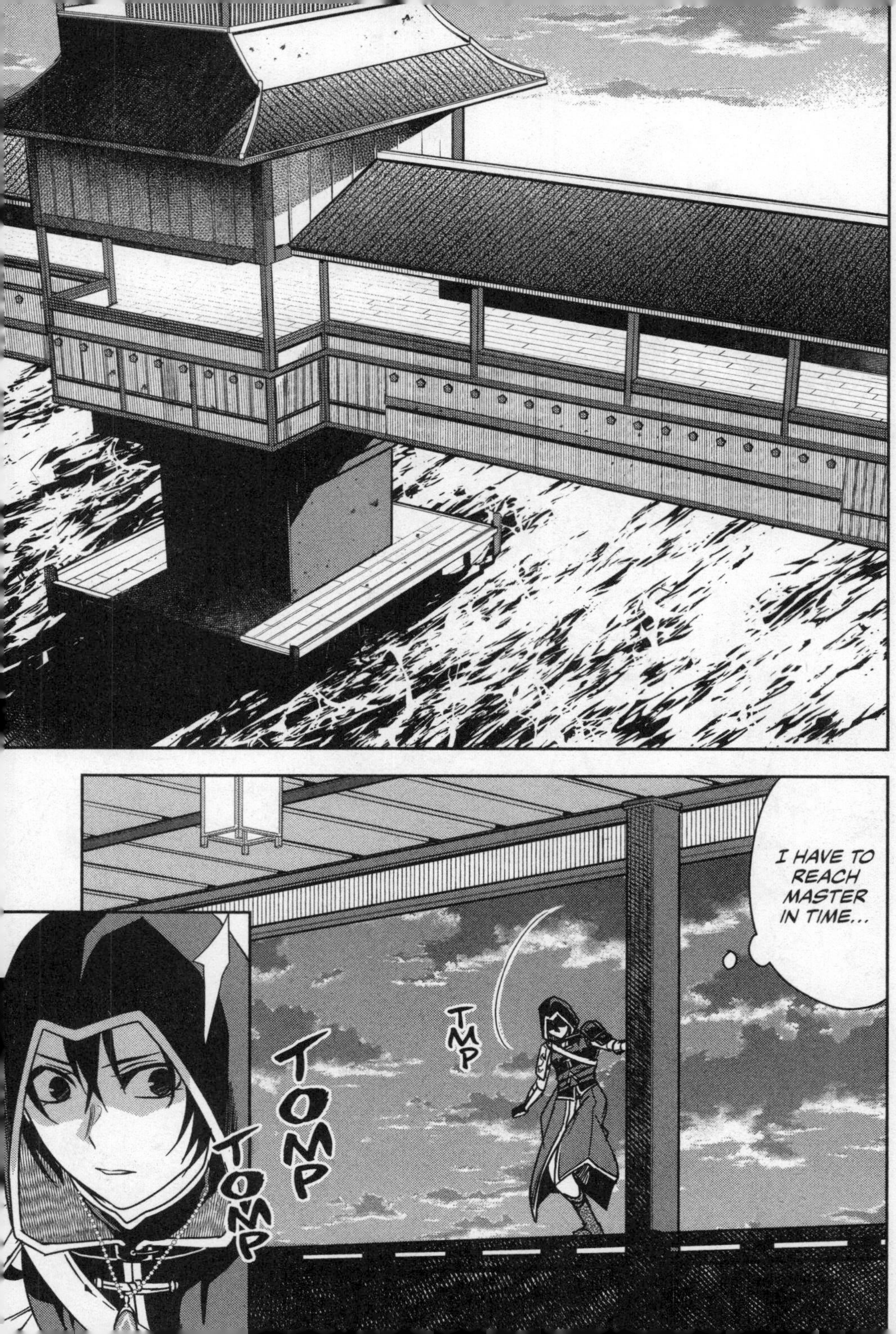
I HAVE TO REACH MASTER IN TIME...
TMP
TOMP
TOMP

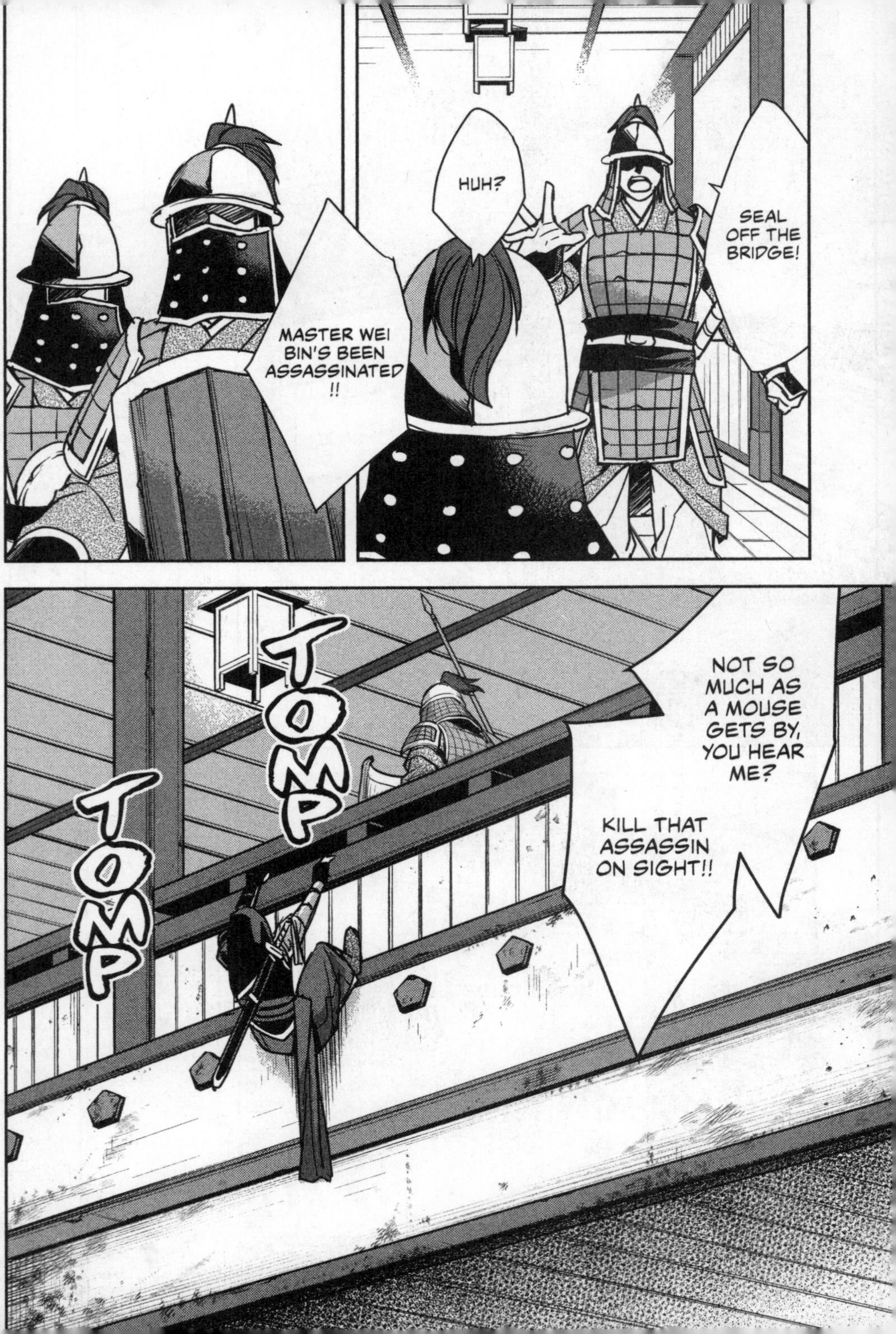
SEAL OFF THE BRIDGE!
HUH?
MASTER WEI BIN'S BEEN ASSASSINATED !!
NOT SO MUCH AS A MOUSE GETS BY, YOU HEAR ME?
KILL THAT ASSASSIN ON SIGHT!!
TOMP
TOMP

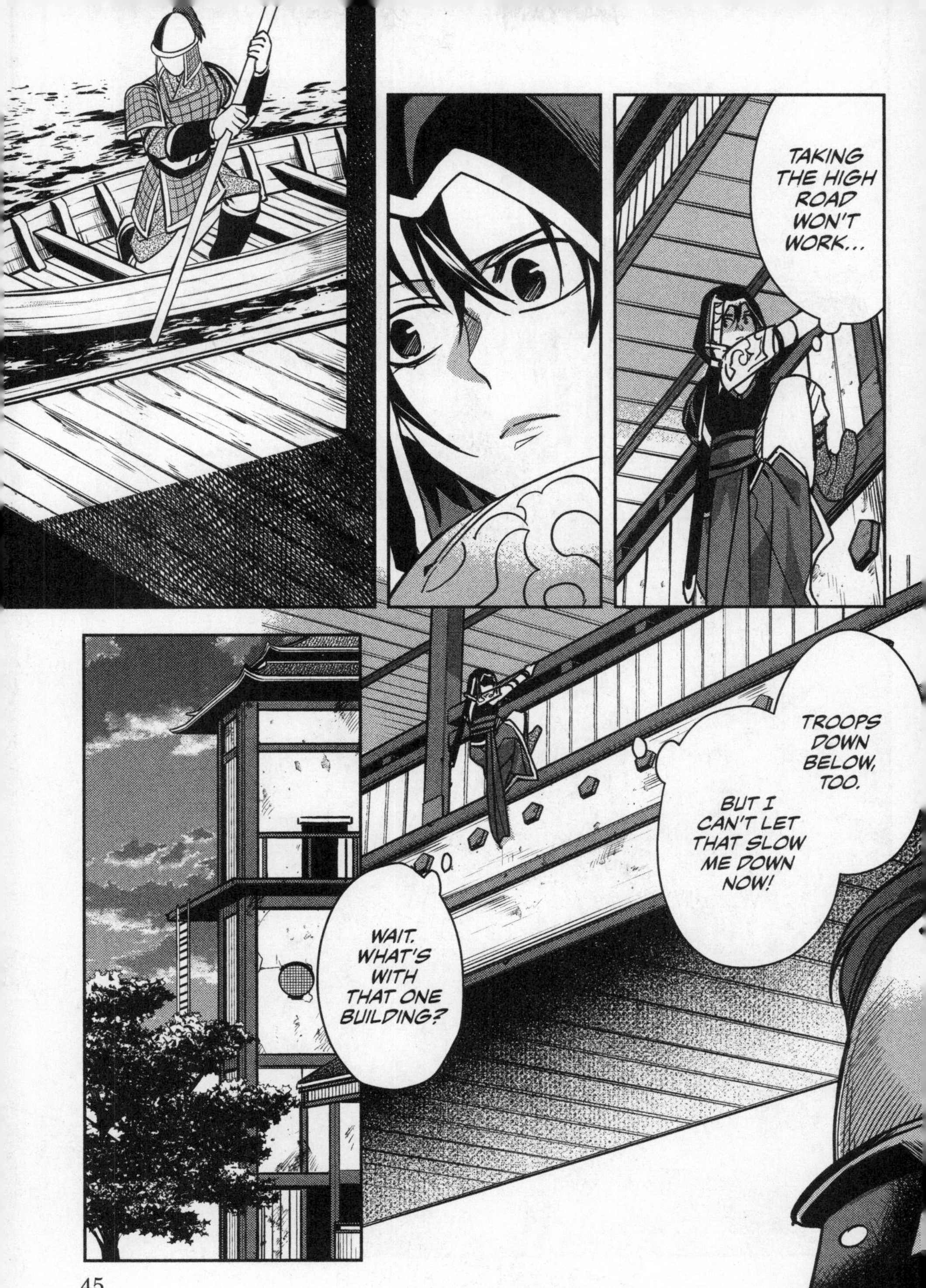
TAKING THE HIGH ROAD WON'T WORK...
TROOPS DOWN BELOW, TOO.
BUT I CAN'T LET THAT SLOW ME DOWN NOW!
WAIT. WHAT'S WITH THAT ONE BUILDING?

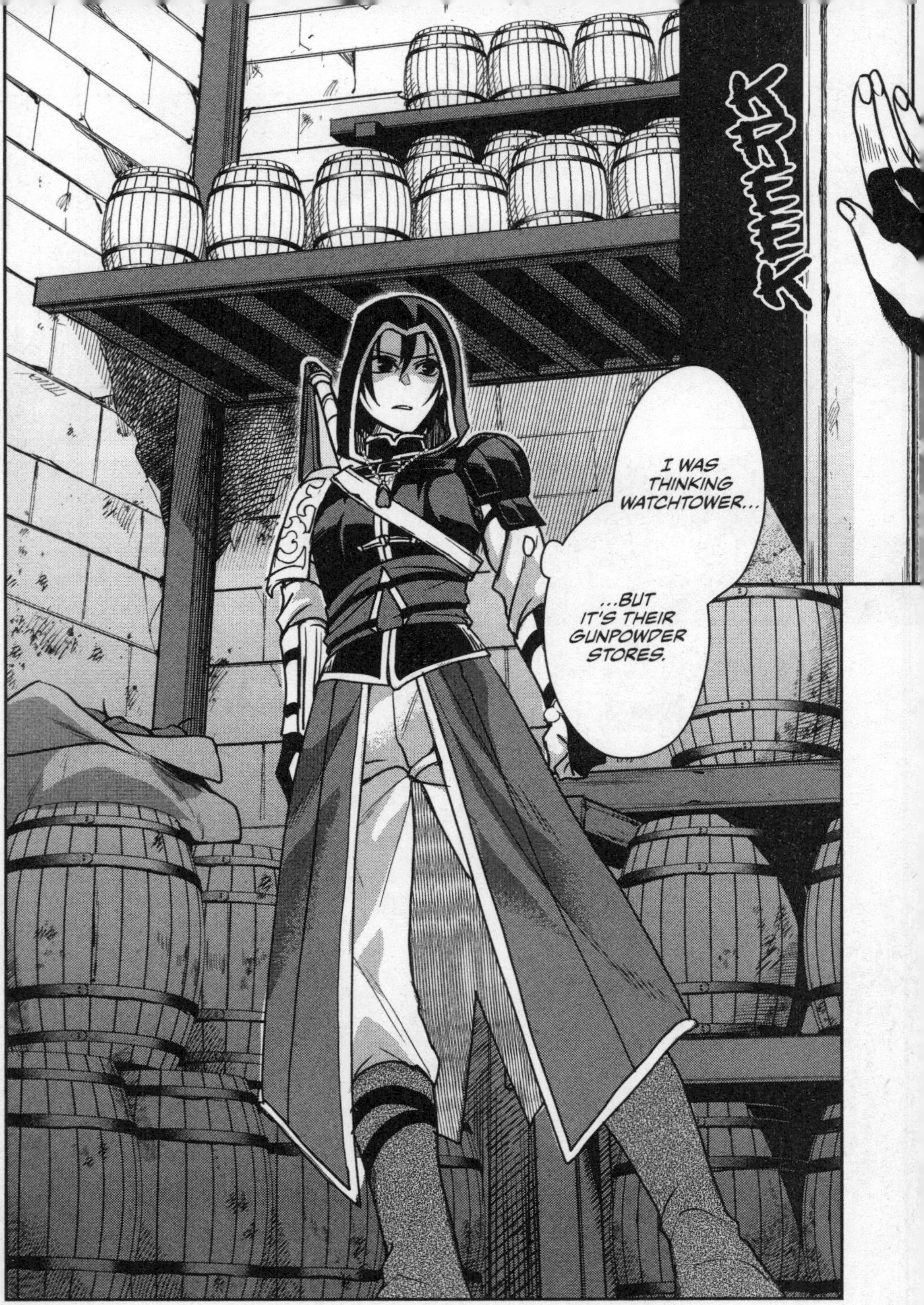
KREEEK
I WAS THINKING WATCHTOWER...
...BUT IT'S THEIR GUNPOWDER STORES.

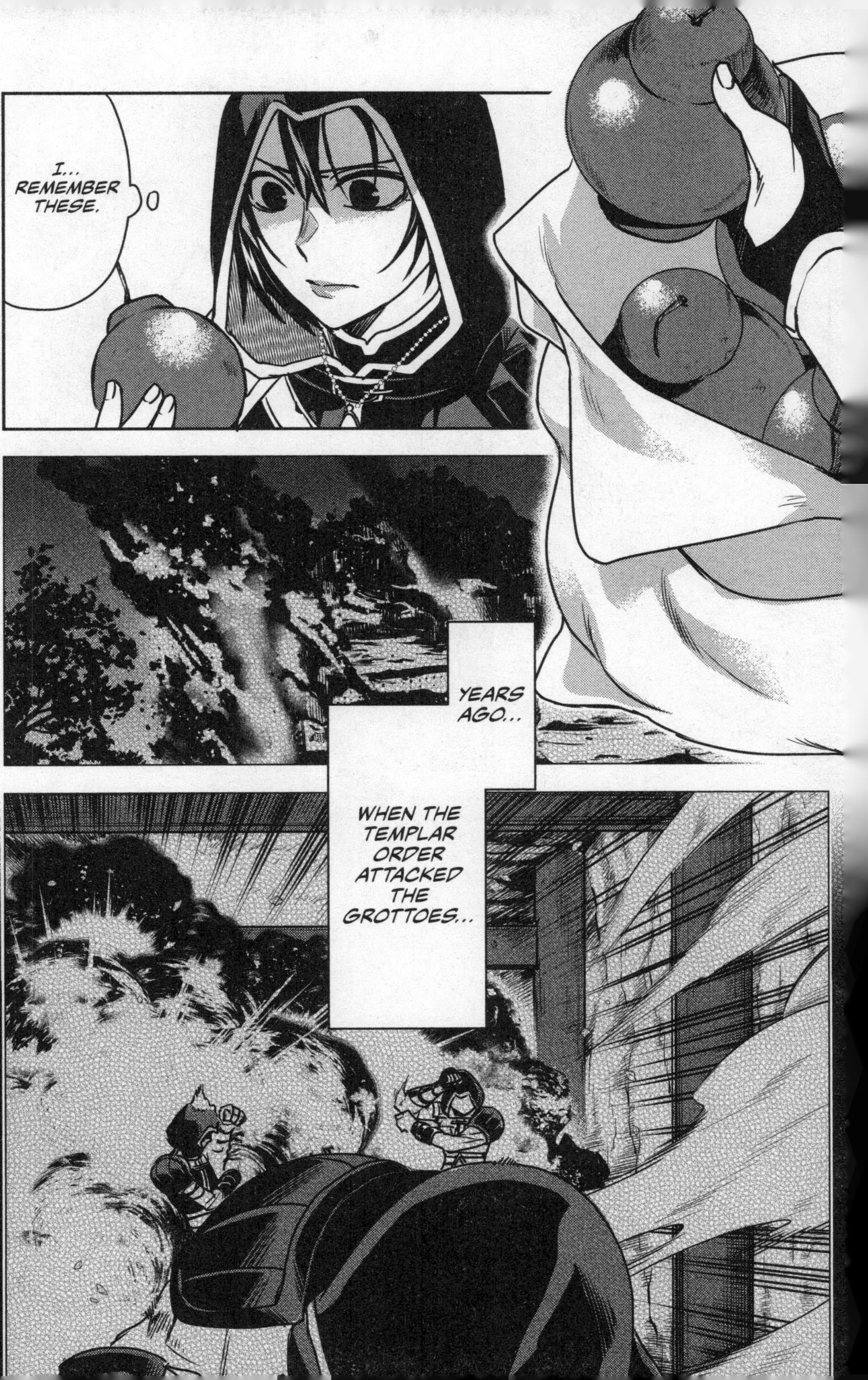
I... REMEMBER THESE.
YEARS AGO...
WHEN THE TEMPLAR ORDER ATTACKED THE GROTTOES...

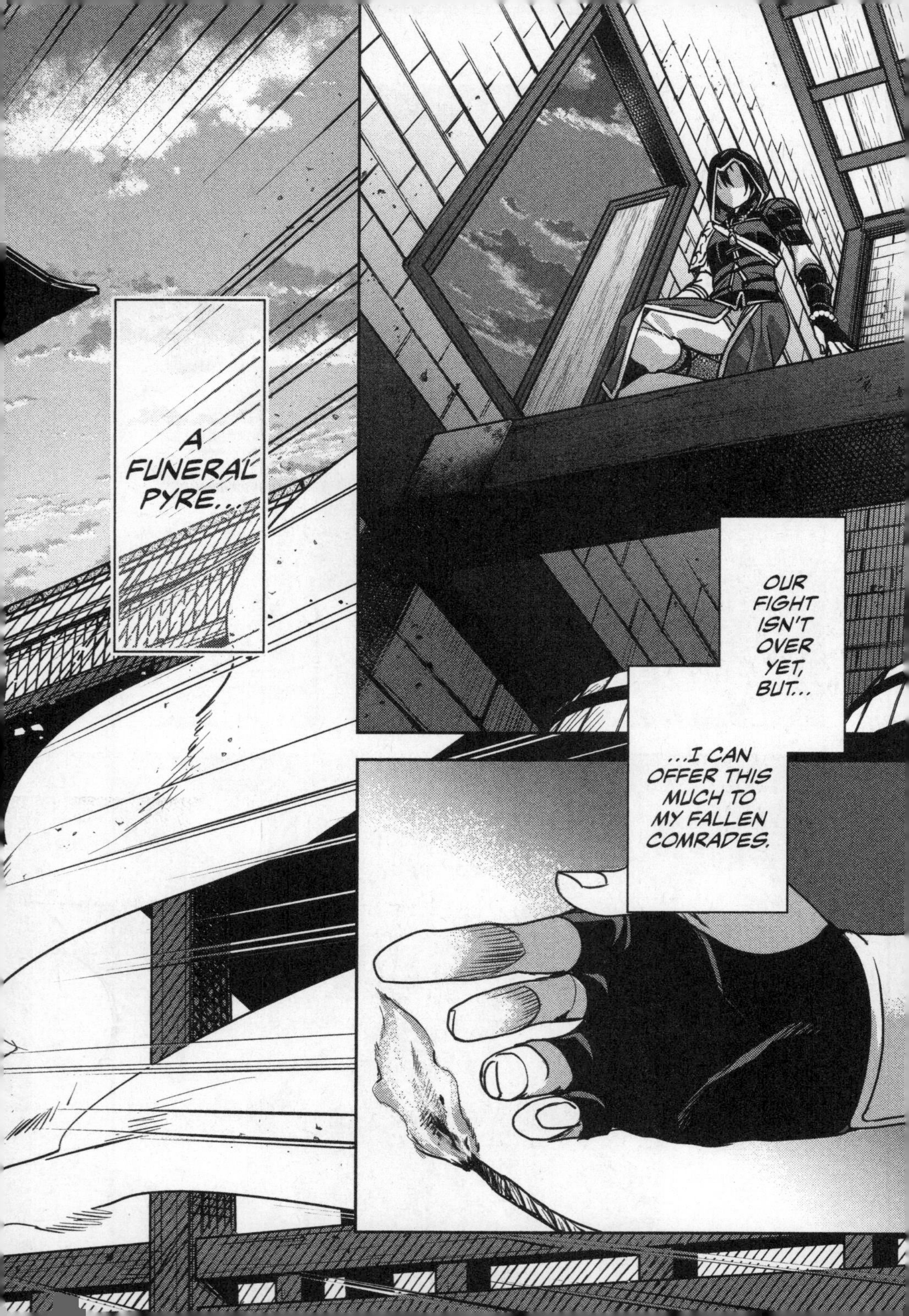
OUR FIGHT ISN'T OVER YET, BUT...
...I CAN OFFER THIS MUCH TO MY FALLEN COMRADES.
A FUNERAL PYRE...

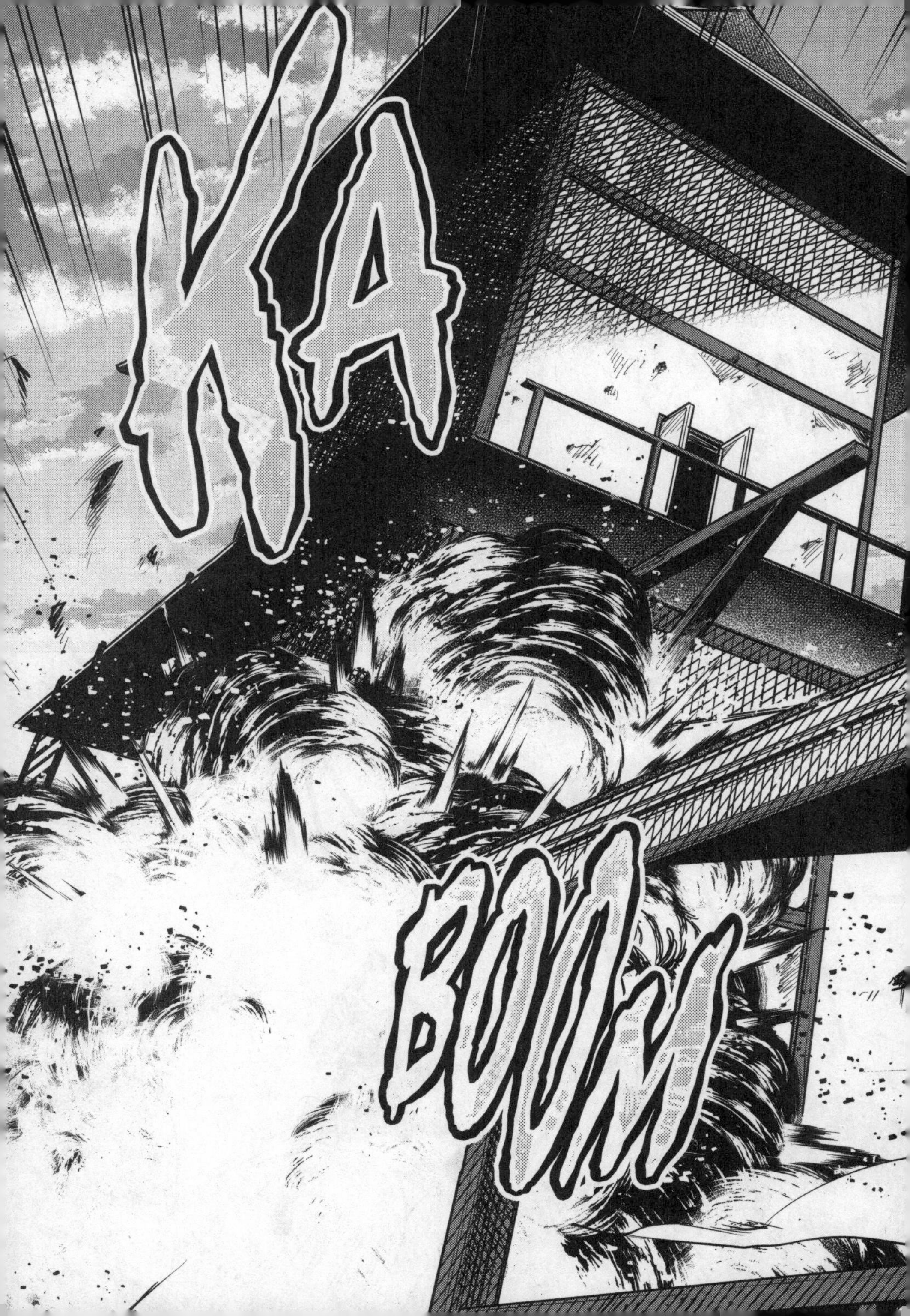
KA
BOOM

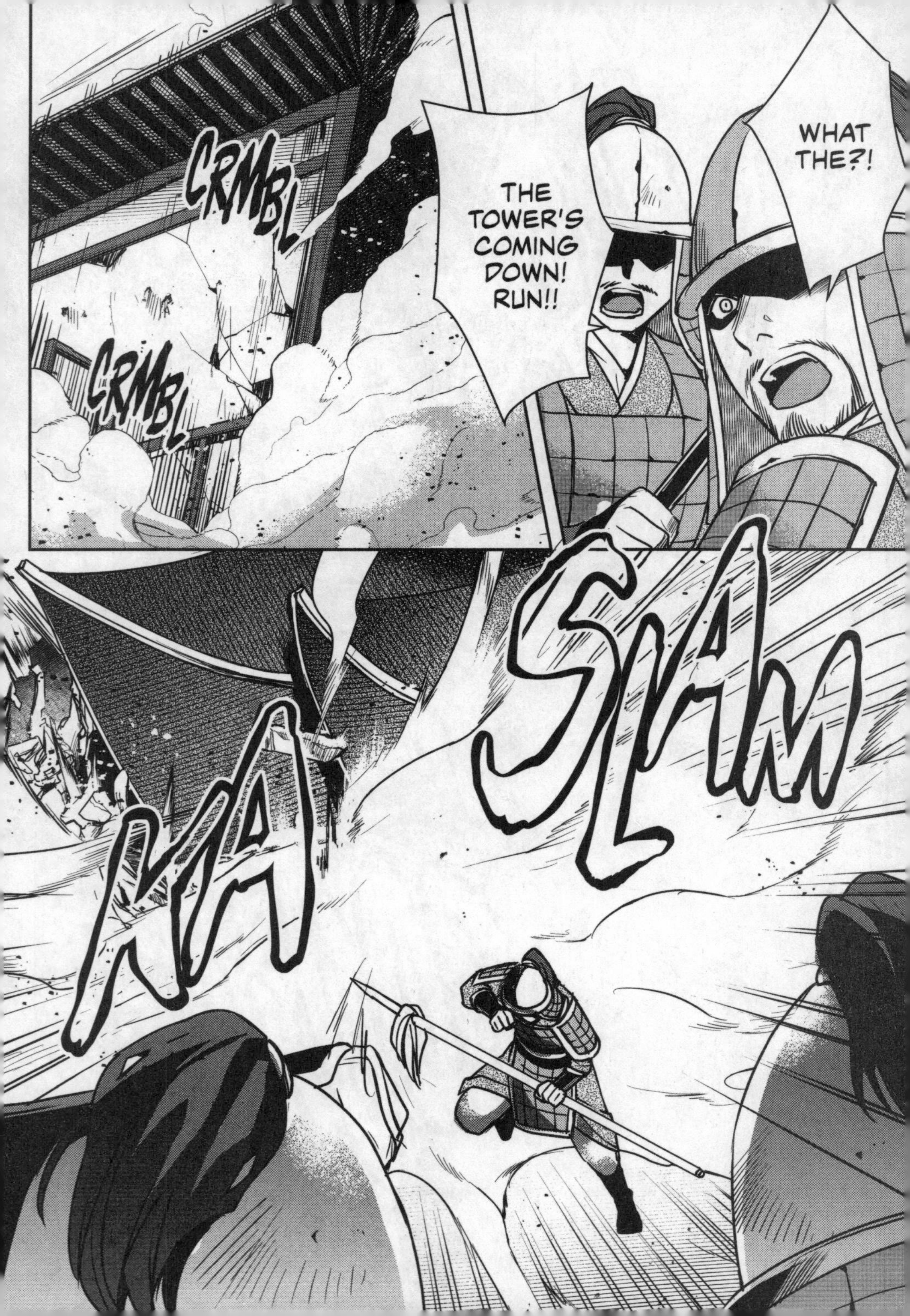
WHAT THE?!
THE TOWER'S COMING DOWN! RUN!!
CRMBL
CRMBL
SLAM

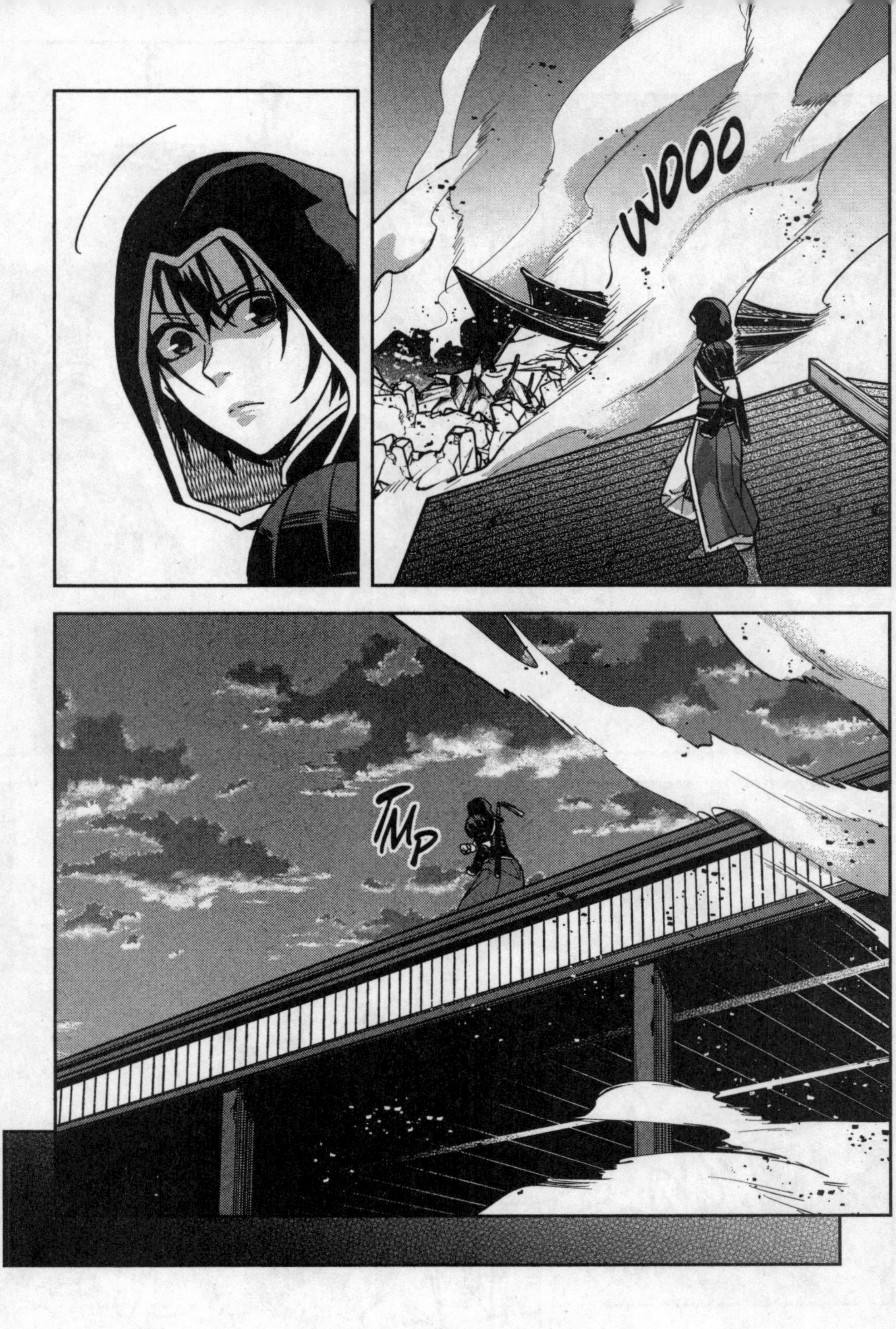
WOOO
TMP

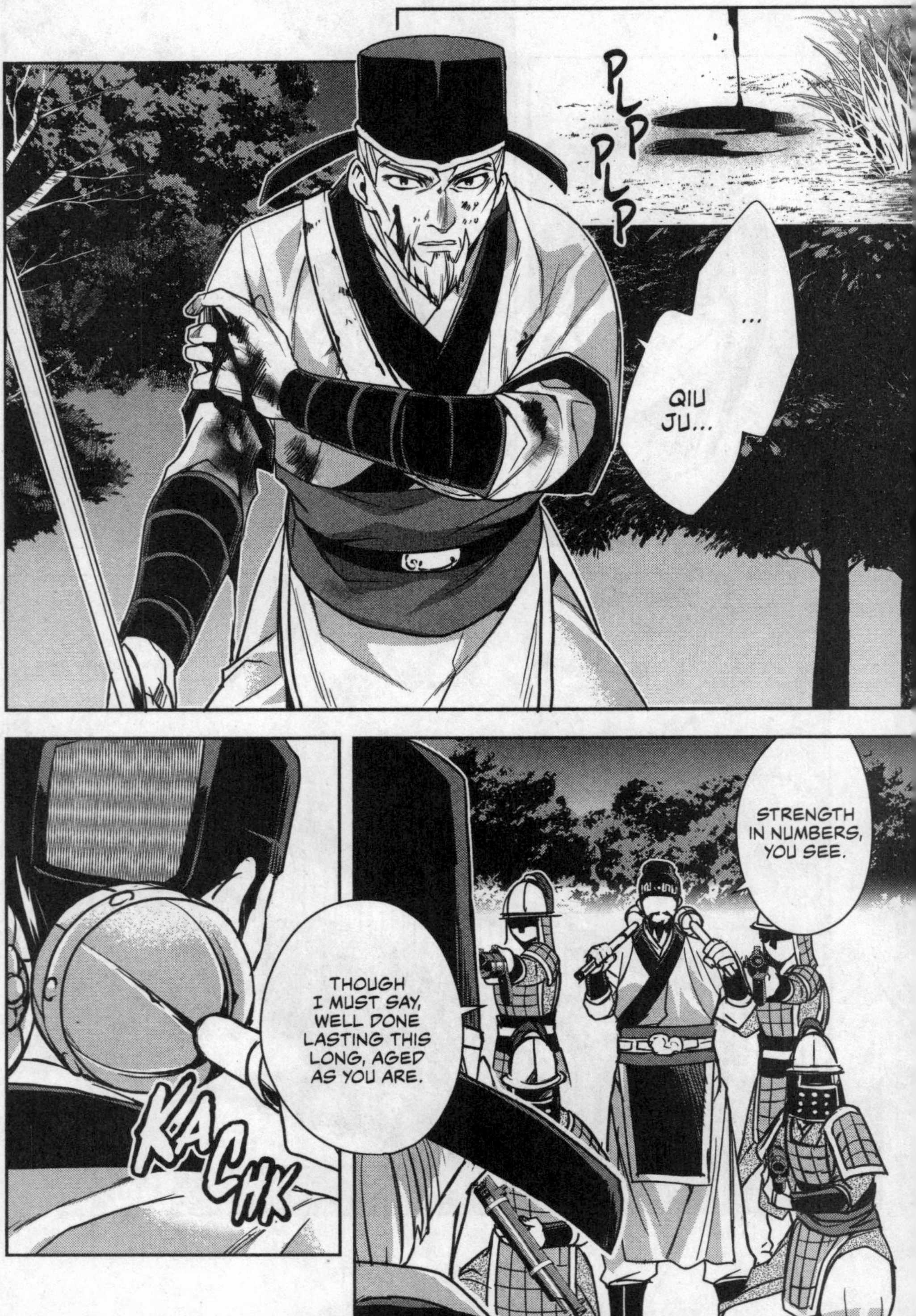
PLP PLP PLP
...
QIU JU...
STRENGTH IN NUMBERS, YOU SEE.
THOUGH I MUST SAY, WELL DONE LASTING THIS LONG, AGED AS YOU ARE.
KACHK

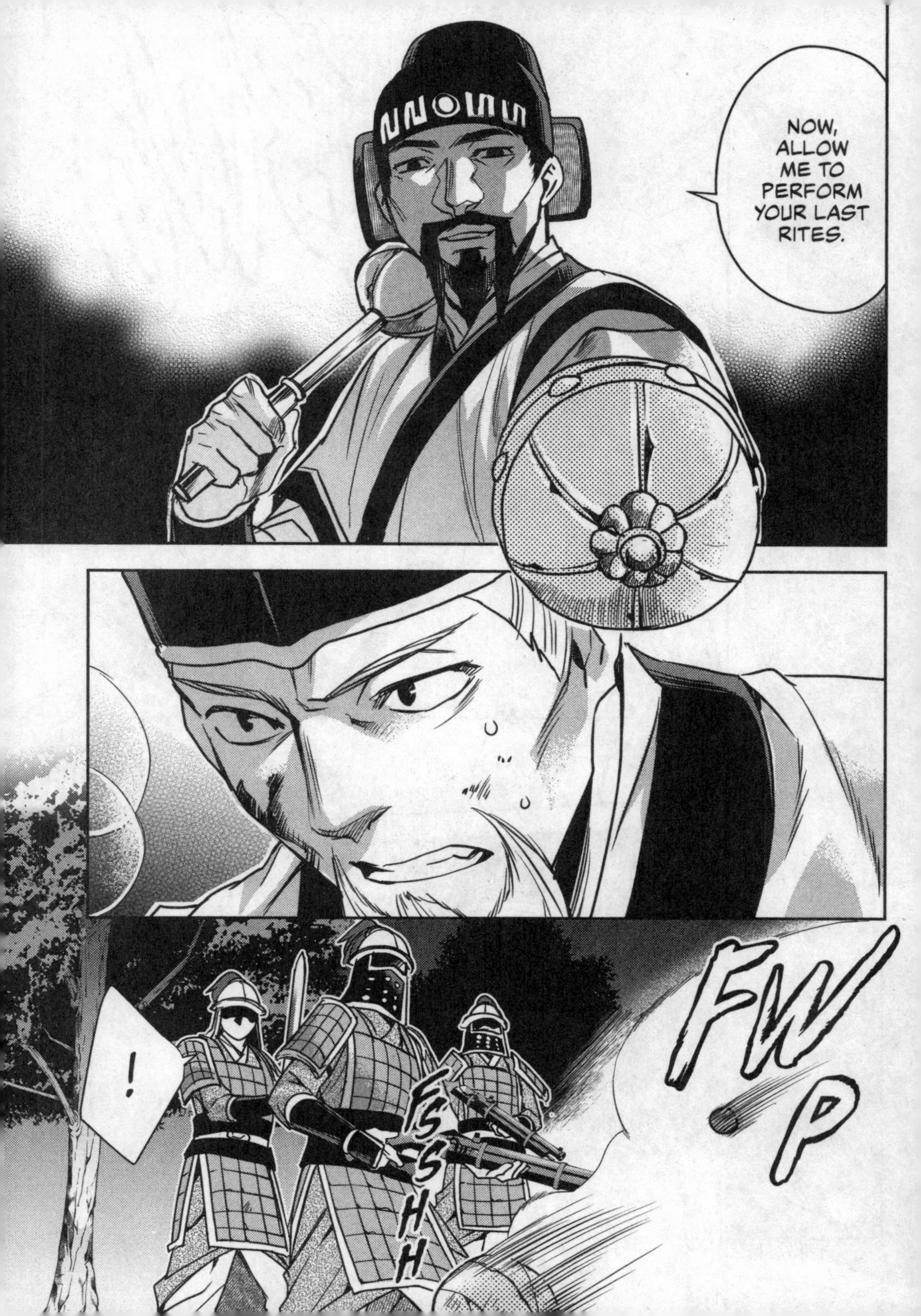
NOW, ALLOW ME TO PERFORM YOUR LAST RITES.
FWP
!
FSSHH

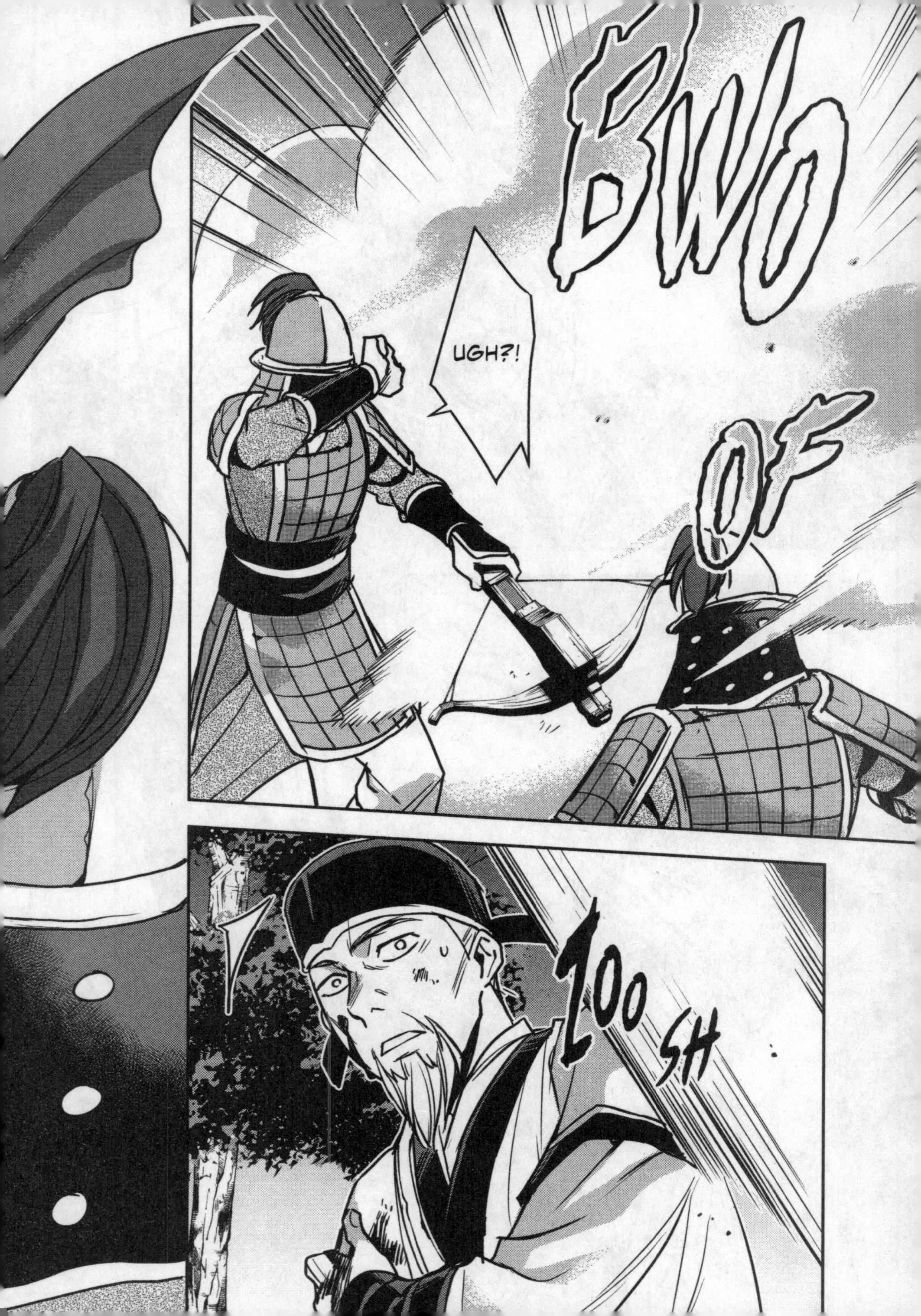
BWO
UGH?!
OF
ZOO SH

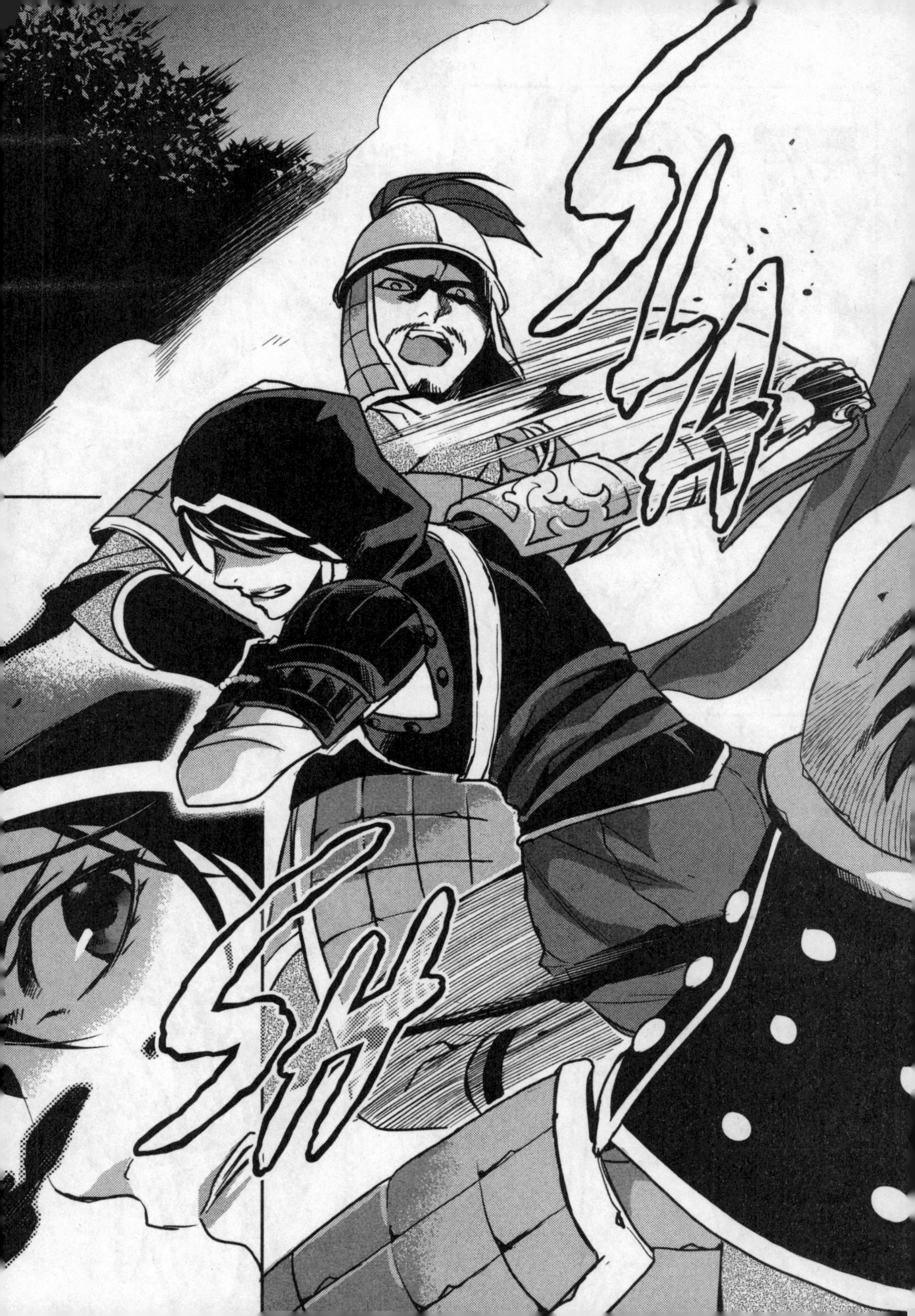

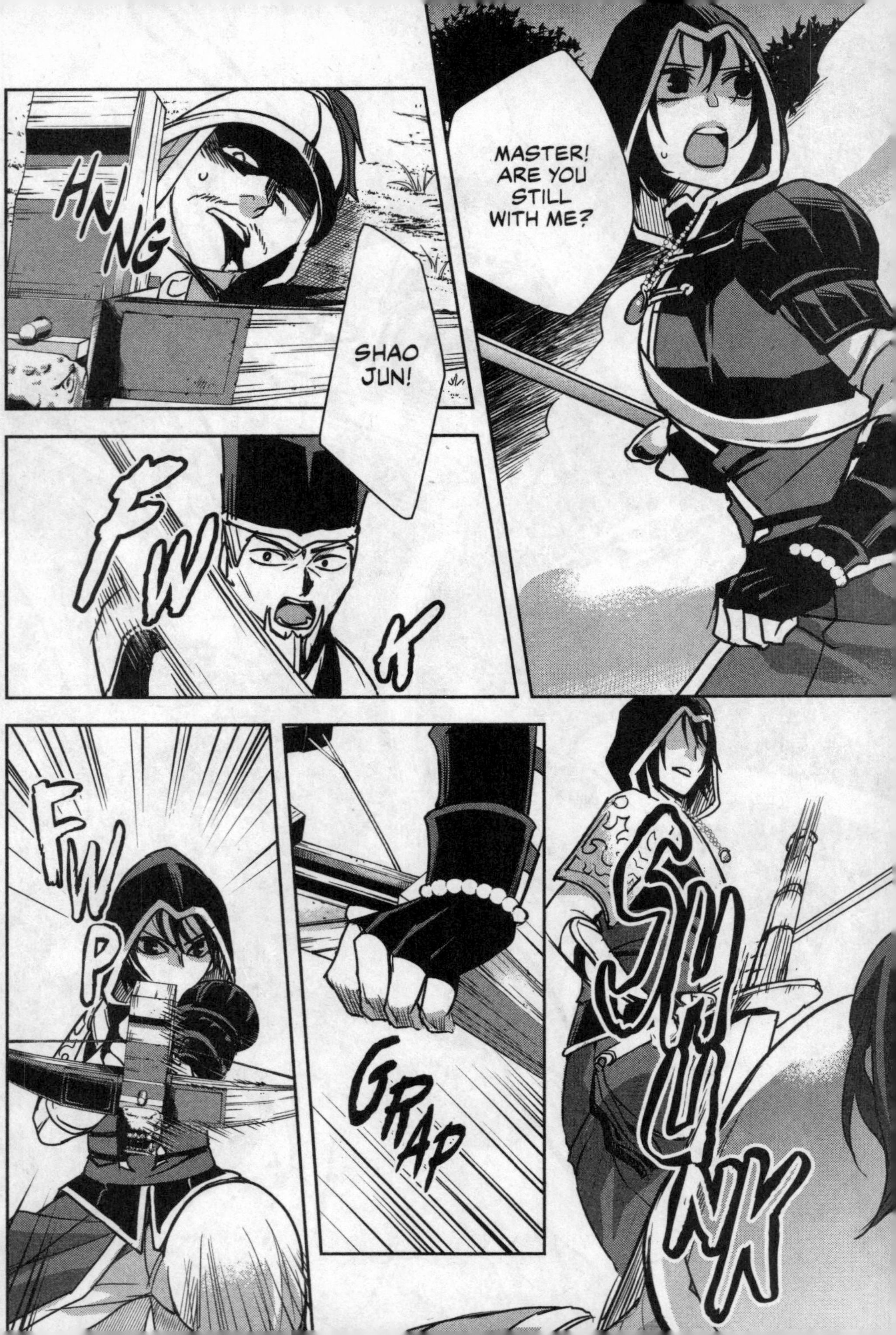
MASTER! ARE YOU STILL WITH ME?
HNNG
SHAO JUN!
FWK
SHUNK
GRAP
FWP

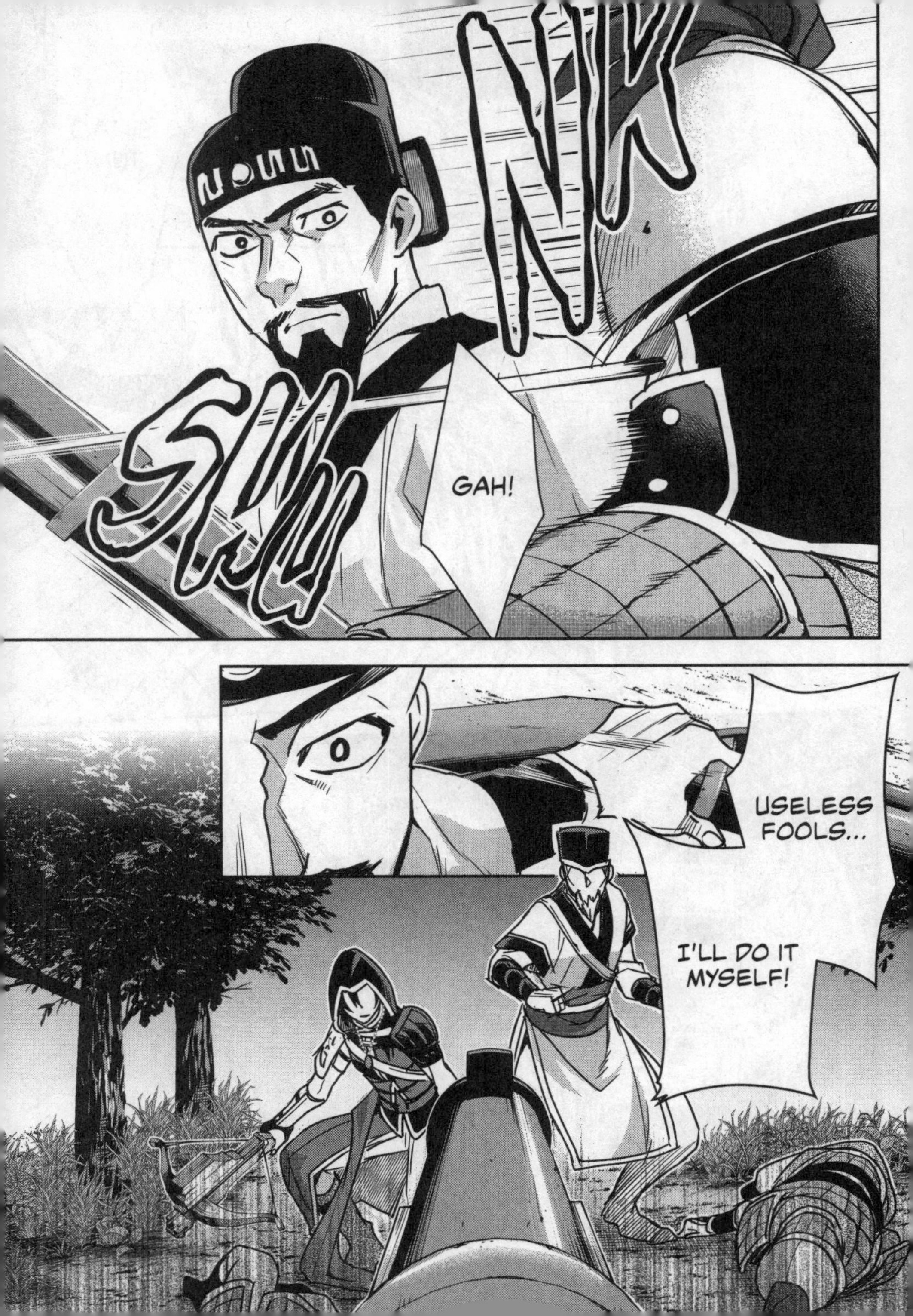
SHNK
GAH!
USELESS FOOLS...
I'LL DO IT MYSELF!

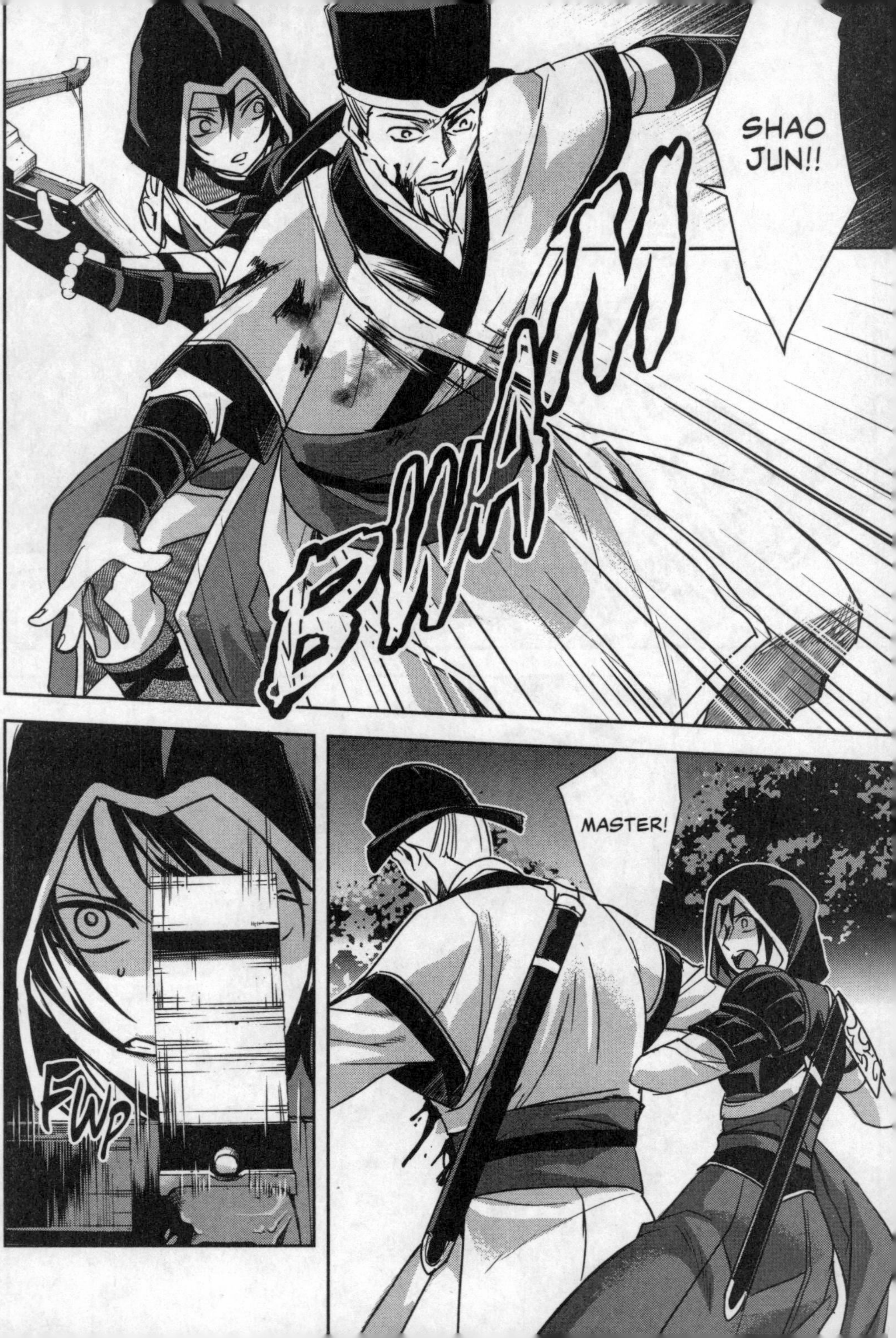
SHAO JUN!!
BWAM
MASTER!
FWP

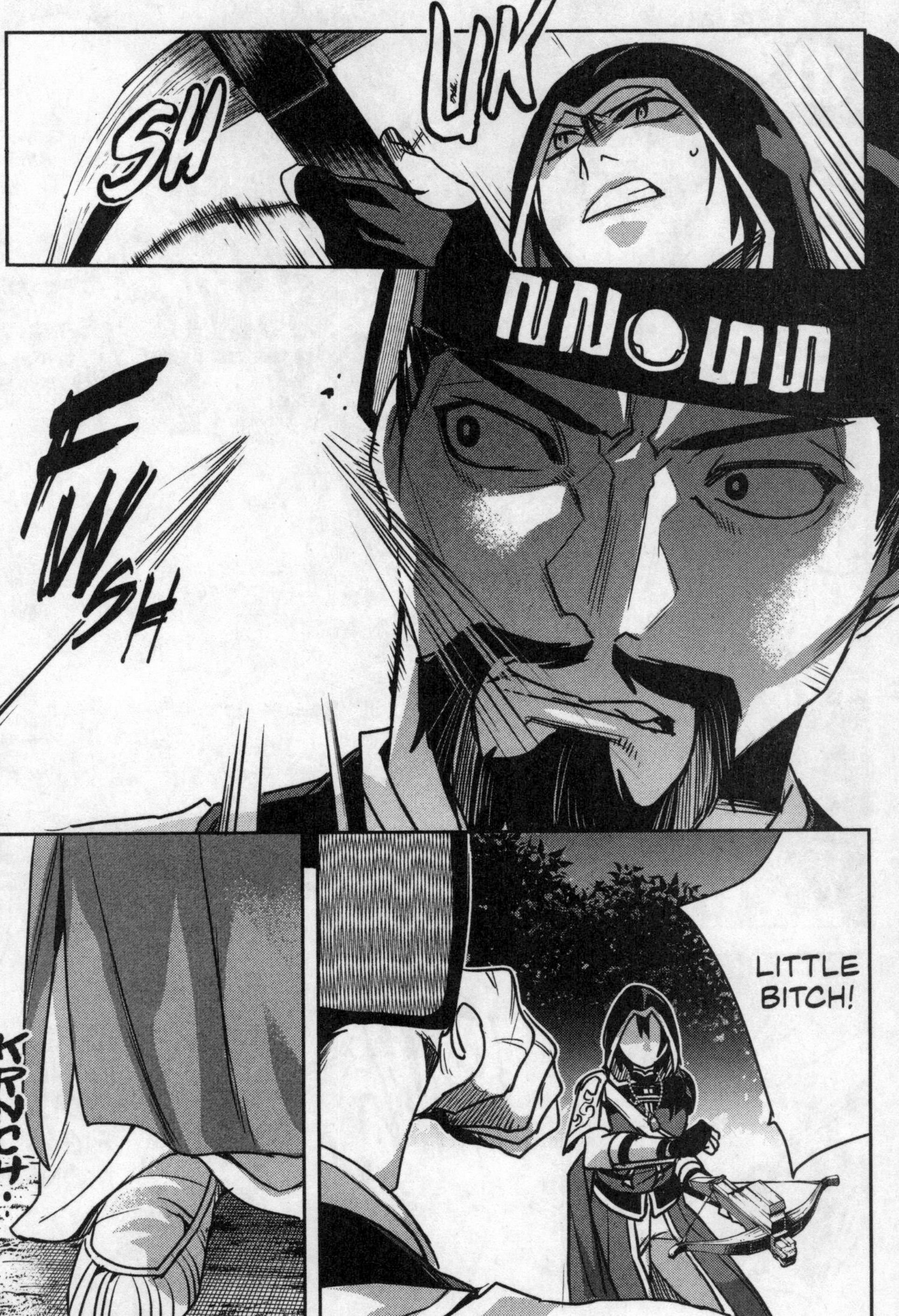
SH UK
FWSH
LITTLE BITCH!
KRNCH!

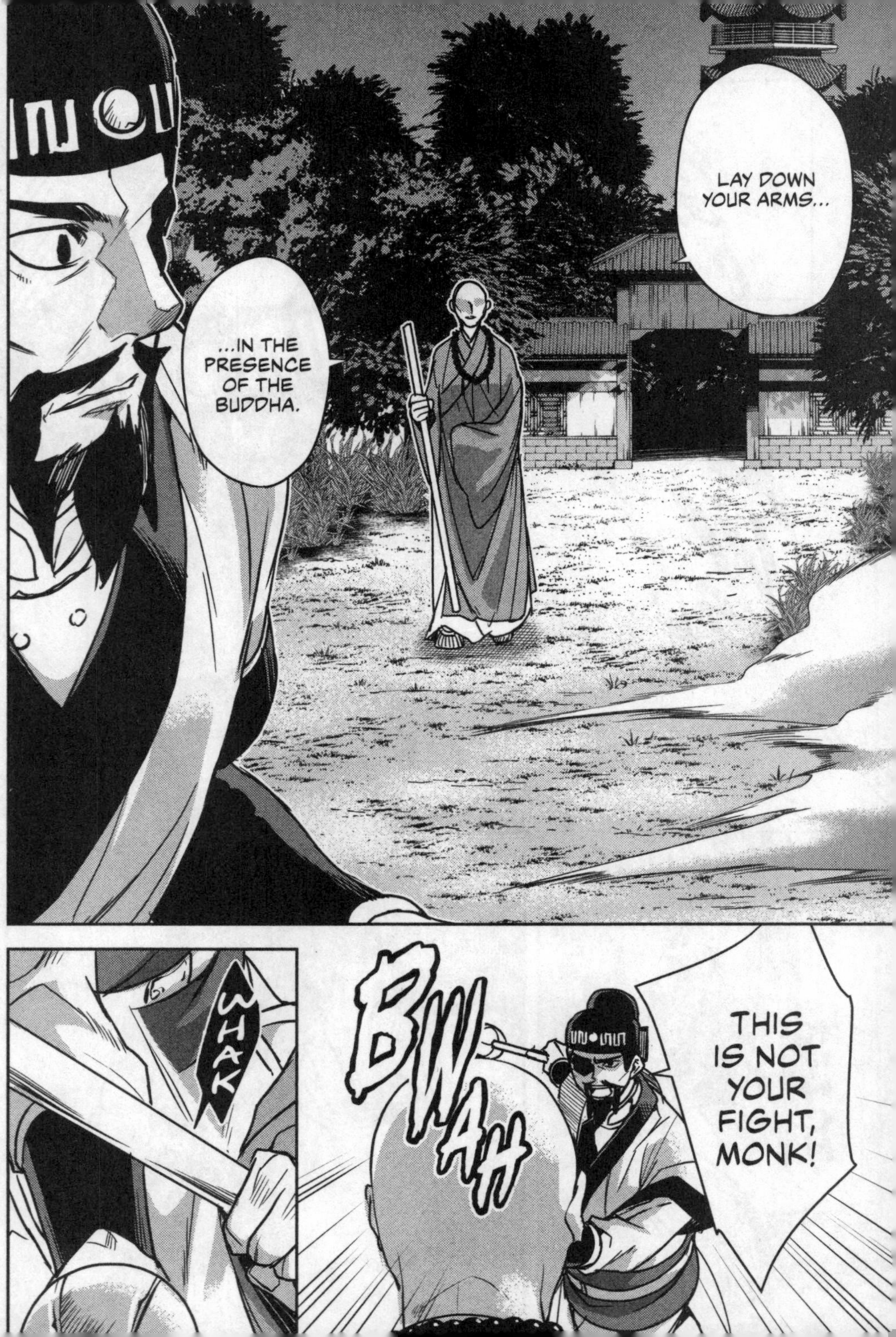
LAY DOWN YOUR ARMS...
...IN THE PRESENCE OF THE BUDDHA.
THIS IS NOT YOUR FIGHT, MONK!
BWAH
WHAK

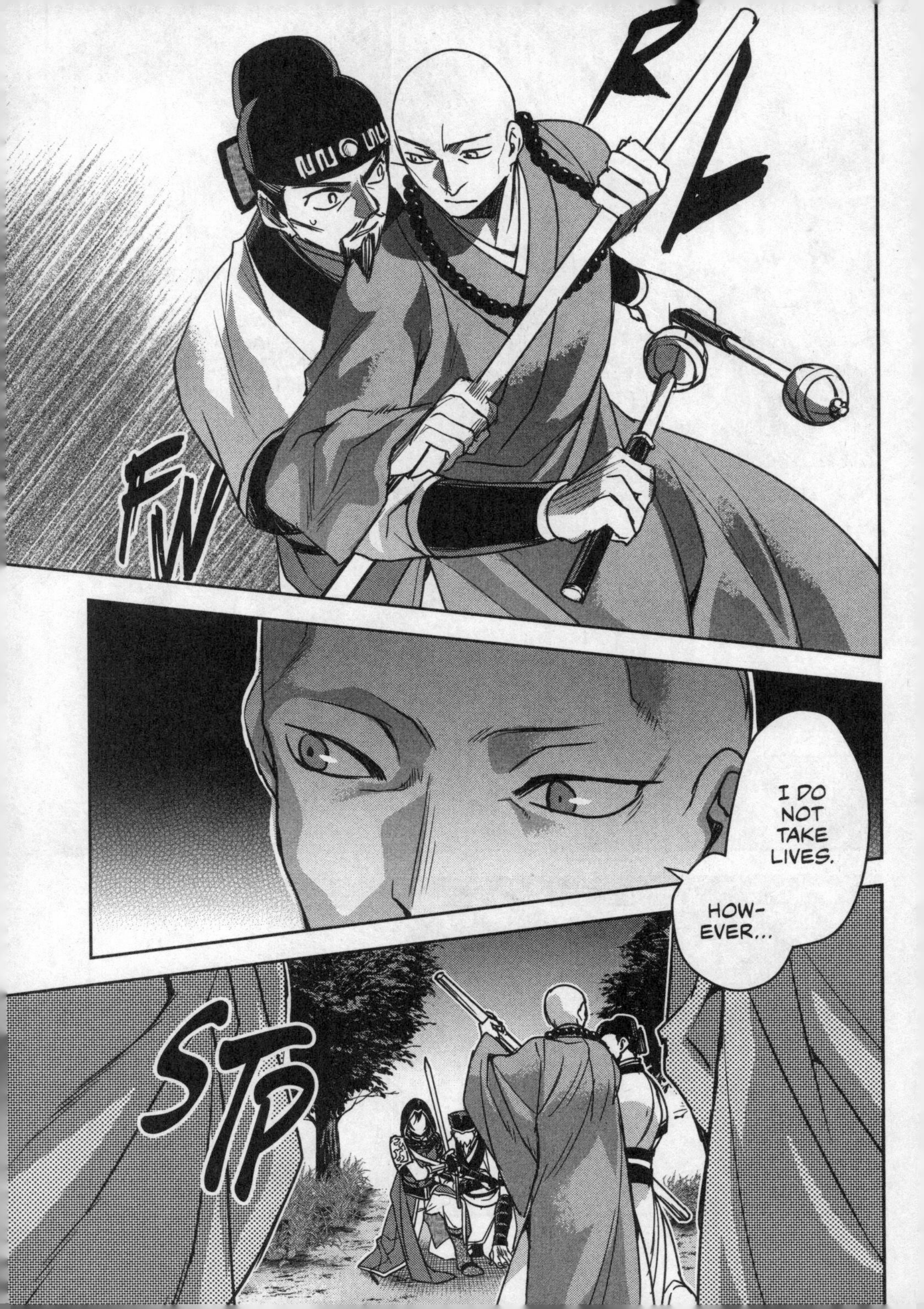
FW
I DO NOT TAKE LIVES.
HOW-EVER...
STP

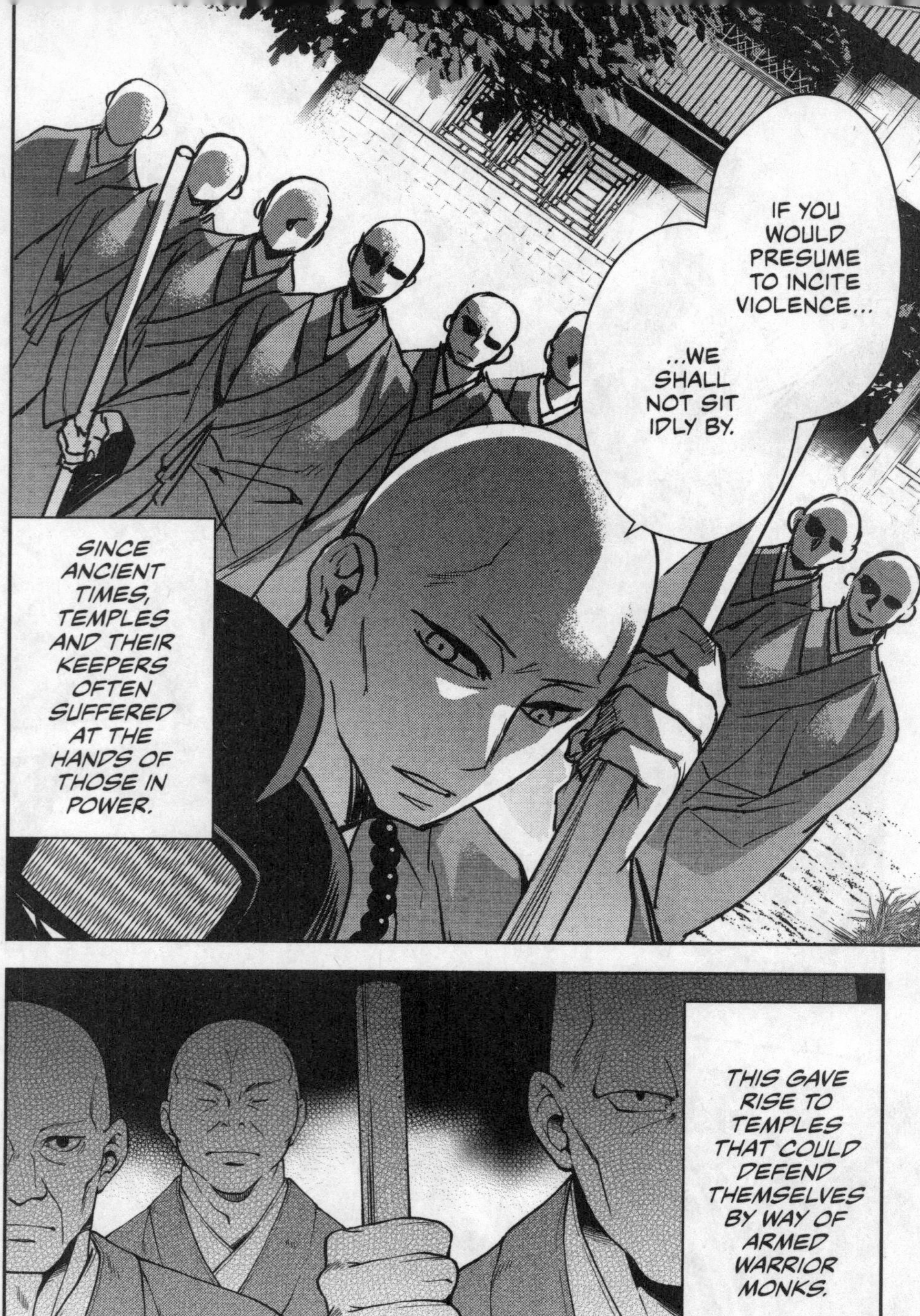
IF YOU WOULD PRESUME TO INCITE VIOLENCE...
...WE SHALL NOT SIT IDLY BY.
SINCE ANCIENT TIMES, TEMPLES AND THEIR KEEPERS OFTEN SUFFERED AT THE HANDS OF THOSE IN POWER.
THIS GAVE RISE TO TEMPLES THAT COULD DEFEND THEMSELVES BY WAY OF ARMED WARRIOR MONKS.

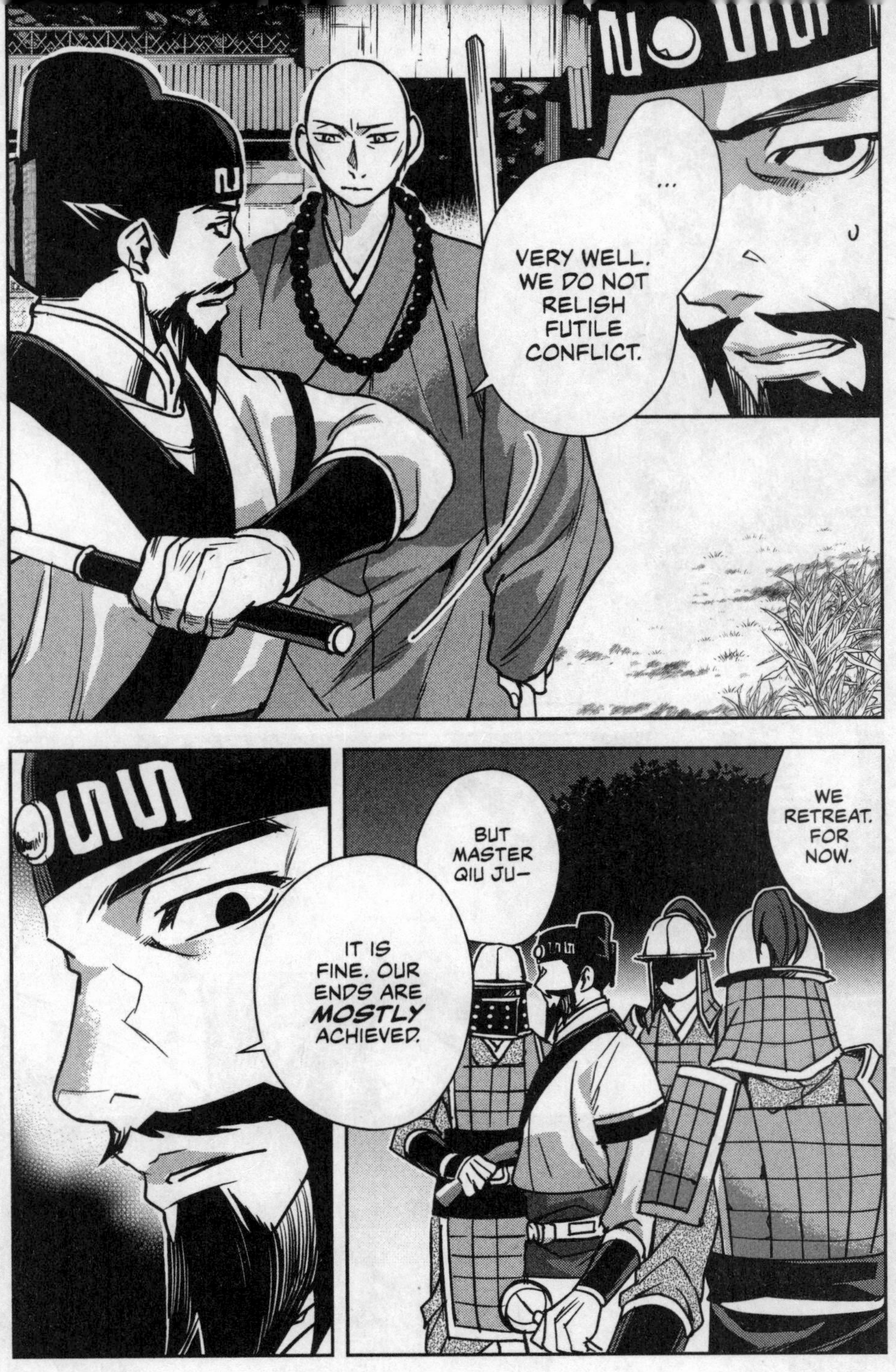
...
VERY WELL. WE DO NOT RELISH FUTILE CONFLICT.
WE RETREAT. FOR NOW.
BUT MASTER QIU JU—
IT IS FINE. OUR ENDS ARE *MOSTLY* ACHIEVED.

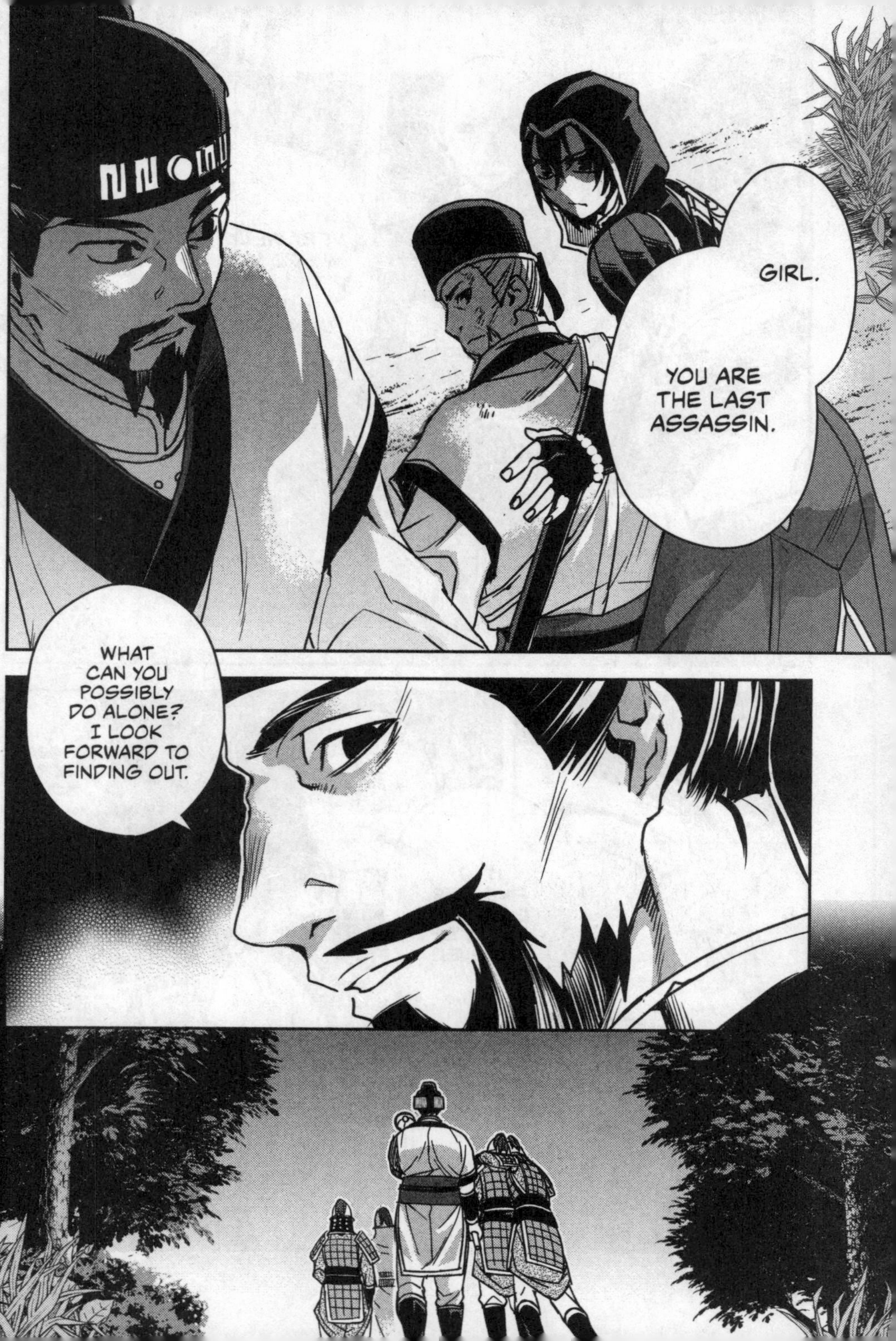
GIRL.
YOU ARE THE LAST ASSASSIN.
WHAT CAN YOU POSSIBLY DO ALONE? I LOOK FORWARD TO FINDING OUT.

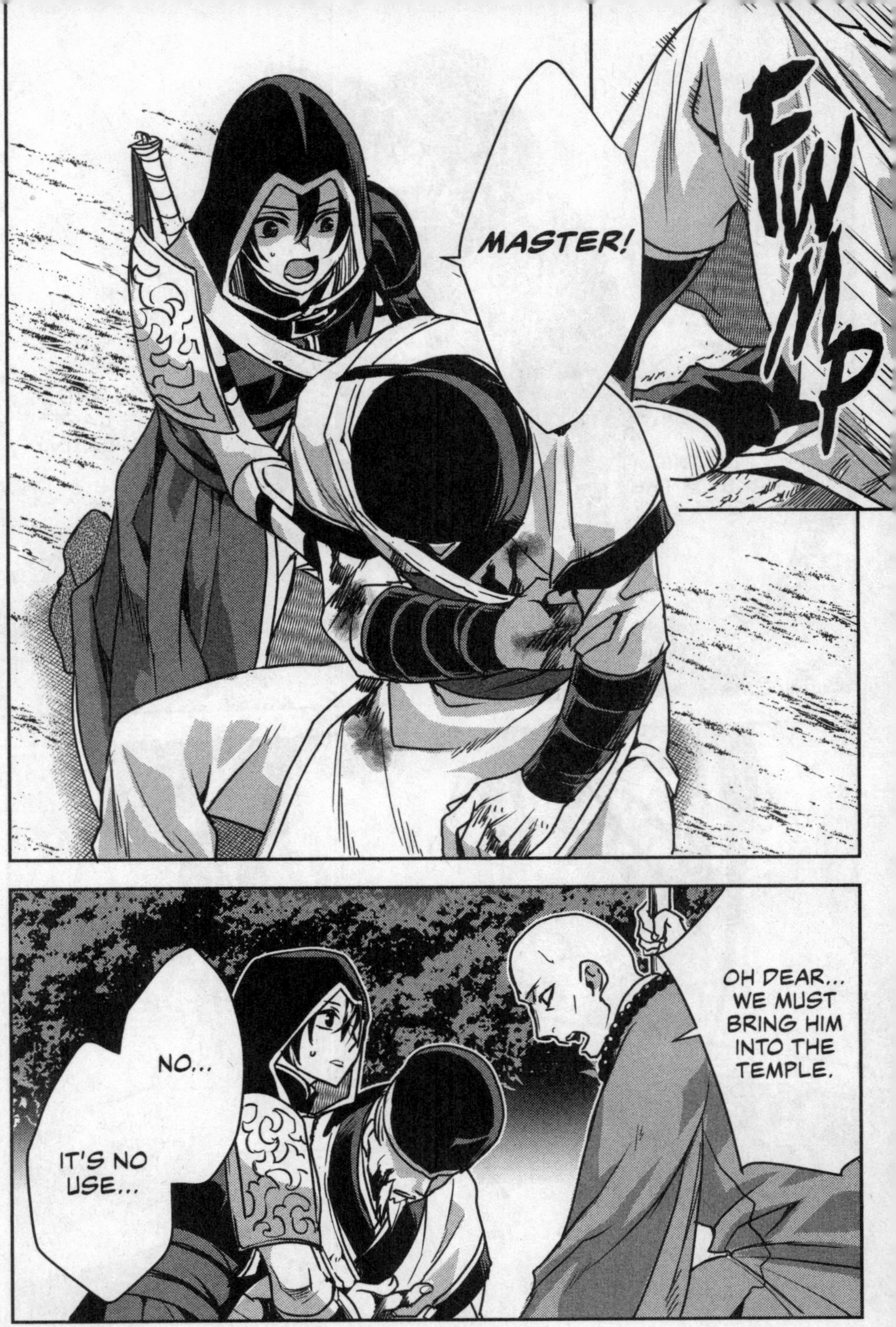
FWUMP
MASTER!
OH DEAR... WE MUST BRING HIM INTO THE TEMPLE.
NO...
IT'S NO USE...

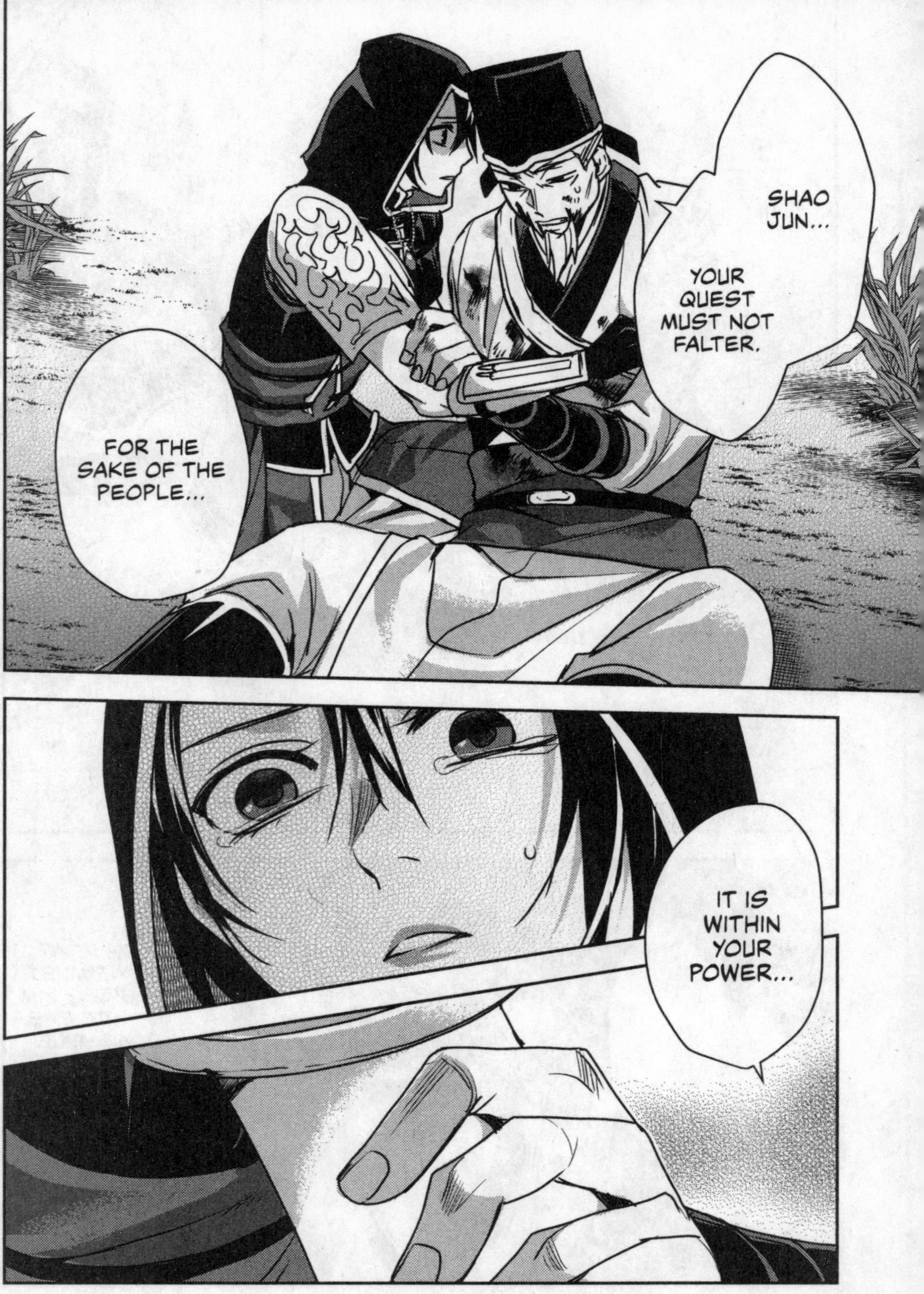
SHAO JUN...
YOUR QUEST MUST NOT FALTER.
FOR THE SAKE OF THE PEOPLE...
IT IS WITHIN YOUR POWER...

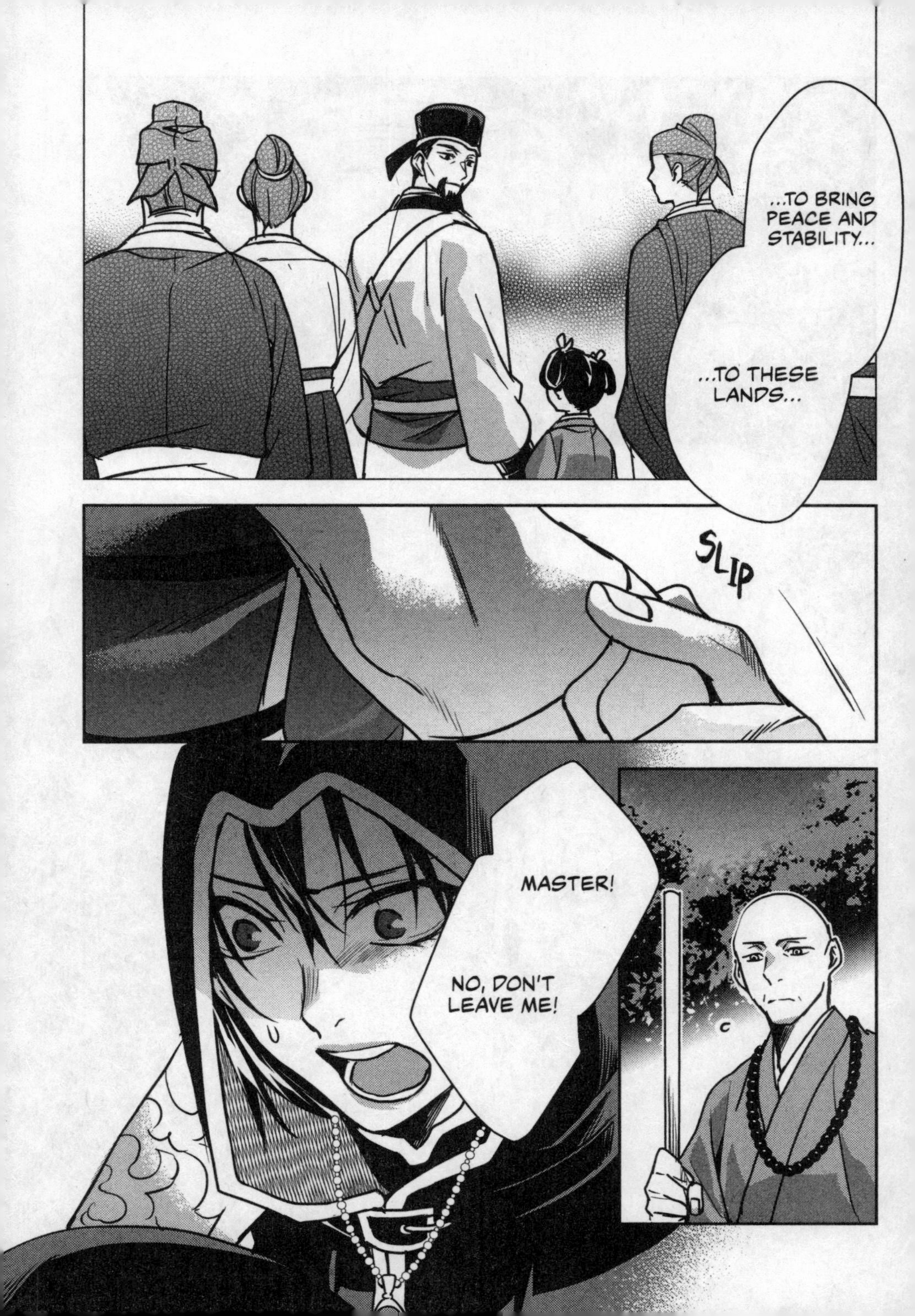
...TO BRING PEACE AND STABILITY...
...TO THESE LANDS...
SLIP
MASTER!
NO, DON'T LEAVE ME!

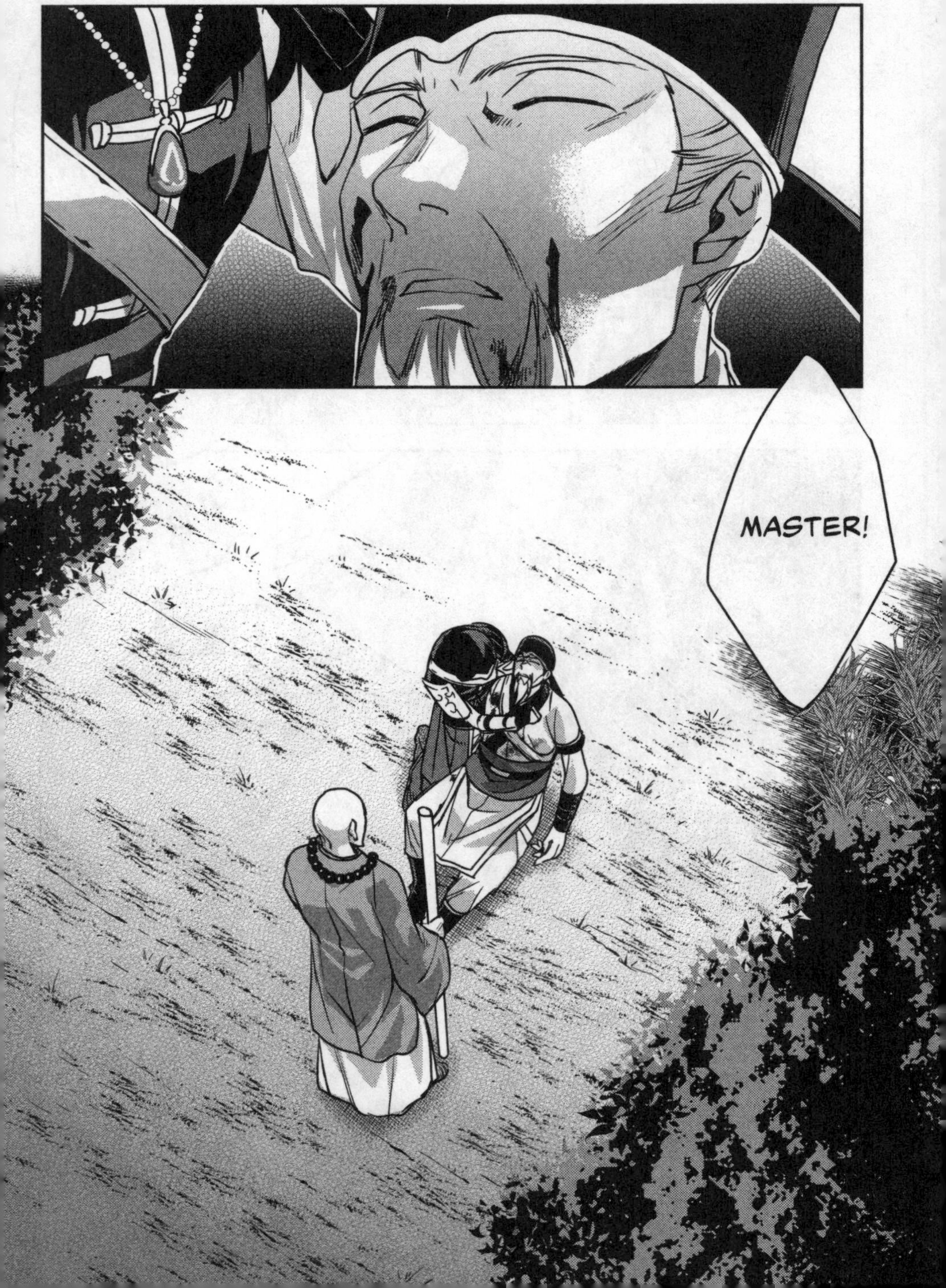
MASTER!

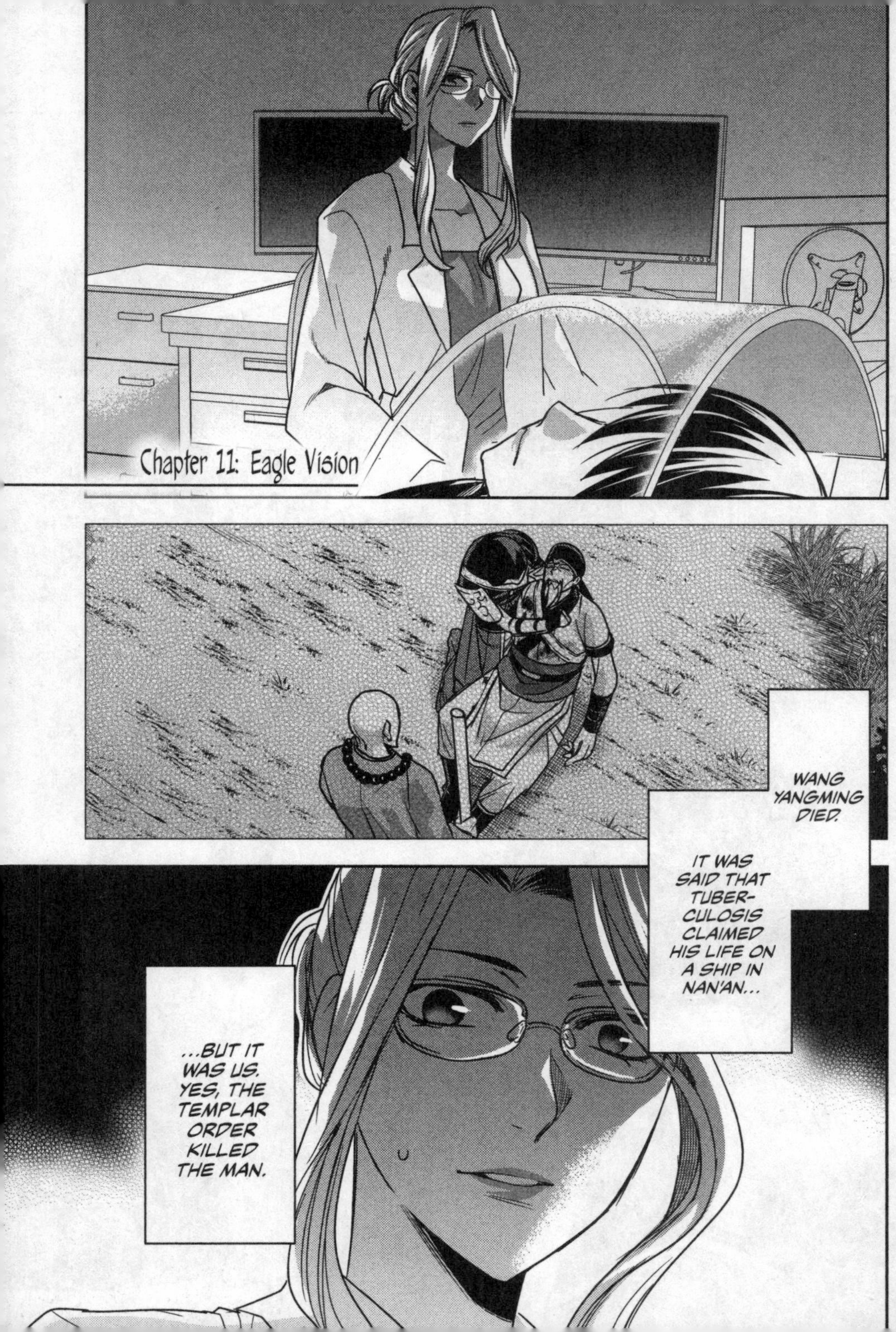
Chapter 11: Eagle Vision
WANG YANGMING DIED.
IT WAS SAID THAT TUBER-CULOSIS CLAIMED HIS LIFE ON A SHIP IN NAN'AN...
...BUT IT WAS US. YES, THE TEMPLAR ORDER KILLED THE MAN.

Chapter 11: Eagle Vision

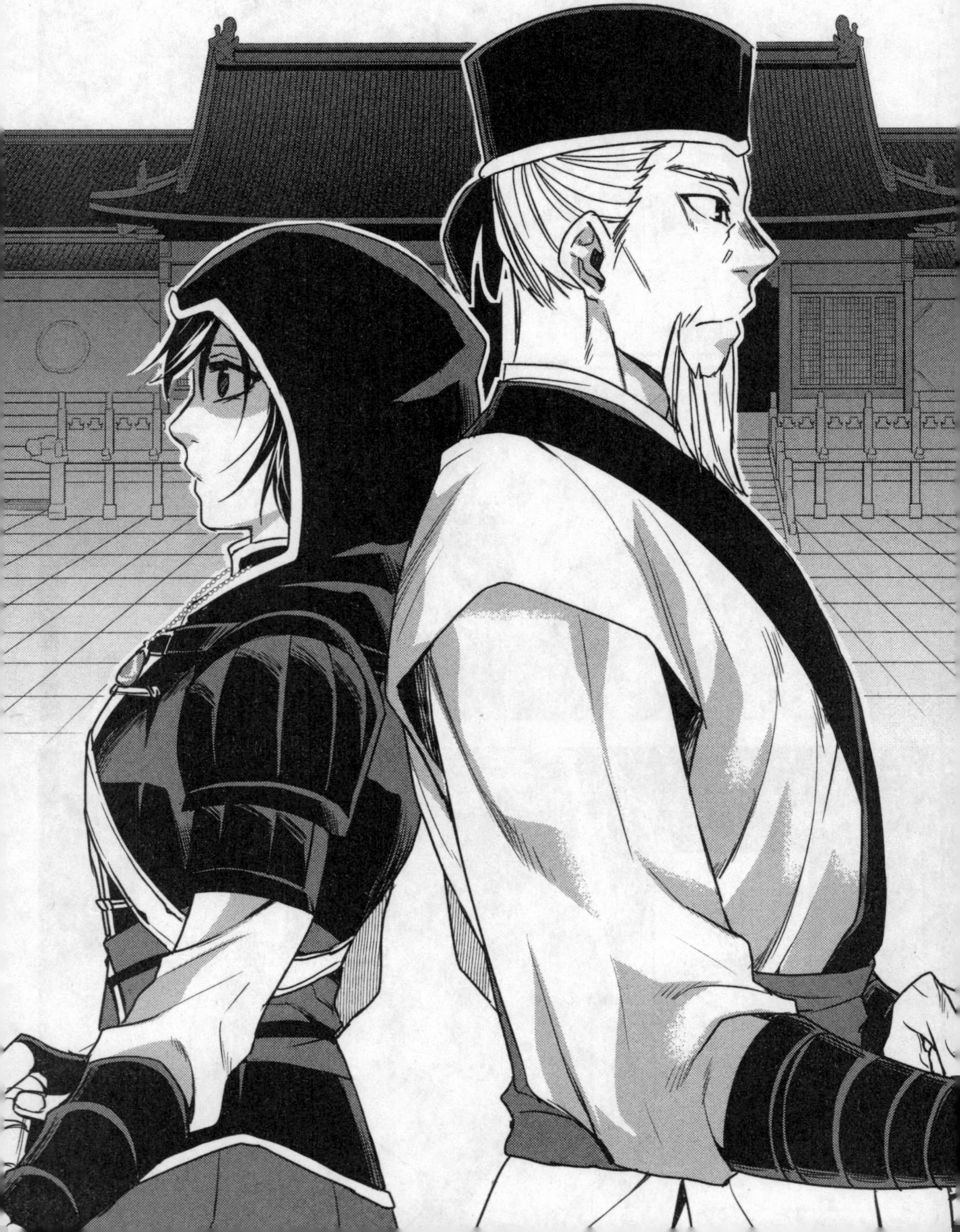

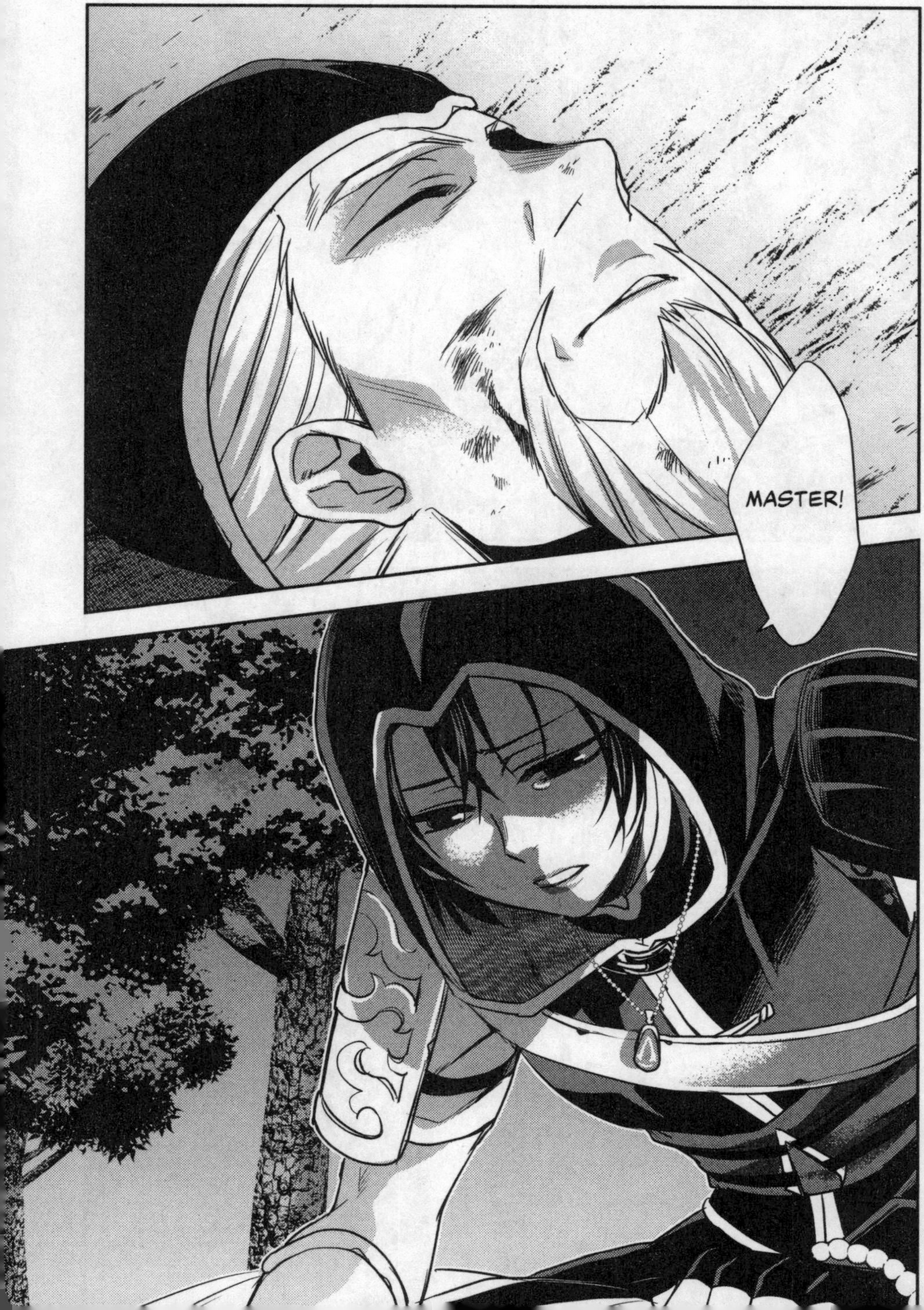
MASTER!

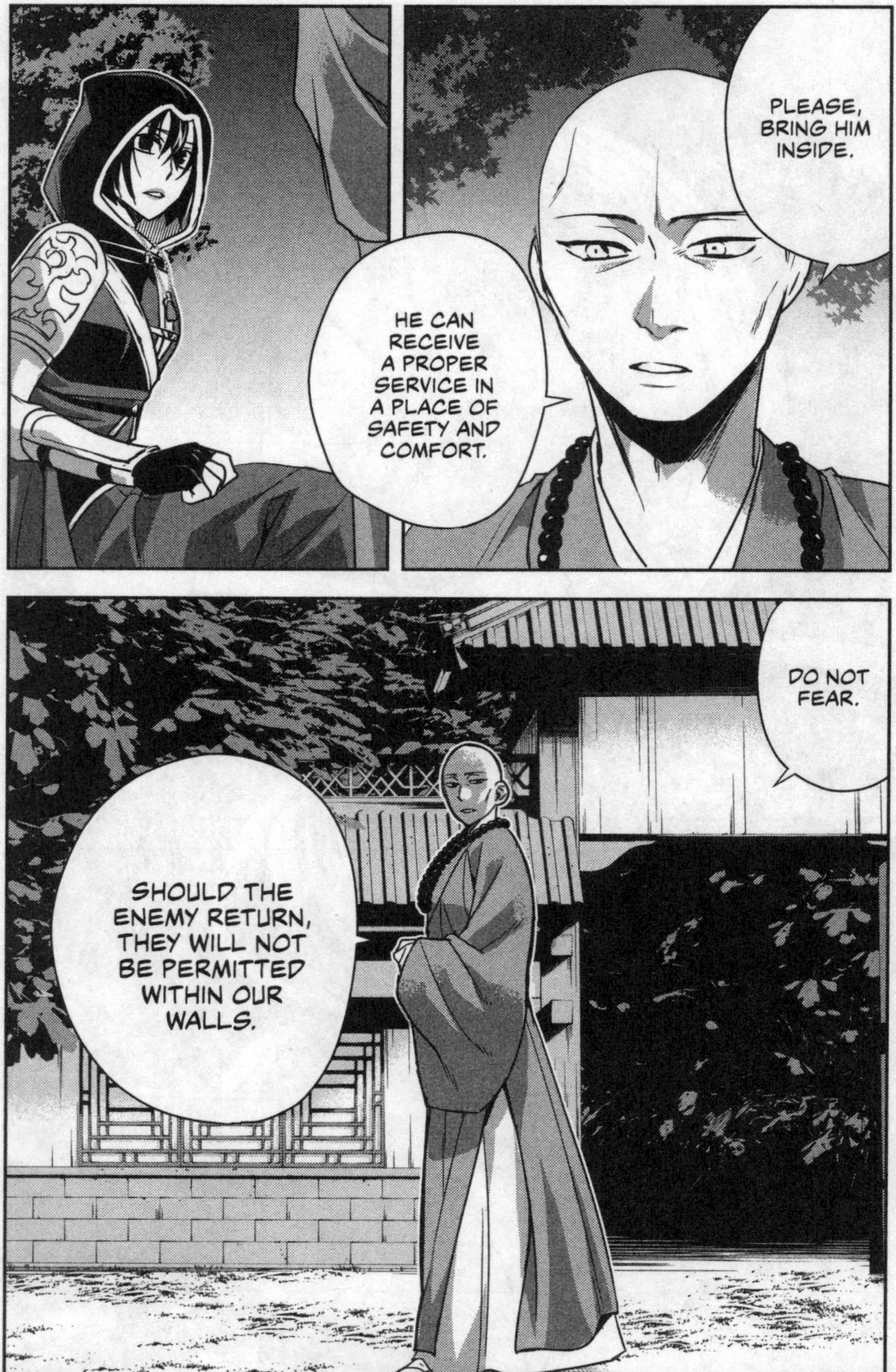
PLEASE, BRING HIM INSIDE.
HE CAN RECEIVE A PROPER SERVICE IN A PLACE OF SAFETY AND COMFORT.
DO NOT FEAR.
SHOULD THE ENEMY RETURN, THEY WILL NOT BE PERMITTED WITHIN OUR WALLS.

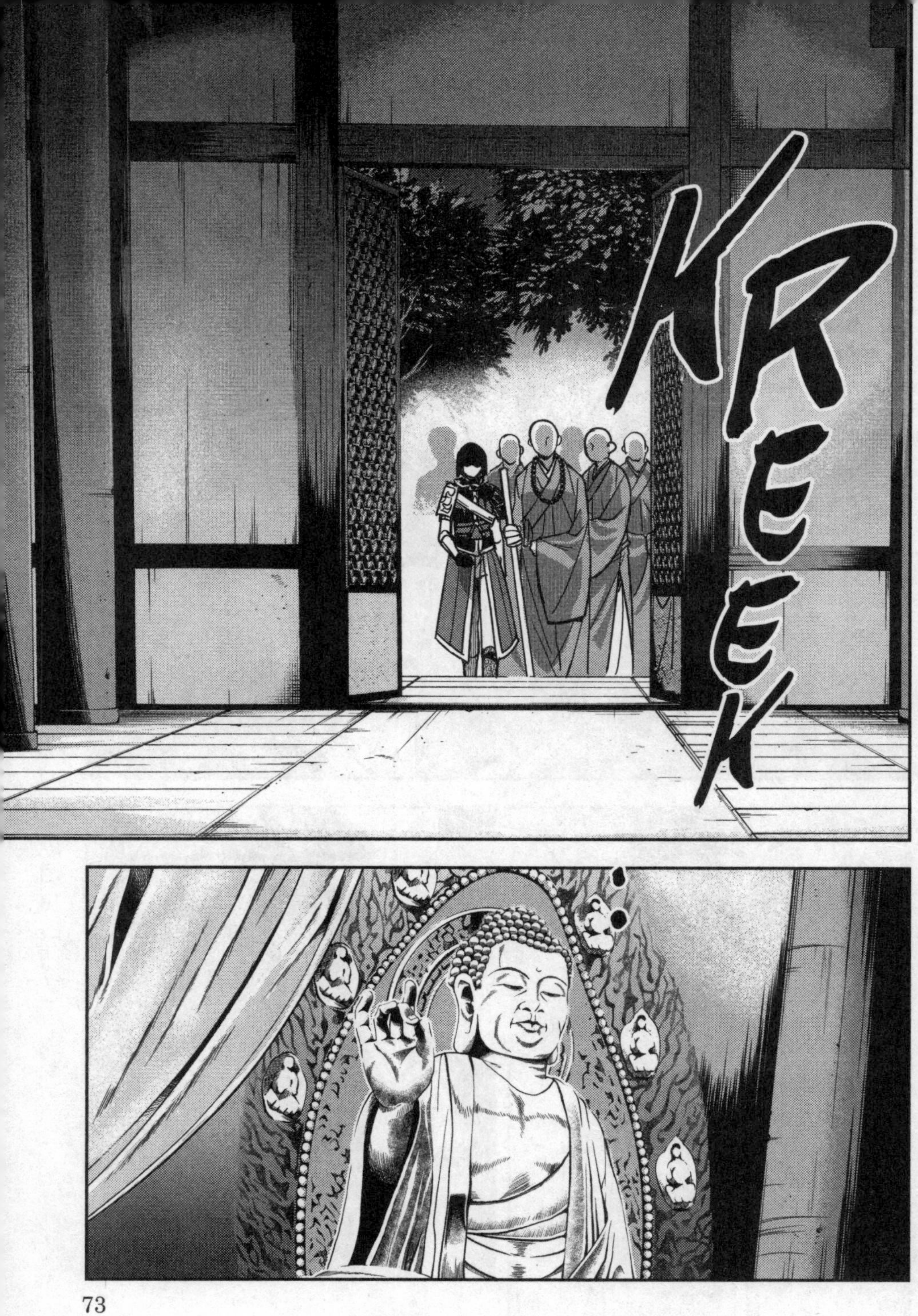
KREEK

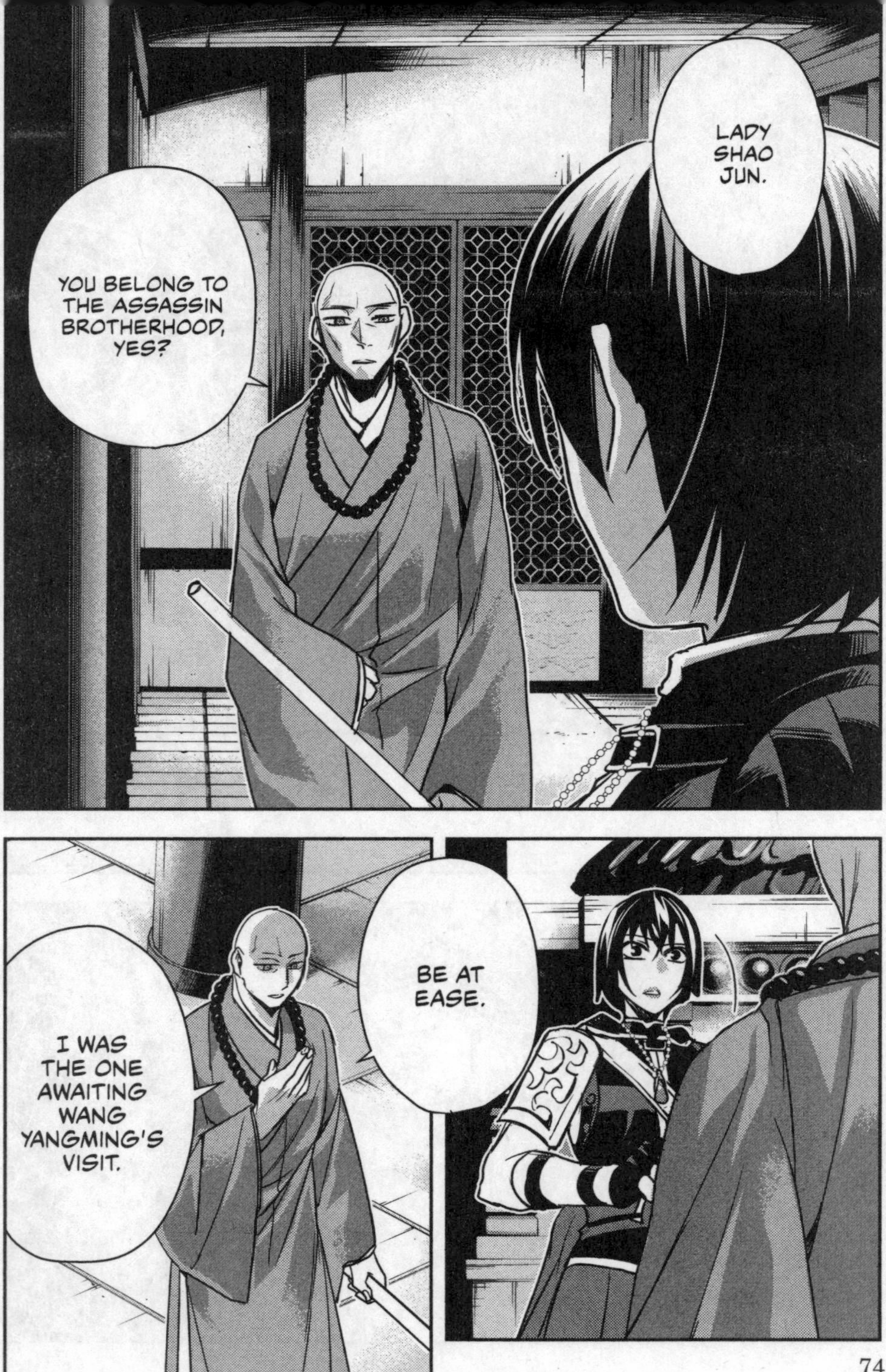
LADY SHAO JUN.
YOU BELONG TO THE ASSASSIN BROTHERHOOD, YES?
BE AT EASE.
I WAS THE ONE AWAITING WANG YANGMING'S VISIT.

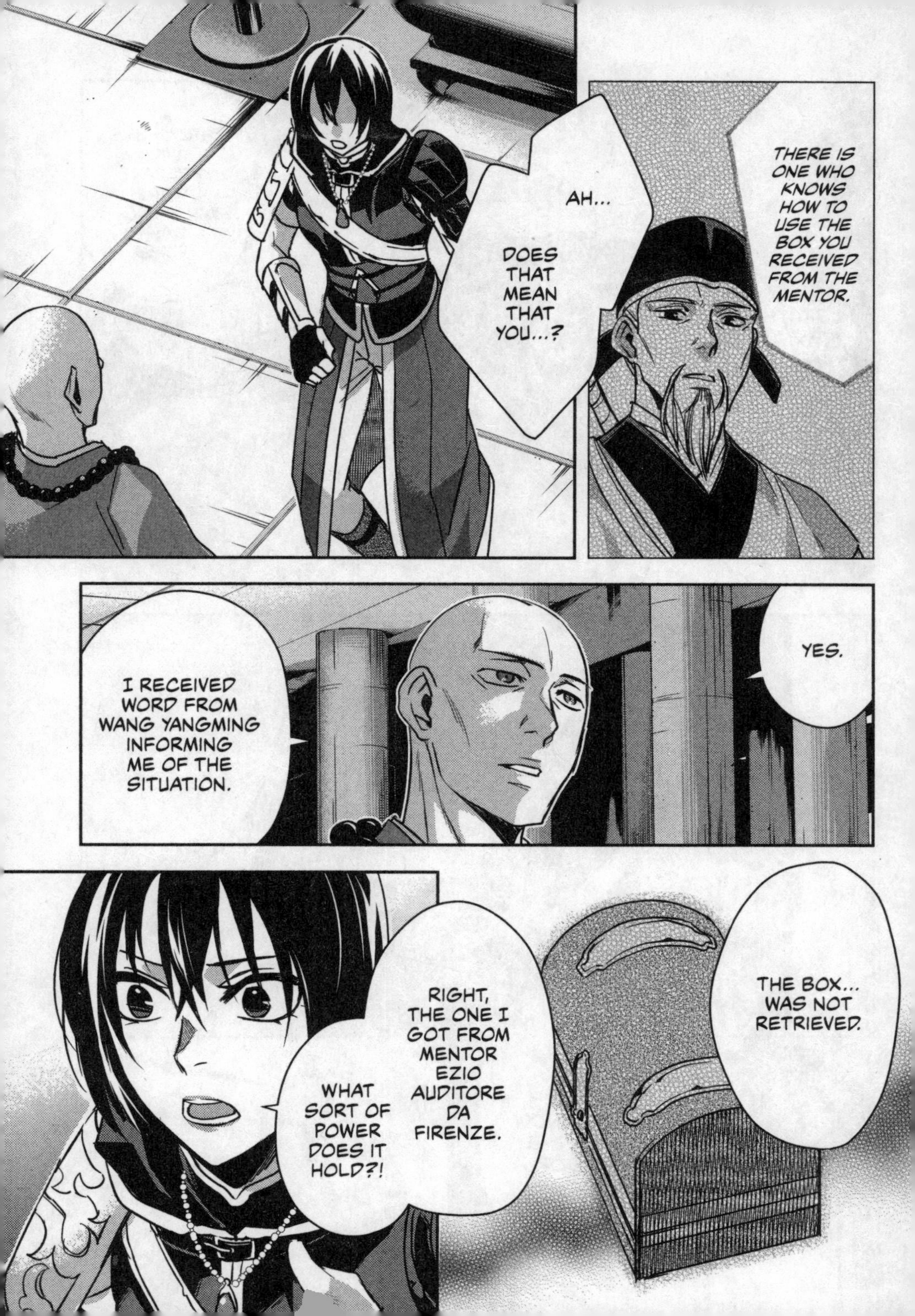
THERE IS ONE WHO KNOWS HOW TO USE THE BOX YOU RECEIVED FROM THE MENTOR.
AH...
DOES THAT MEAN THAT YOU...?
YES.
I RECEIVED WORD FROM WANG YANGMING INFORMING ME OF THE SITUATION.
THE BOX... WAS NOT RETRIEVED.
RIGHT, THE ONE I GOT FROM MENTOR EZIO AUDITORE DA FIRENZE.
WHAT SORT OF POWER DOES IT HOLD?!

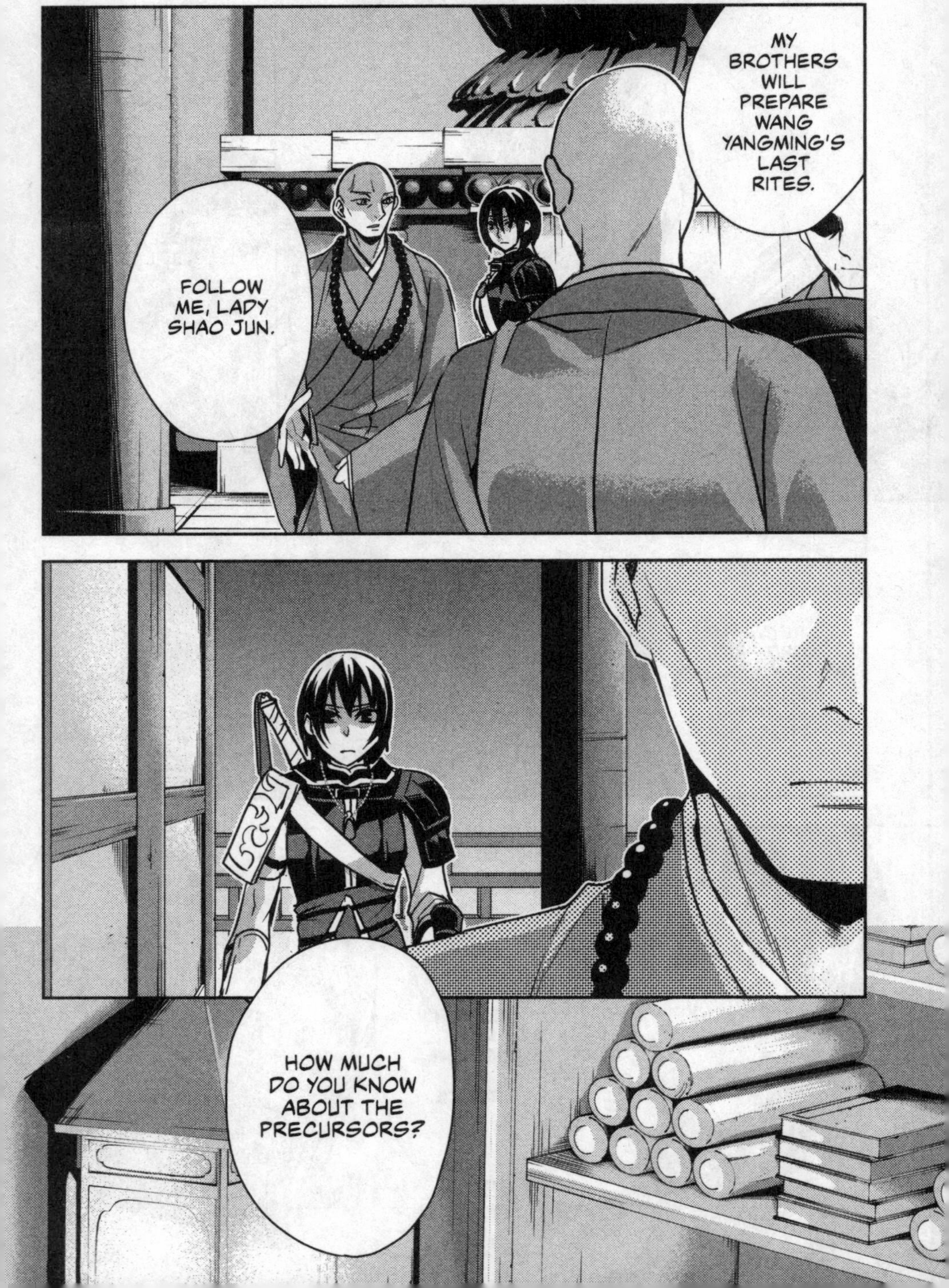
MY BROTHERS WILL PREPARE WANG YANGMING'S LAST RITES.
FOLLOW ME, LADY SHAO JUN.
HOW MUCH DO YOU KNOW ABOUT THE PRECURSORS?

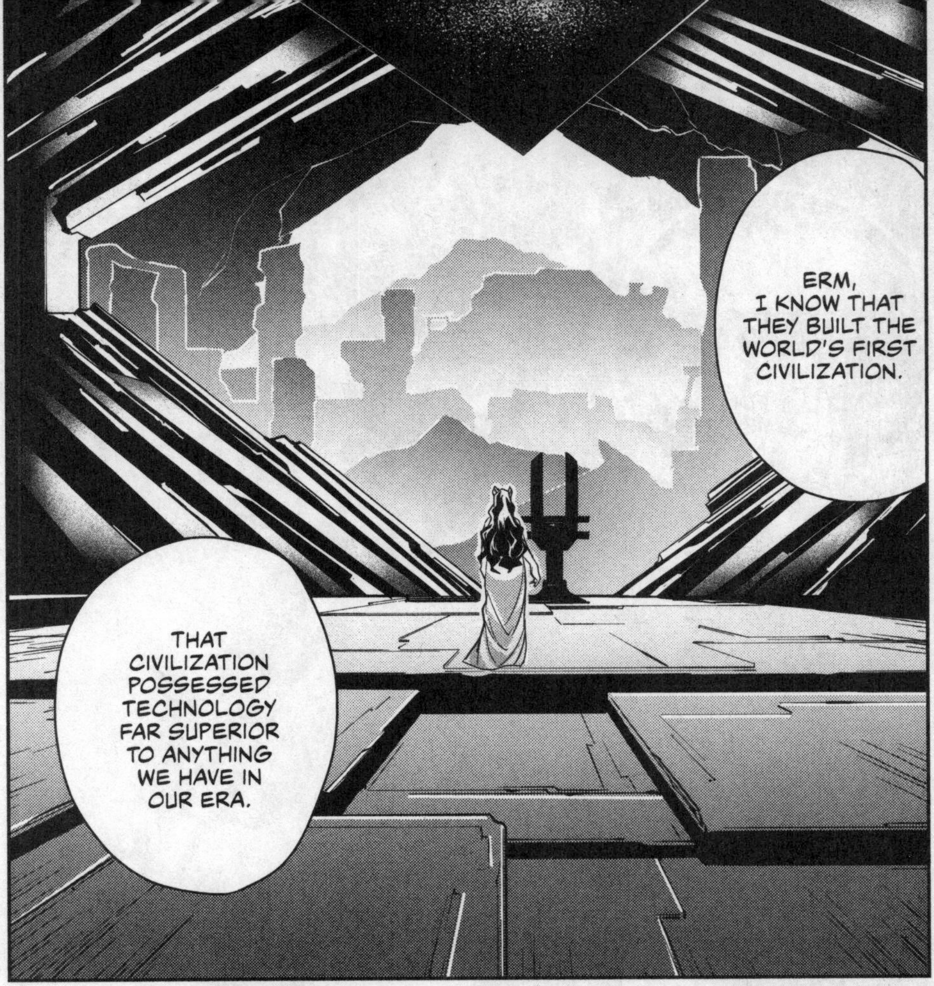
ERM, I KNOW THAT THEY BUILT THE WORLD'S FIRST CIVILIZATION.
THAT CIVILIZATION POSSESSED TECHNOLOGY FAR SUPERIOR TO ANYTHING WE HAVE IN OUR ERA.

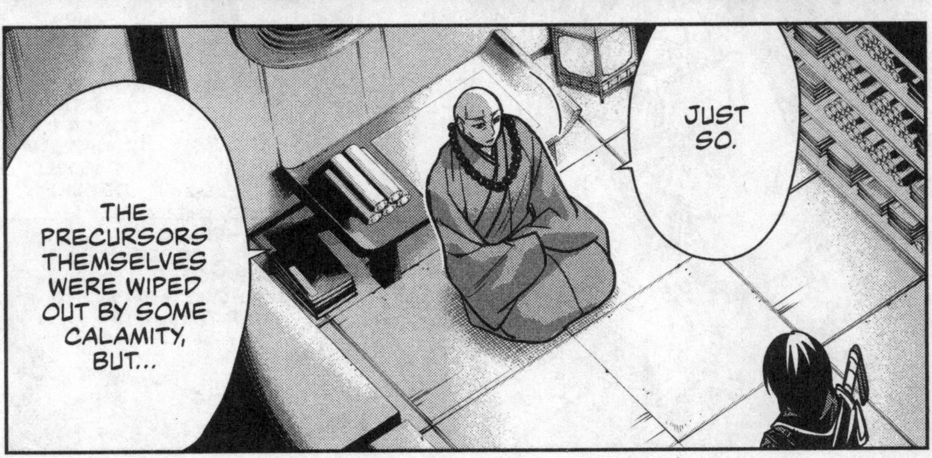
JUST SO.
THE PRECURSORS THEMSELVES WERE WIPED OUT BY SOME CALAMITY, BUT...

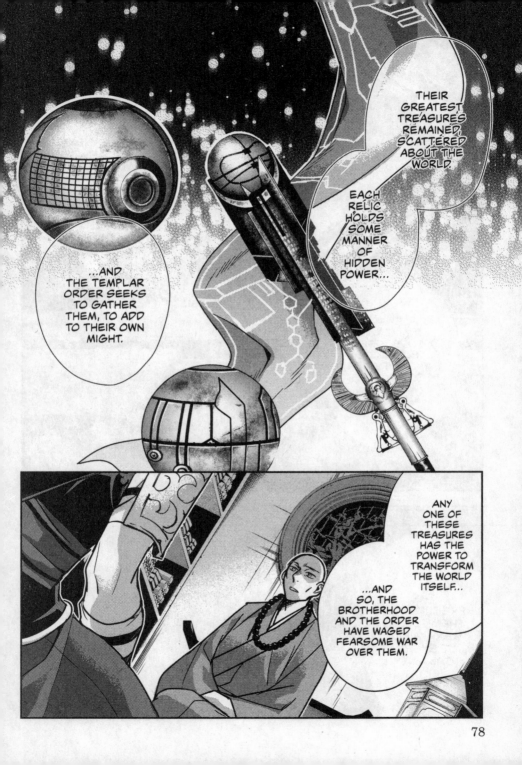

THEIR GREATEST TREASURES REMAINED, SCATTERED ABOUT THE WORLD.

EACH RELIC HOLDS SOME MANNER OF HIDDEN POWER...

...AND THE TEMPLAR ORDER SEEKS TO GATHER THEM, TO ADD TO THEIR OWN MIGHT.

ANY ONE OF THESE TREASURES HAS THE POWER TO TRANSFORM THE WORLD ITSELF...

...AND SO, THE BROTHERHOOD AND THE ORDER HAVE WAGED FEARSOME WAR OVER THEM.

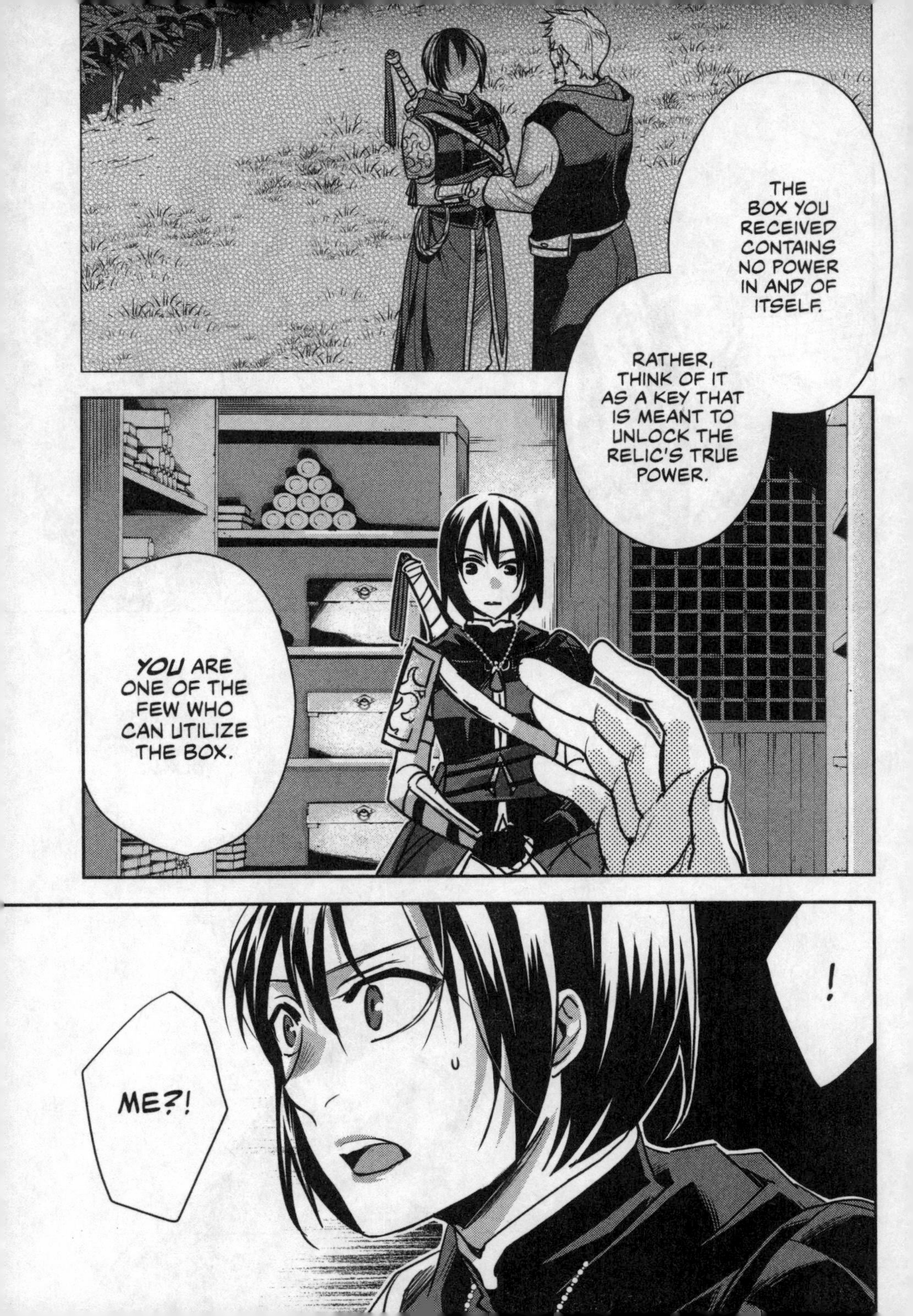
THE BOX YOU RECEIVED CONTAINS NO POWER IN AND OF ITSELF.
RATHER, THINK OF IT AS A KEY THAT IS MEANT TO UNLOCK THE RELIC'S TRUE POWER.
YOU ARE ONE OF THE FEW WHO CAN UTILIZE THE BOX.
!
ME?!

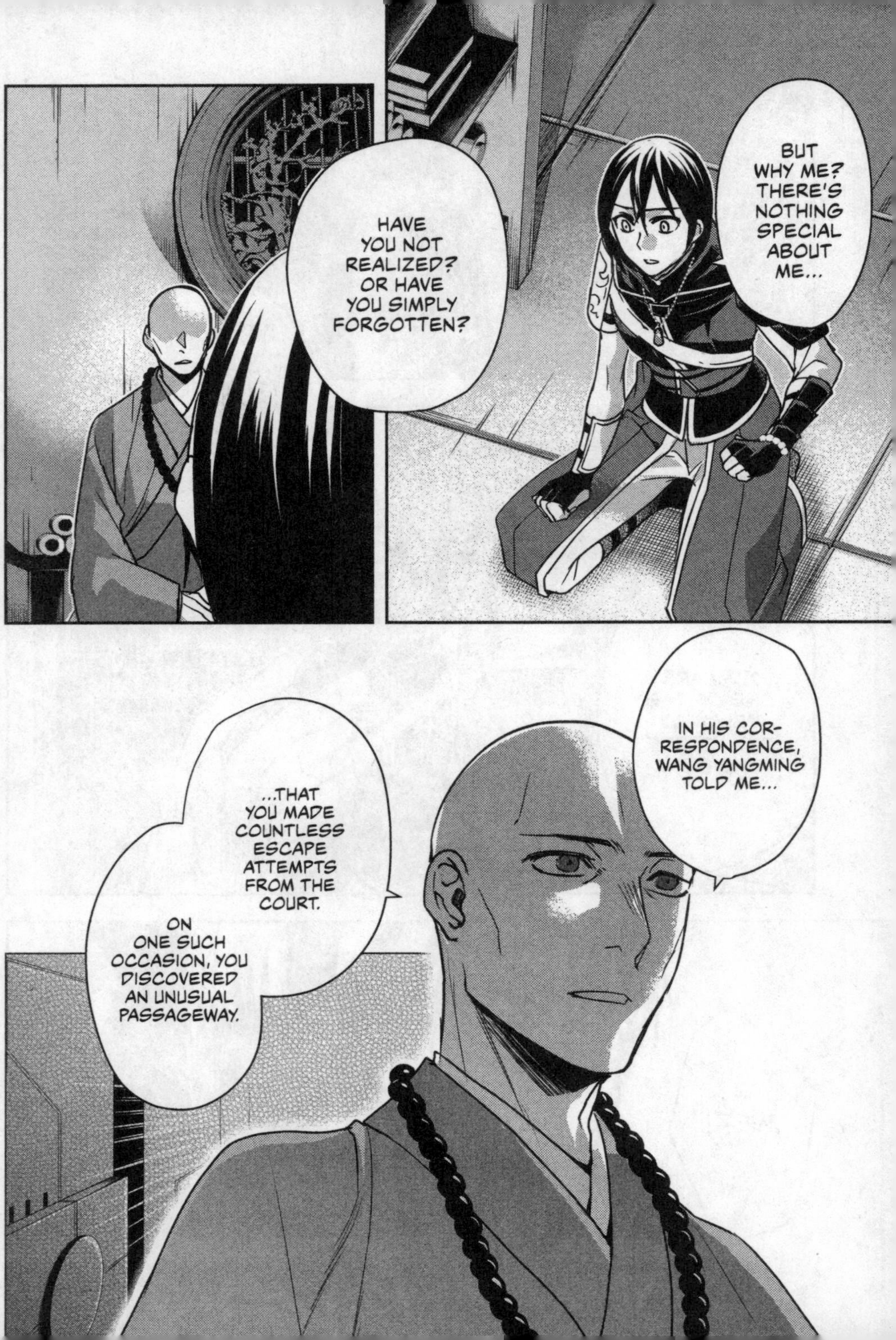
BUT WHY ME? THERE'S NOTHING SPECIAL ABOUT ME...
HAVE YOU NOT REALIZED? OR HAVE YOU SIMPLY FORGOTTEN?
IN HIS COR-RESPONDENCE, WANG YANGMING TOLD ME...
...THAT YOU MADE COUNTLESS ESCAPE ATTEMPTS FROM THE COURT.
ON ONE SUCH OCCASION, YOU DISCOVERED AN UNUSUAL PASSAGEWAY.

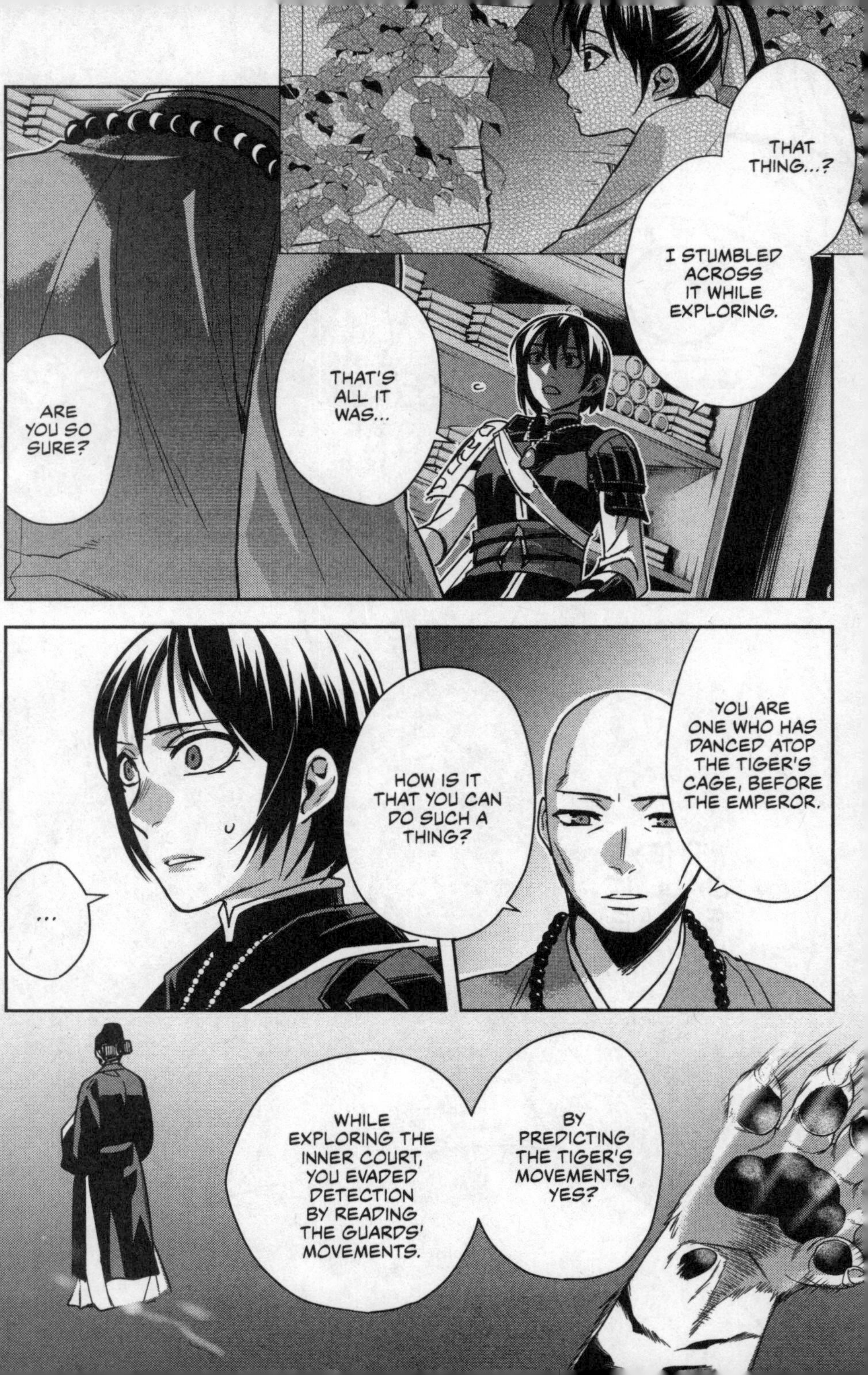
THAT THING...?
I STUMBLED ACROSS IT WHILE EXPLORING.
THAT'S ALL IT WAS...
ARE YOU SO SURE?
YOU ARE ONE WHO HAS DANCED ATOP THE TIGER'S CAGE, BEFORE THE EMPEROR.
HOW IS IT THAT YOU CAN DO SUCH A THING?
...
BY PREDICTING THE TIGER'S MOVEMENTS, YES?
WHILE EXPLORING THE INNER COURT, YOU EVADED DETECTION BY READING THE GUARDS' MOVEMENTS.

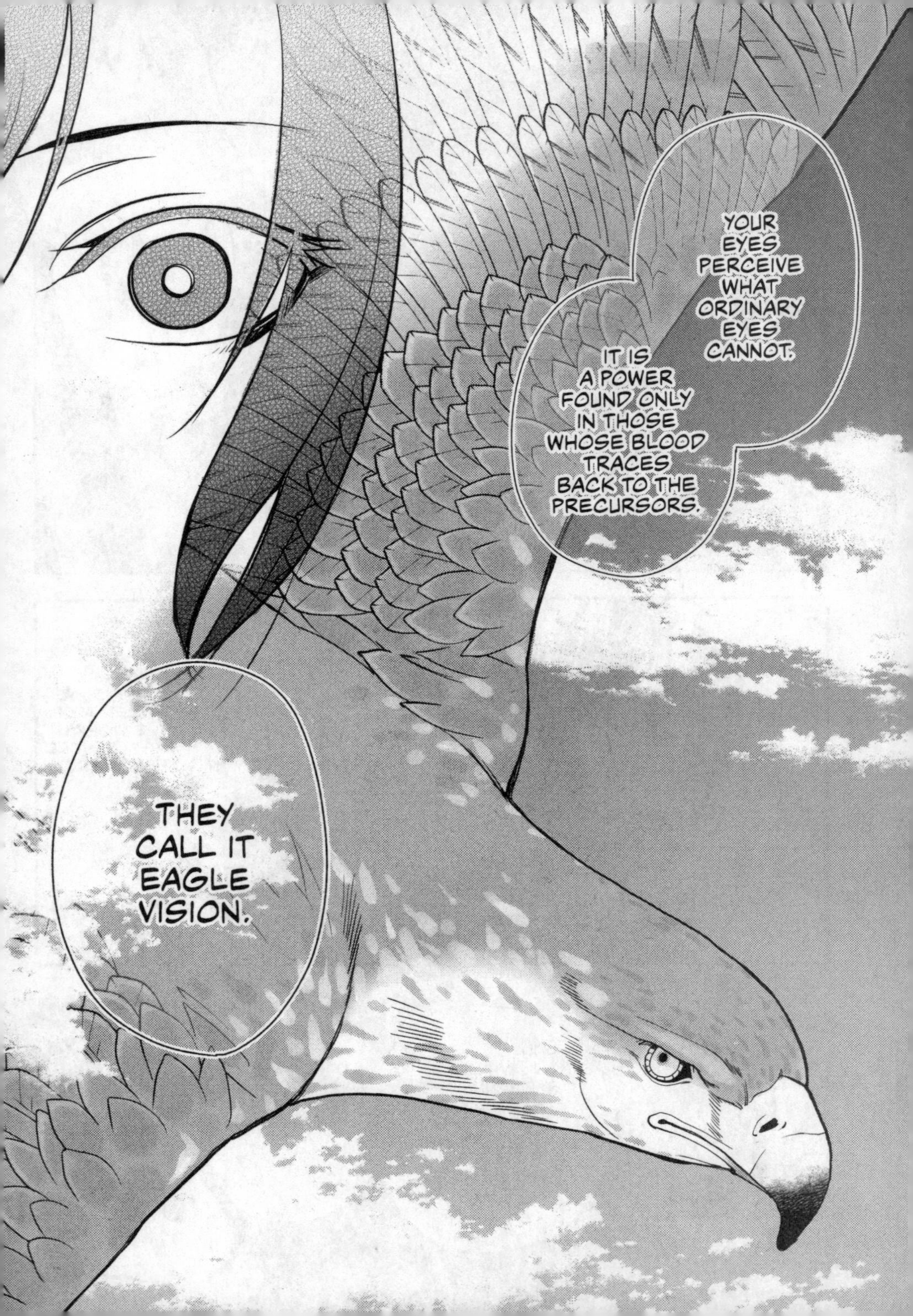
YOUR EYES PERCEIVE WHAT ORDINARY EYES CANNOT.
IT IS A POWER FOUND ONLY IN THOSE WHOSE BLOOD TRACES BACK TO THE PRECURSORS.
THEY CALL IT EAGLE VISION.

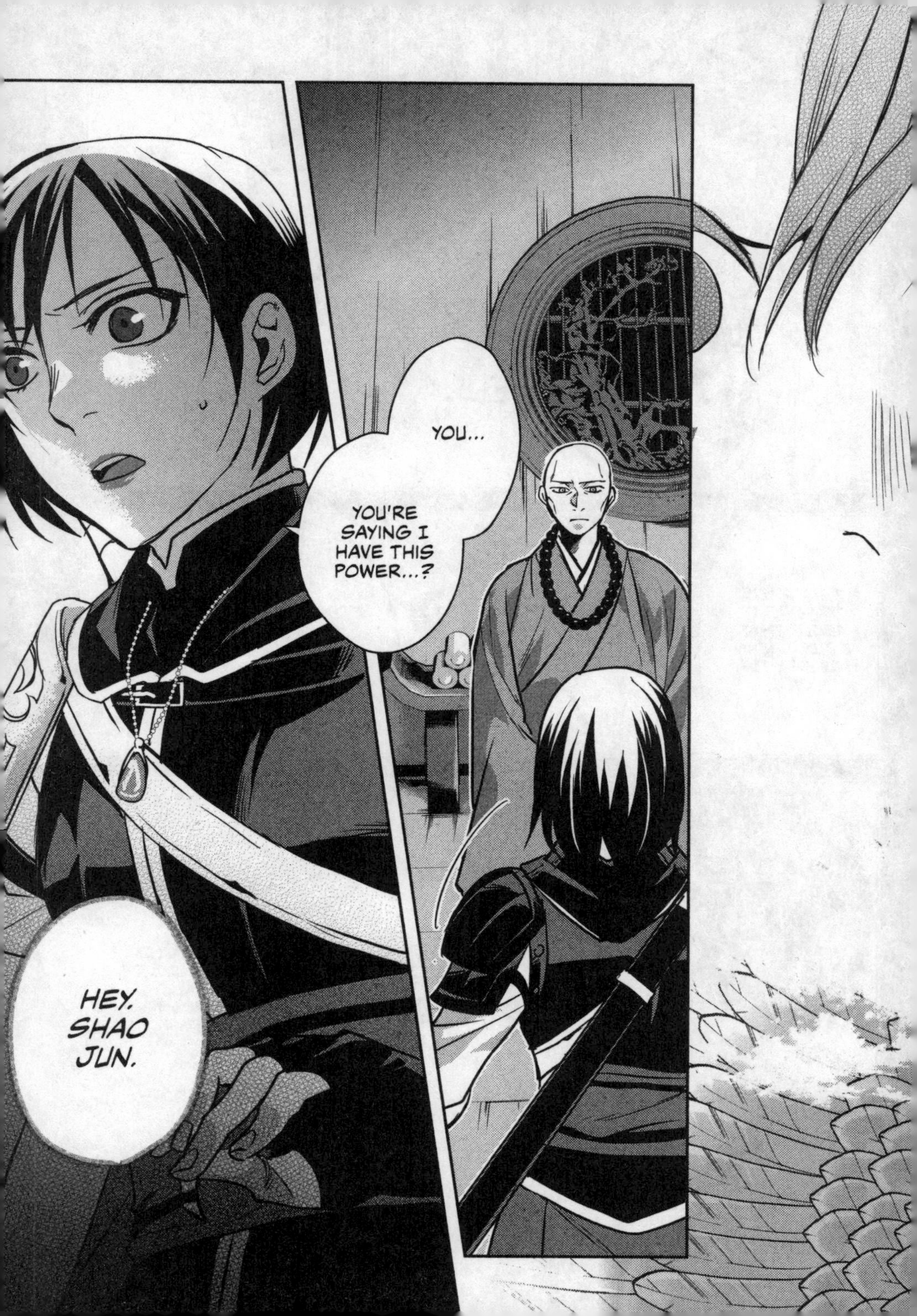
YOU...
YOU'RE SAYING I HAVE THIS POWER...?
HEY. SHAO JUN.

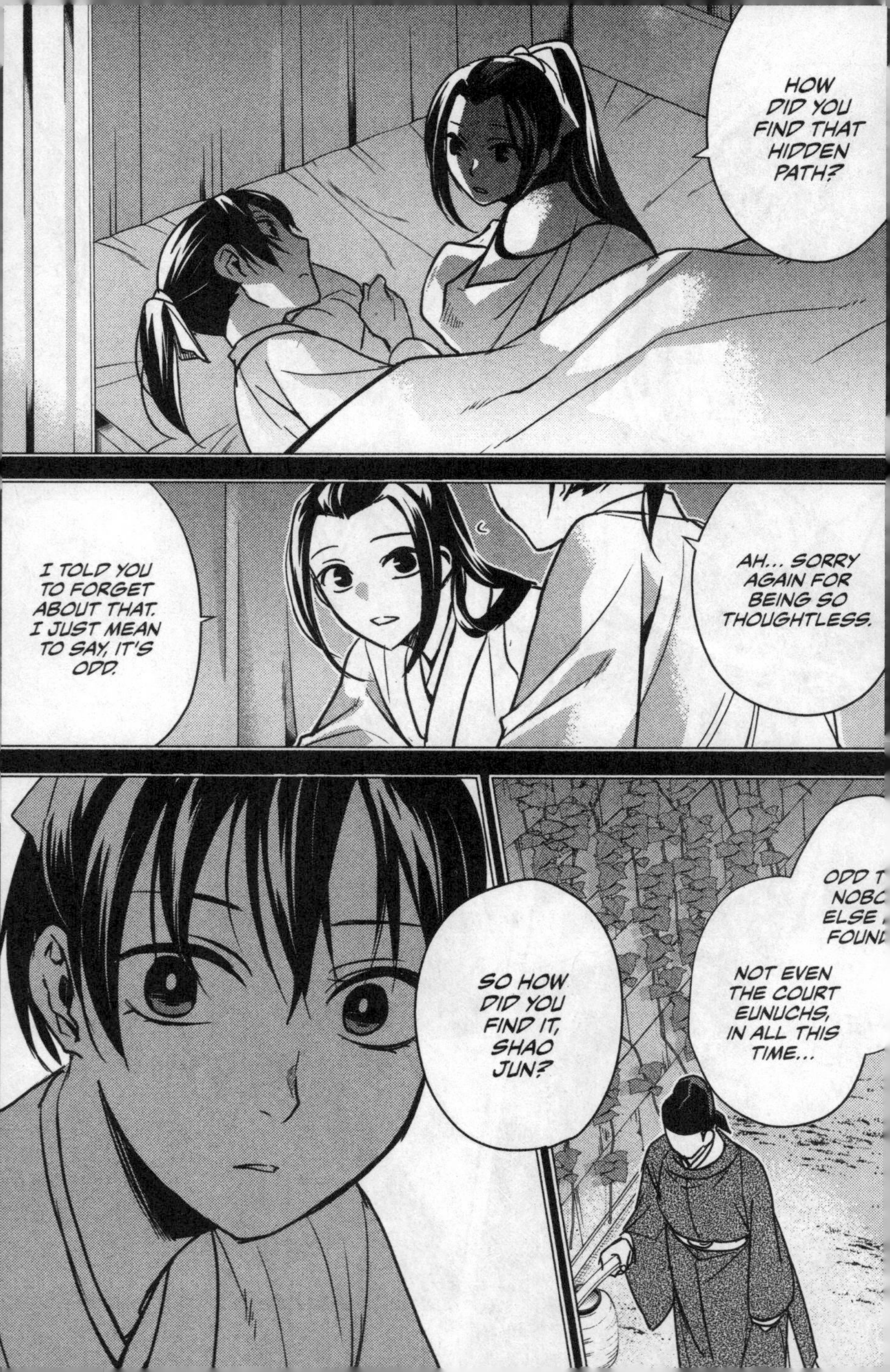
HOW DID YOU FIND THAT HIDDEN PATH?
AH... SORRY AGAIN FOR BEING SO THOUGHTLESS.
I TOLD YOU TO FORGET ABOUT THAT. I JUST MEAN TO SAY, IT'S ODD.
ODD T NOBO ELSE FOUND
NOT EVEN THE COURT EUNUCHS, IN ALL THIS TIME...
SO HOW DID YOU FIND IT, SHAO JUN?

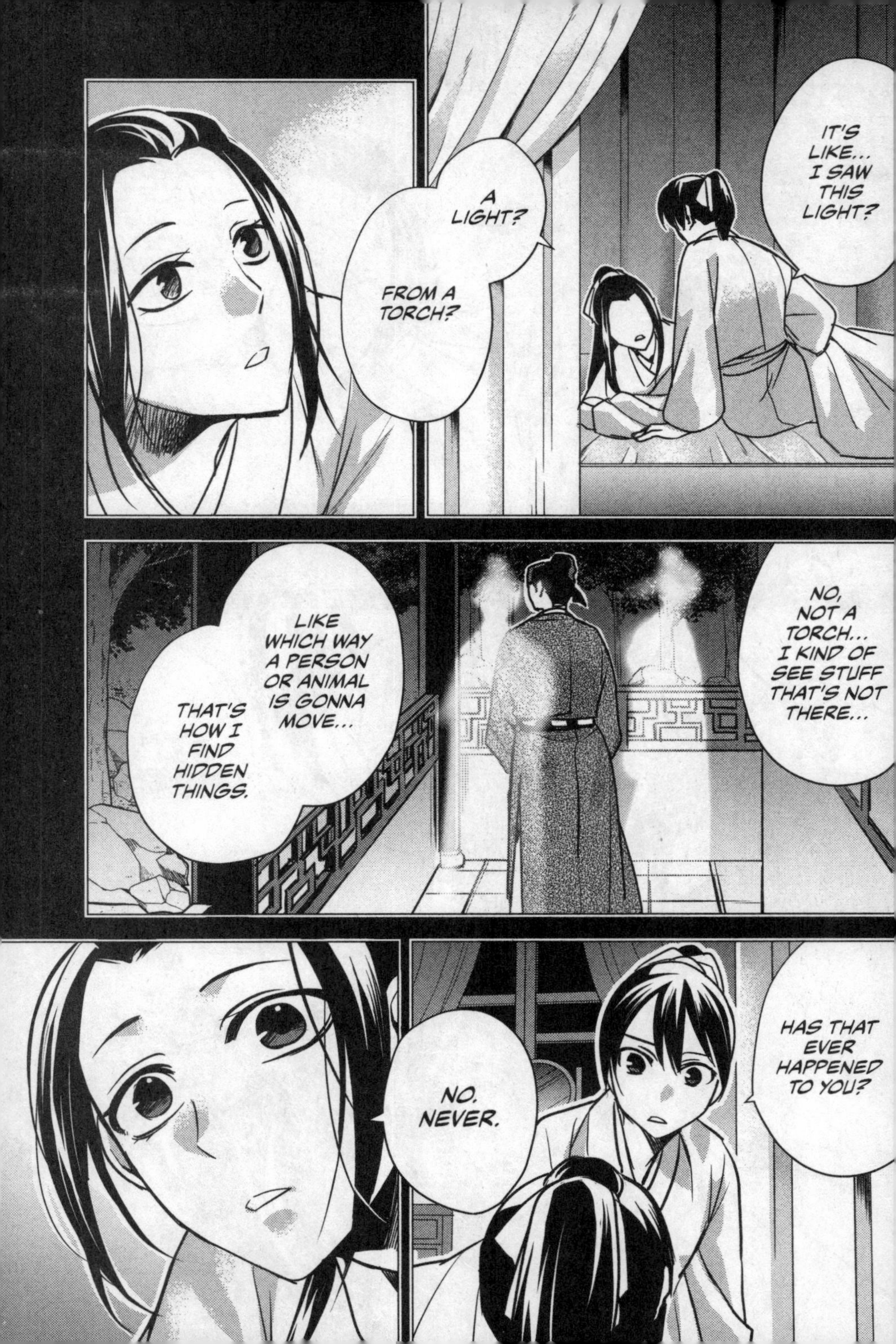
IT'S LIKE... I SAW THIS LIGHT?
A LIGHT?
FROM A TORCH?
NO, NOT A TORCH... I KIND OF SEE STUFF THAT'S NOT THERE...
LIKE WHICH WAY A PERSON OR ANIMAL IS GONNA MOVE...
THAT'S HOW I FIND HIDDEN THINGS.
HAS THAT EVER HAPPENED TO YOU?
NO. NEVER.

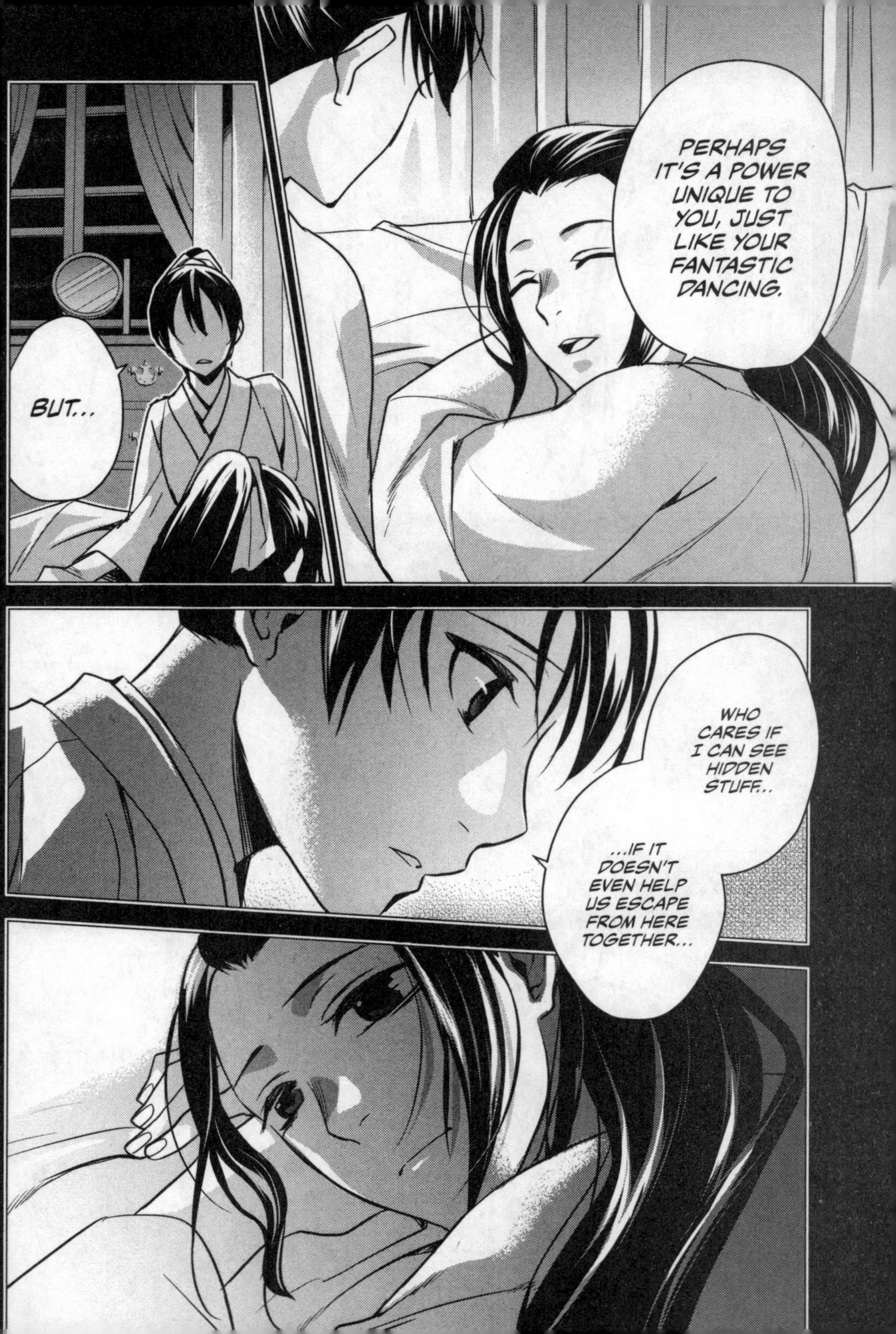
PERHAPS IT'S A POWER UNIQUE TO YOU, JUST LIKE YOUR FANTASTIC DANCING.
BUT...
WHO CARES IF I CAN SEE HIDDEN STUFF...
...IF IT DOESN'T EVEN HELP US ESCAPE FROM HERE TOGETHER...

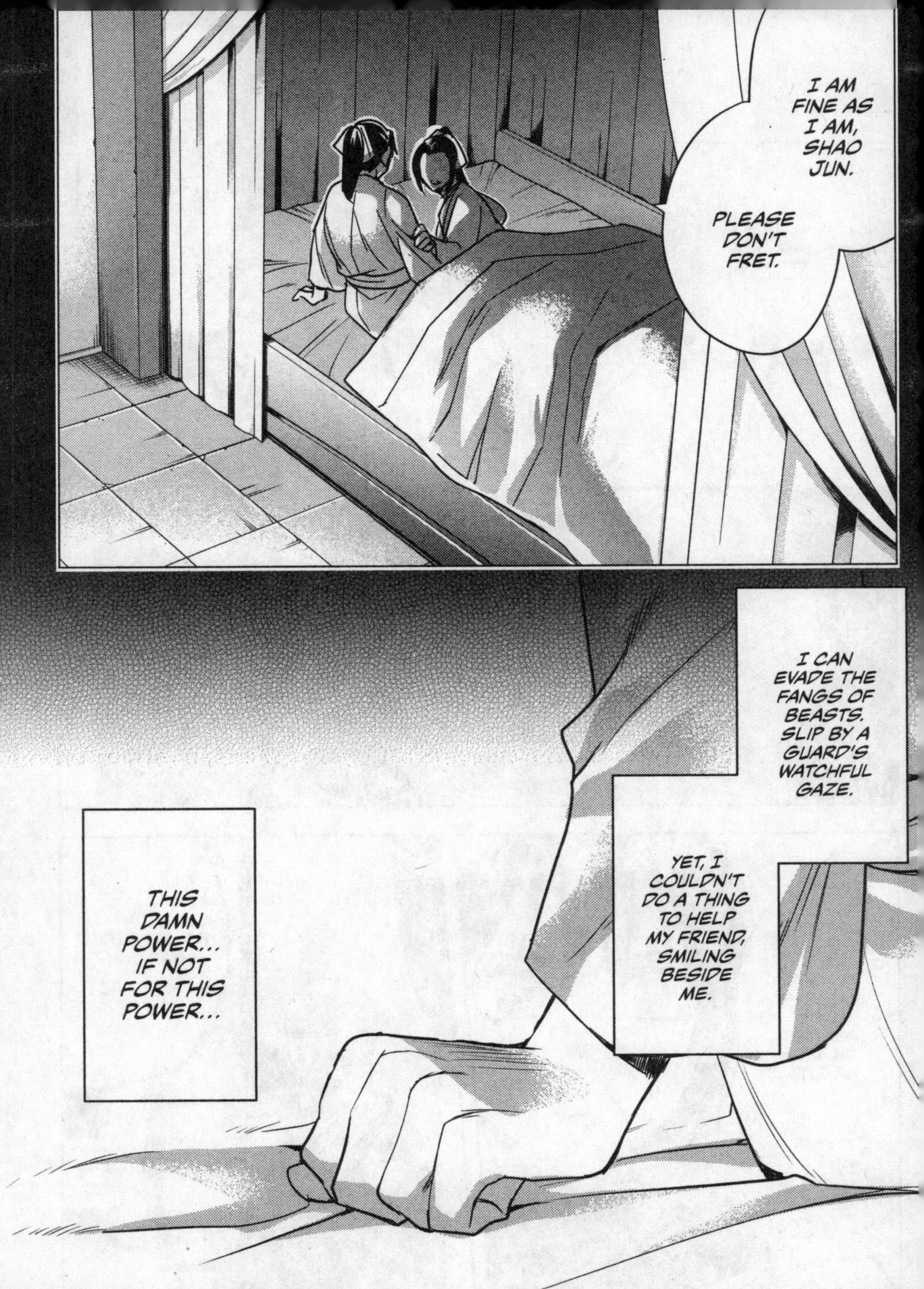
I AM FINE AS I AM, SHAO JUN.
PLEASE DON'T FRET.
I CAN EVADE THE FANGS OF BEASTS. SLIP BY A GUARD'S WATCHFUL GAZE.
YET, I COULDN'T DO A THING TO HELP MY FRIEND, SMILING BESIDE ME.
THIS DAMN POWER... IF NOT FOR THIS POWER...

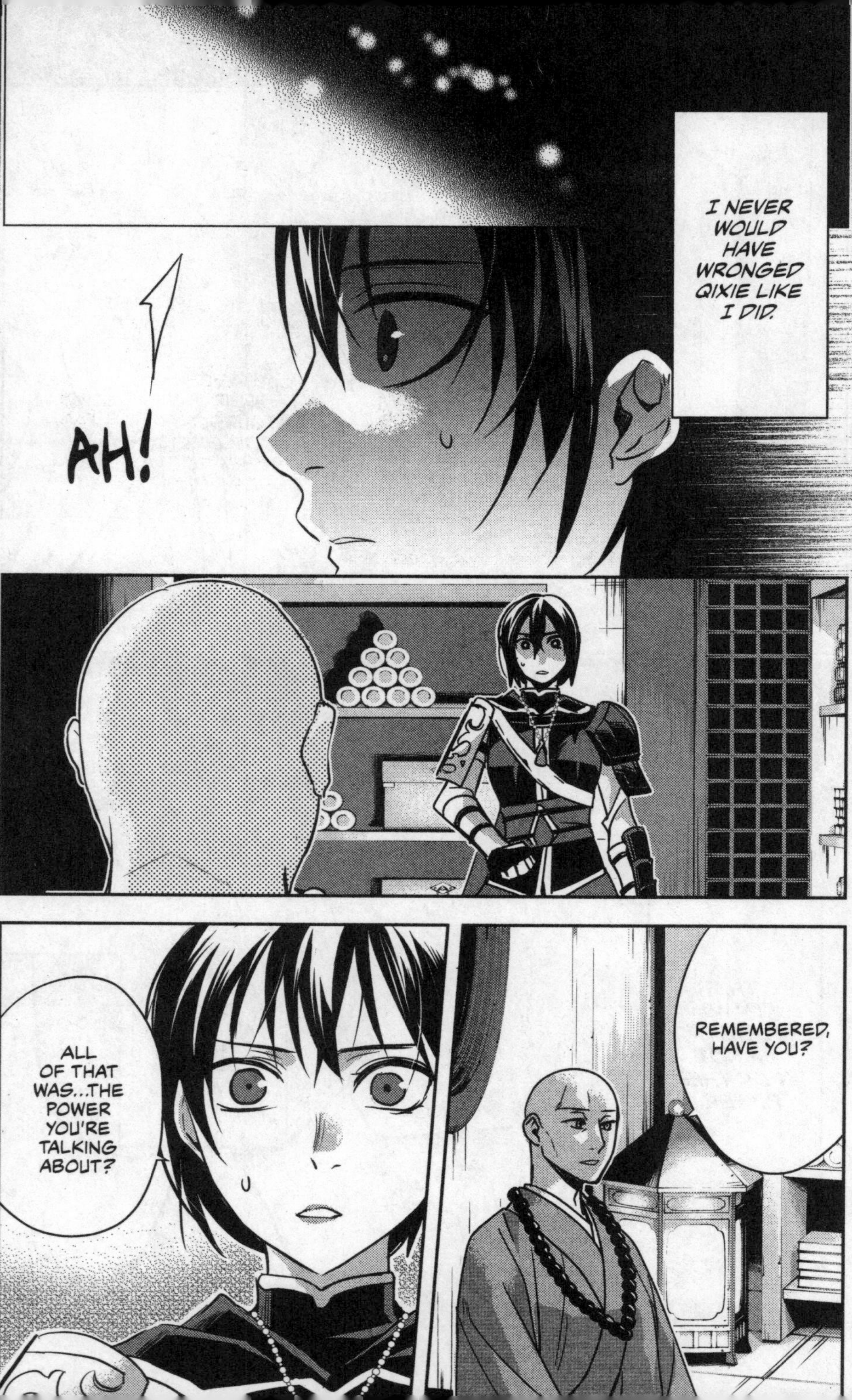
I NEVER WOULD HAVE WRONGED QIXIE LIKE I DID.
AH!
REMEMBERED, HAVE YOU?
ALL OF THAT WAS...THE POWER YOU'RE TALKING ABOUT?

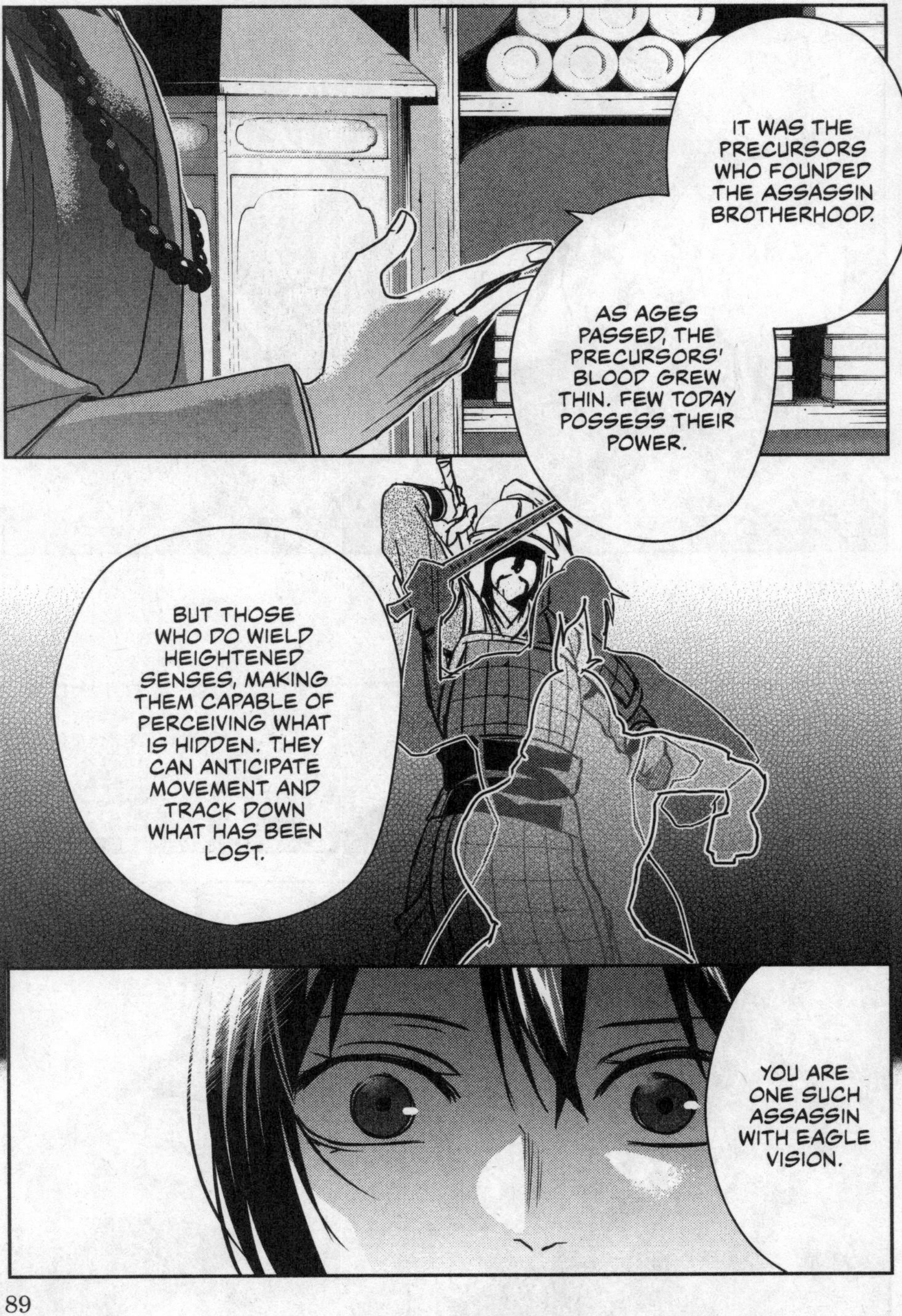
IT WAS THE PRECURSORS WHO FOUNDED THE ASSASSIN BROTHERHOOD.
AS AGES PASSED, THE PRECURSORS' BLOOD GREW THIN. FEW TODAY POSSESS THEIR POWER.
BUT THOSE WHO DO WIELD HEIGHTENED SENSES, MAKING THEM CAPABLE OF PERCEIVING WHAT IS HIDDEN. THEY CAN ANTICIPATE MOVEMENT AND TRACK DOWN WHAT HAS BEEN LOST.
YOU ARE ONE SUCH ASSASSIN WITH EAGLE VISION.

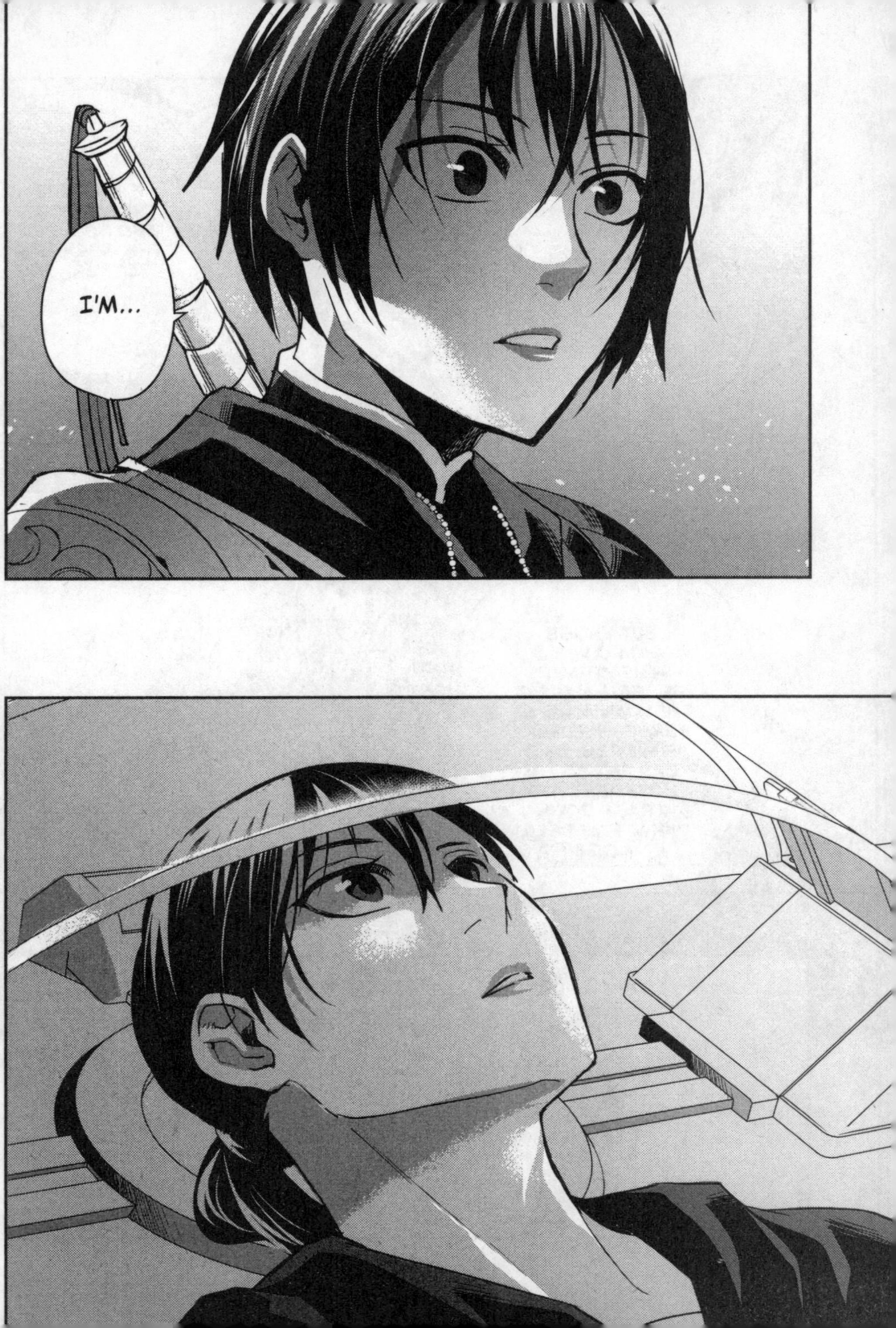
I'M...

THAT'S ALL FOR NOW.

HOW ARE YOU FEELING?

TIRED, I SUPPOSE? LET'S TAKE A BREAK.

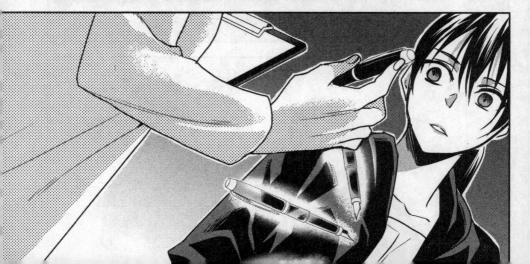

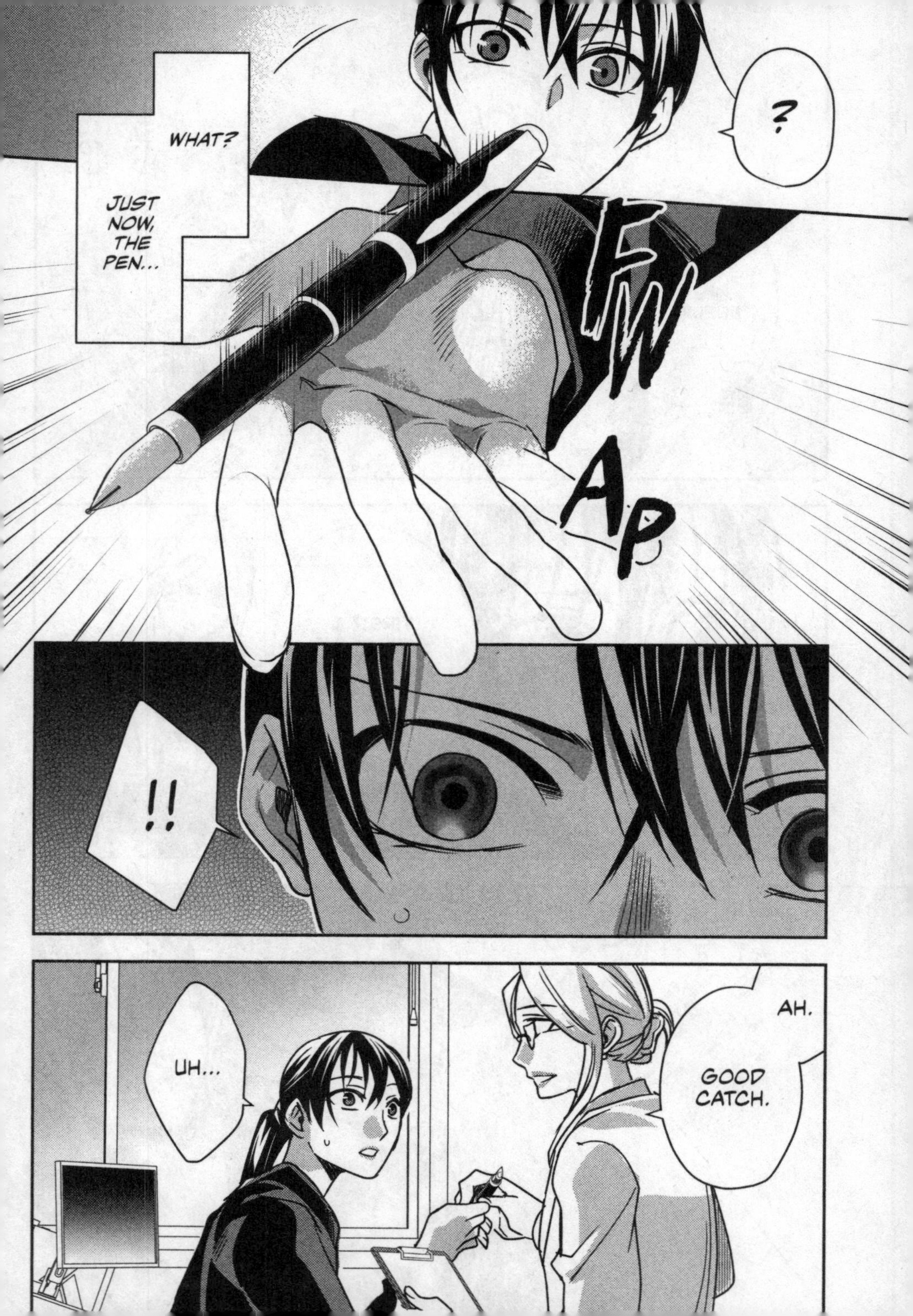
?
WHAT?
JUST NOW, THE PEN...
FWAP
!!
AH.
GOOD CATCH.
UH...

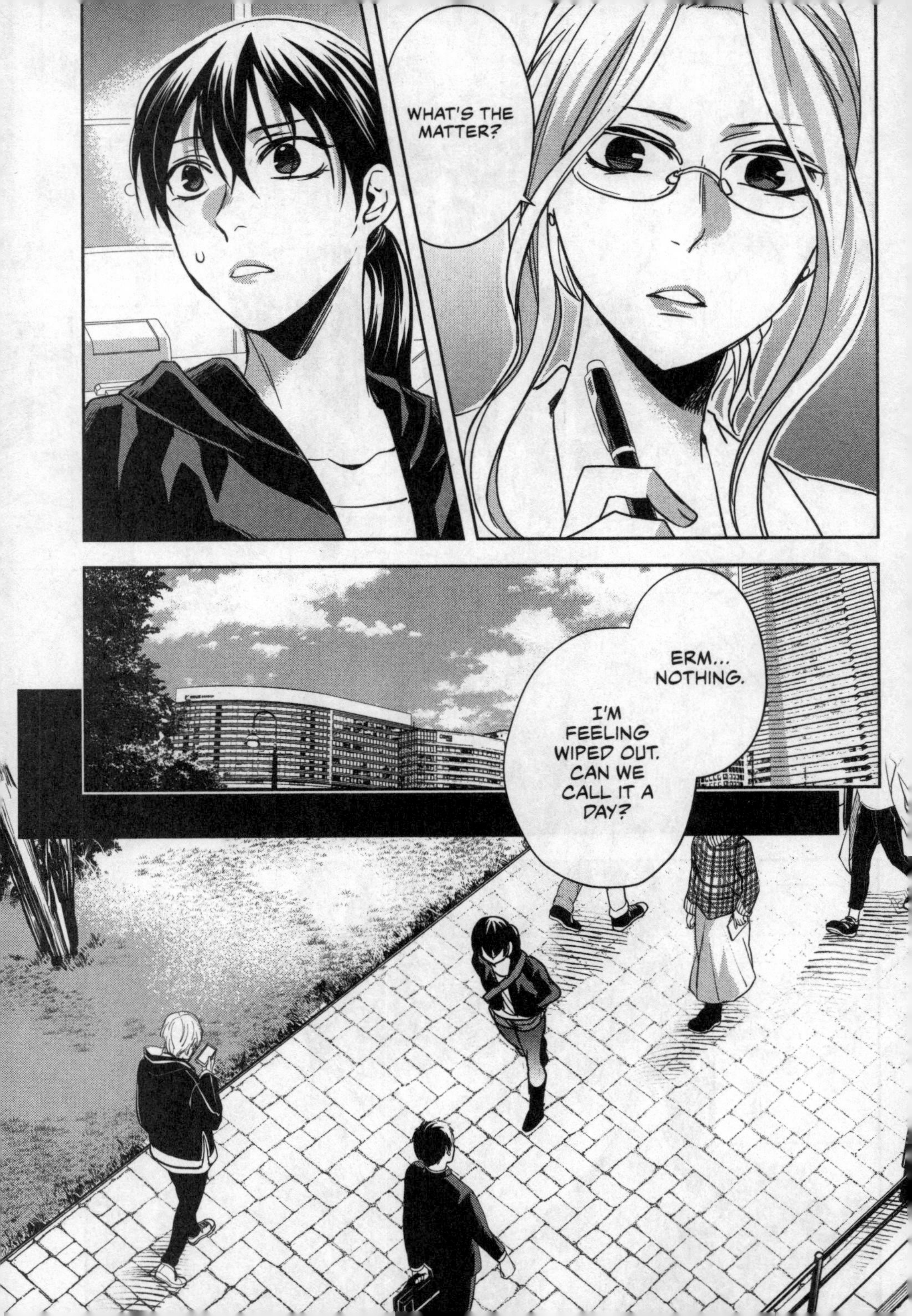
WHAT'S THE MATTER?
ERM... NOTHING.
I'M FEELING WIPED OUT. CAN WE CALL IT A DAY?

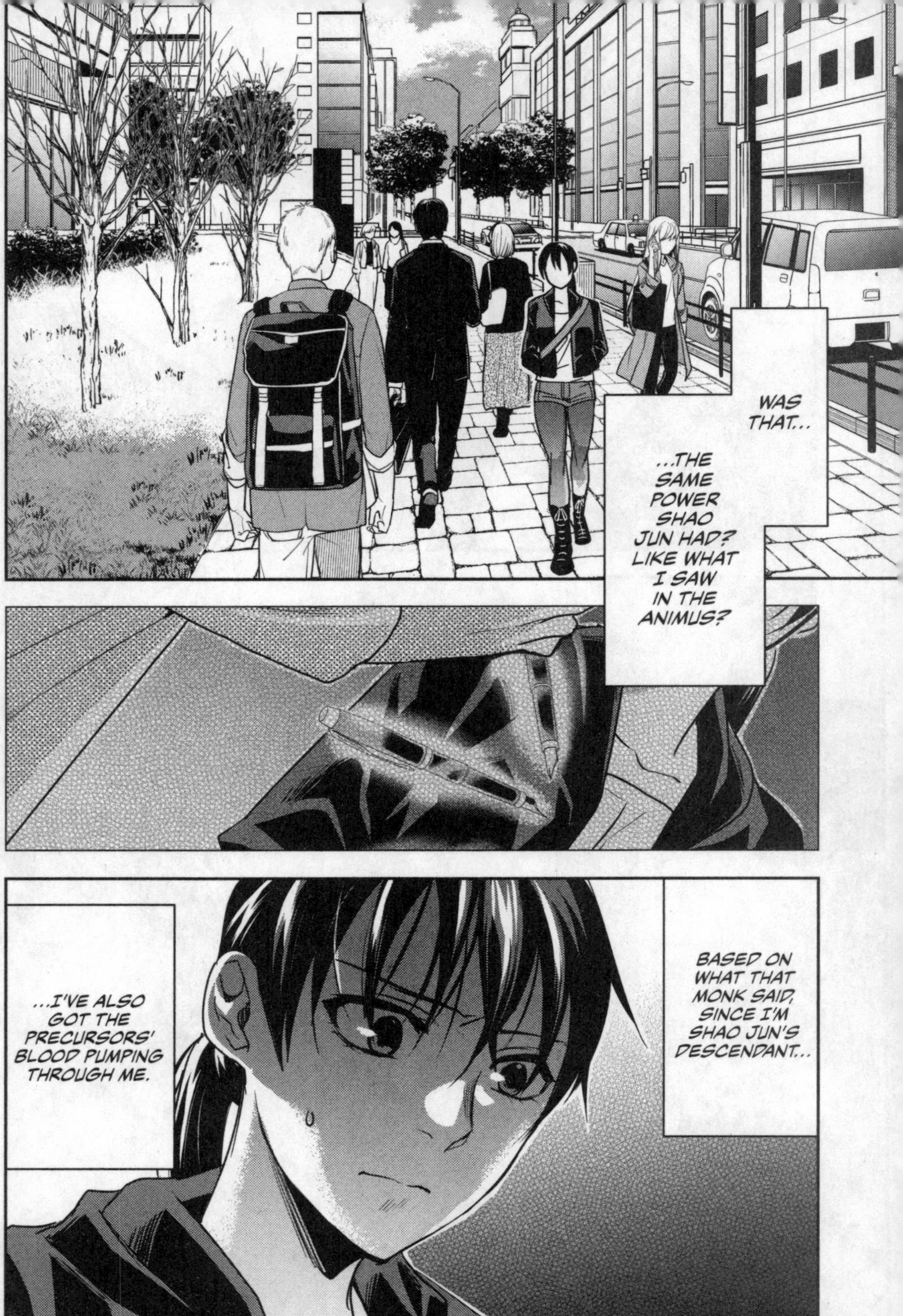
WAS THAT...
...THE SAME POWER SHAO JUN HAD? LIKE WHAT I SAW IN THE ANIMUS?
BASED ON WHAT THAT MONK SAID, SINCE I'M SHAO JUN'S DESCENDANT...
...I'VE ALSO GOT THE PRECURSORS' BLOOD PUMPING THROUGH ME.

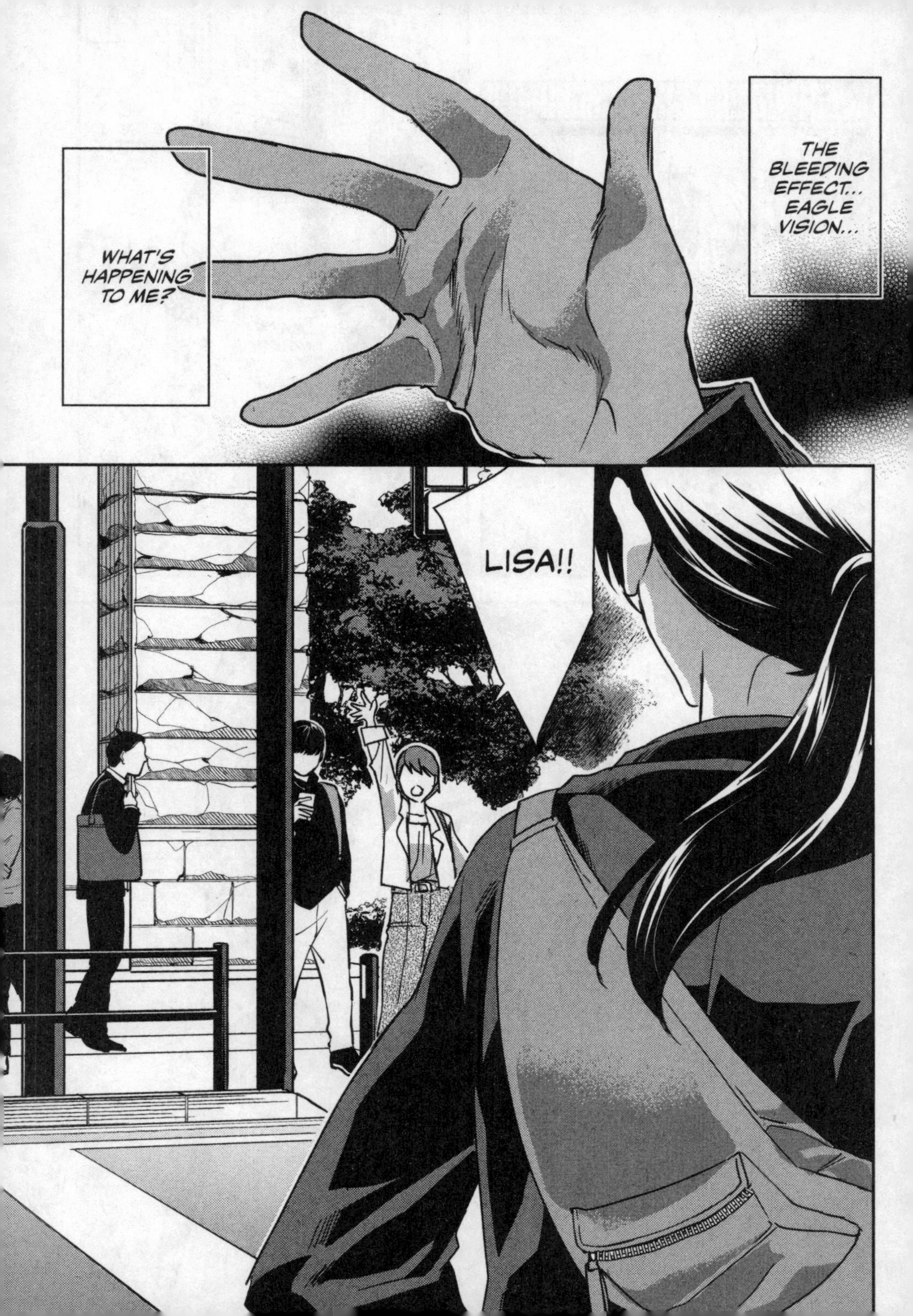
THE BLEEDING EFFECT... EAGLE VISION...
WHAT'S HAPPENING TO ME?
LISA!!

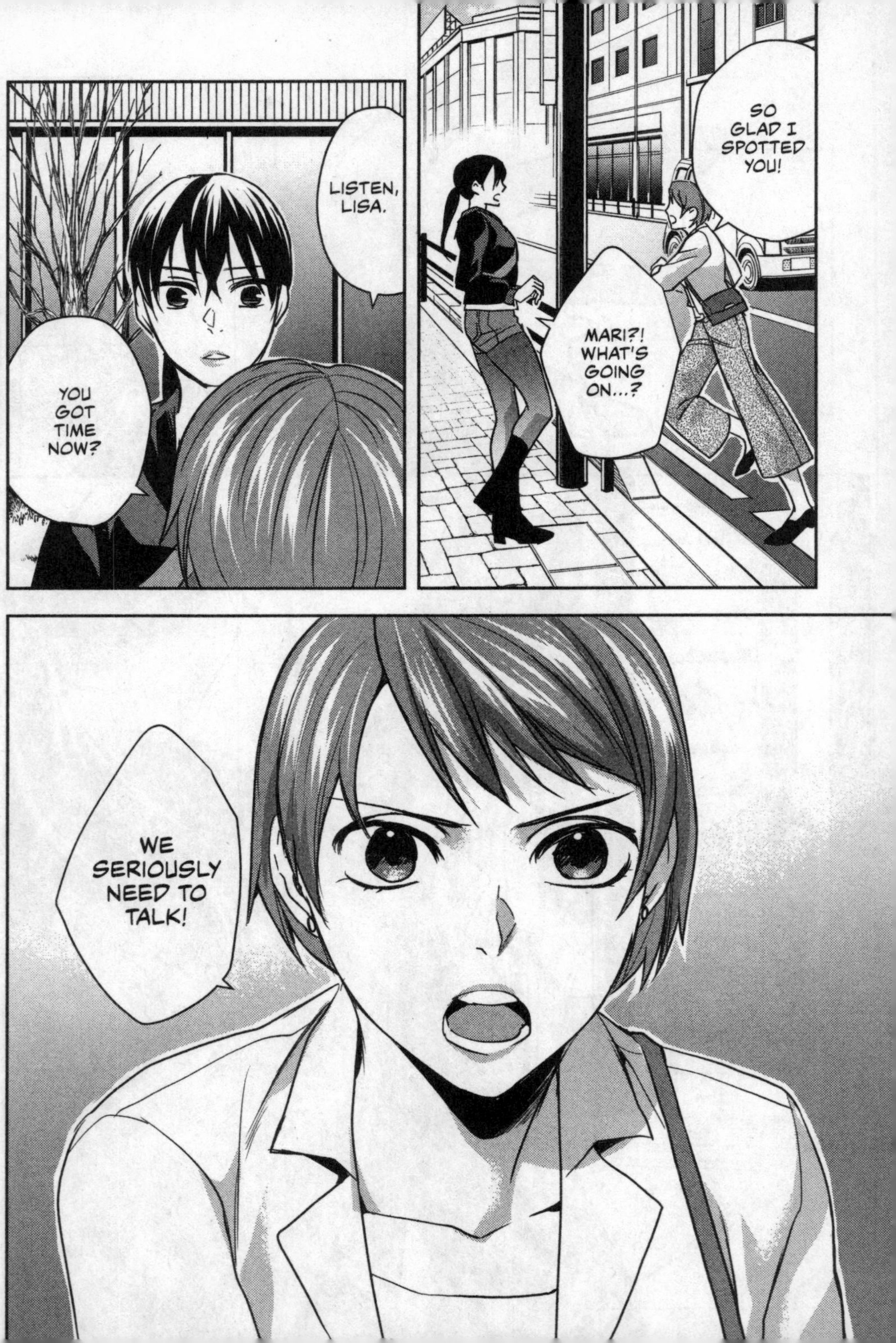
SO GLAD I SPOTTED YOU!
MARI?! WHAT'S GOING ON...?
LISTEN, LISA.
YOU GOT TIME NOW?
WE SERIOUSLY NEED TO TALK!

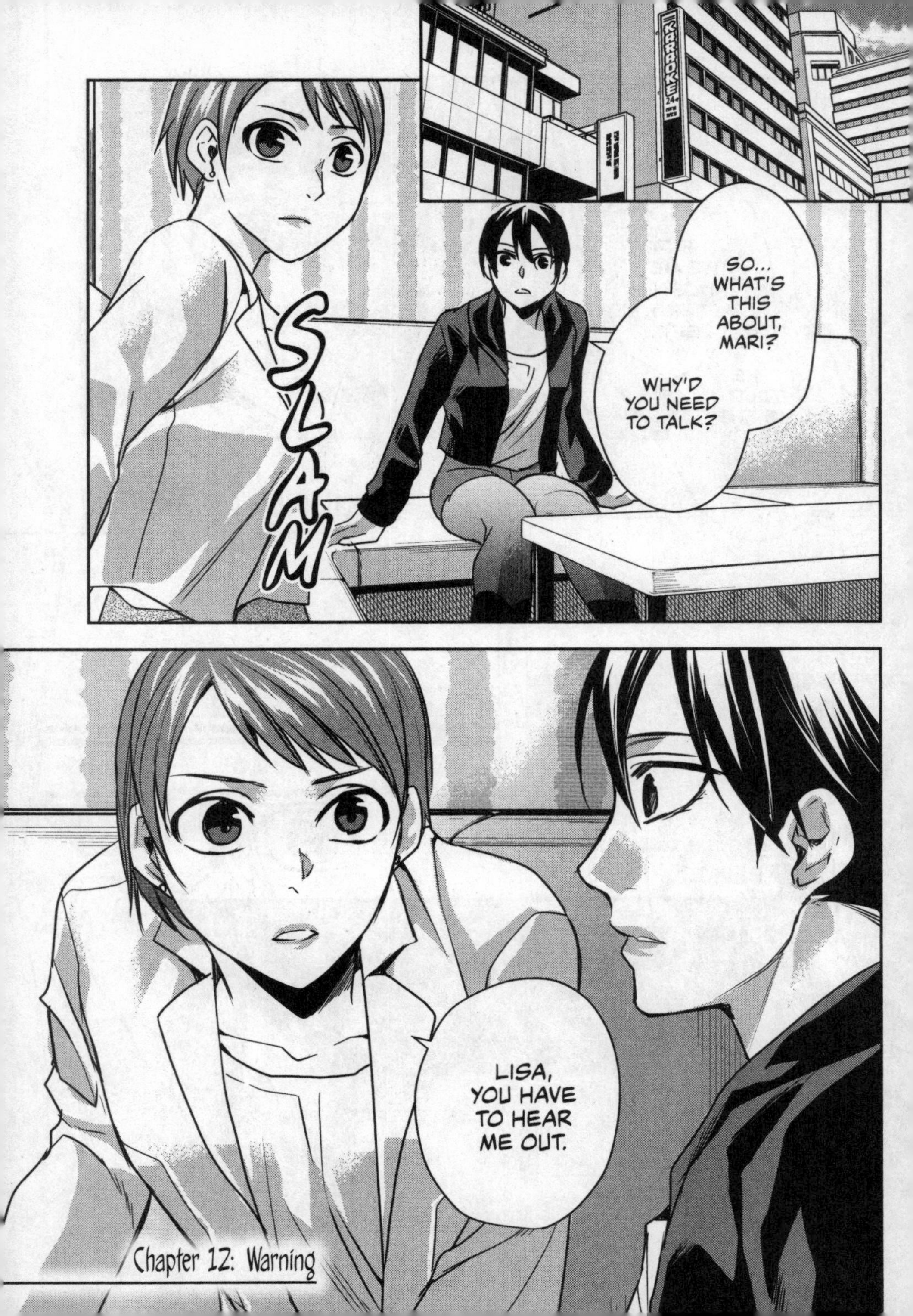
KARAOKE
SO... WHAT'S THIS ABOUT, MARI?
WHY'D YOU NEED TO TALK?
SLAM
LISA, YOU HAVE TO HEAR ME OUT.
Chapter 12: Warning

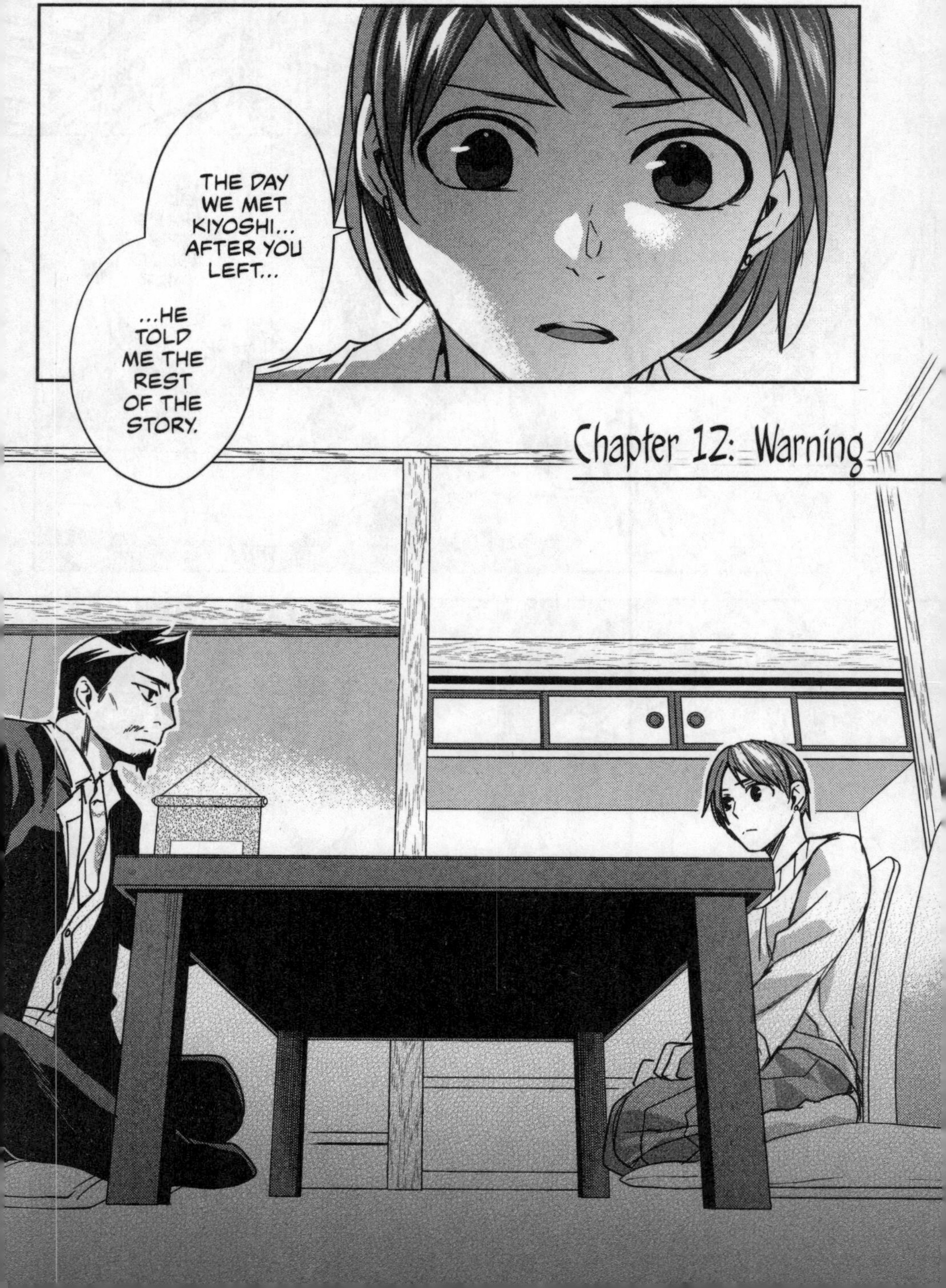
THE DAY WE MET KIYOSHI... AFTER YOU LEFT...
...HE TOLD ME THE REST OF THE STORY.
Chapter 12: Warning

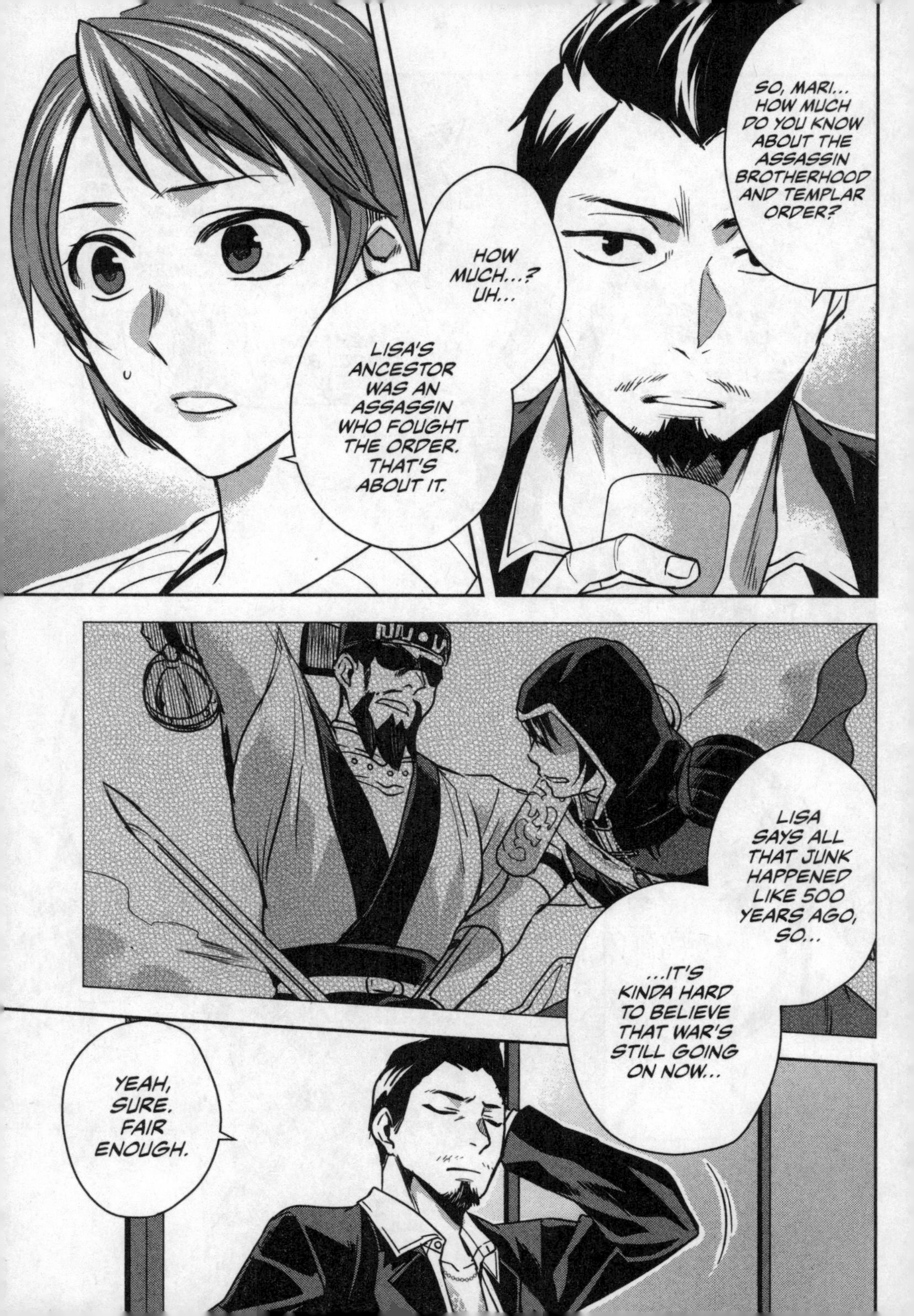
SO, MARI... HOW MUCH DO YOU KNOW ABOUT THE ASSASSIN BROTHERHOOD AND TEMPLAR ORDER?
HOW MUCH...? UH...
LISA'S ANCESTOR WAS AN ASSASSIN WHO FOUGHT THE ORDER. THAT'S ABOUT IT.
LISA SAYS ALL THAT JUNK HAPPENED LIKE 500 YEARS AGO, SO...
...IT'S KINDA HARD TO BELIEVE THAT WAR'S STILL GOING ON NOW...
YEAH, SURE. FAIR ENOUGH.

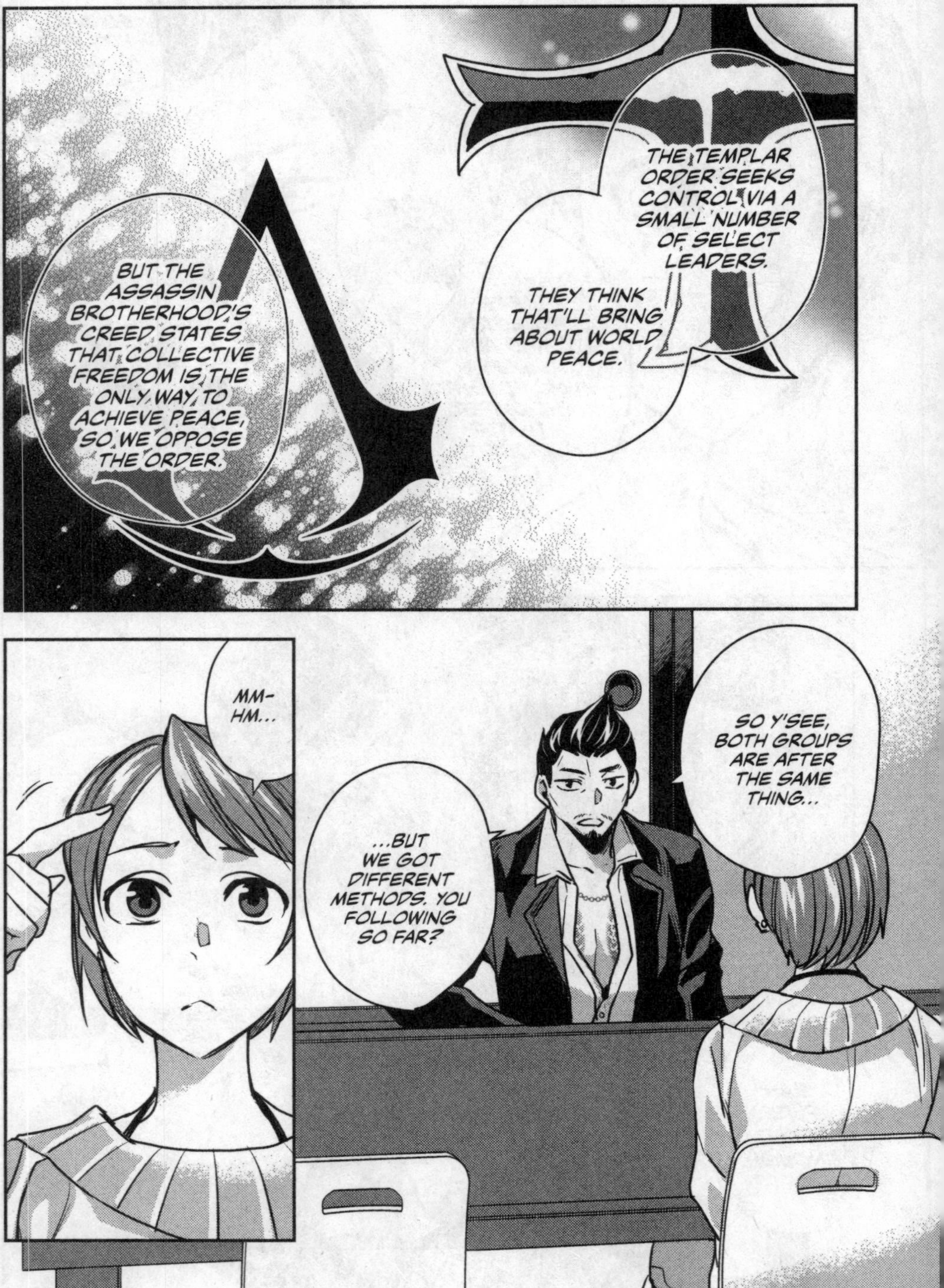
THE TEMPLAR ORDER SEEKS CONTROL VIA A SMALL NUMBER OF SELECT LEADERS.
THEY THINK THAT'LL BRING ABOUT WORLD PEACE.
BUT THE ASSASSIN BROTHERHOOD'S CREED STATES THAT COLLECTIVE FREEDOM IS THE ONLY WAY TO ACHIEVE PEACE, SO WE OPPOSE THE ORDER.
SO Y'SEE, BOTH GROUPS ARE AFTER THE SAME THING...
...BUT WE GOT DIFFERENT METHODS. YOU FOLLOWING SO FAR?
MM-HM...

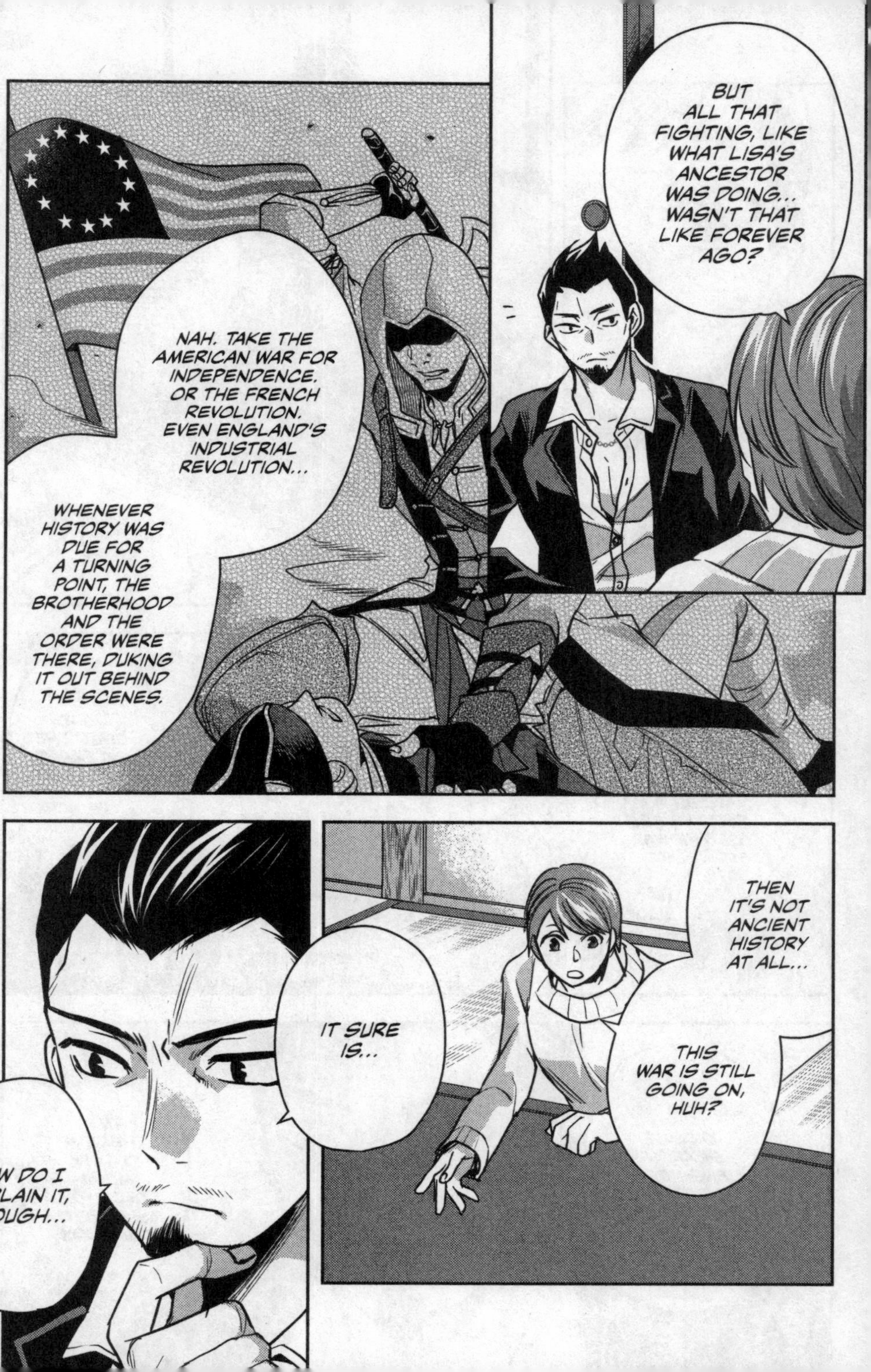
BUT ALL THAT FIGHTING, LIKE WHAT LISA'S ANCESTOR WAS DOING... WASN'T THAT LIKE FOREVER AGO?
NAH. TAKE THE AMERICAN WAR FOR INDEPENDENCE. OR THE FRENCH REVOLUTION. EVEN ENGLAND'S INDUSTRIAL REVOLUTION...
WHENEVER HISTORY WAS DUE FOR A TURNING POINT, THE BROTHERHOOD AND THE ORDER WERE THERE, DUKING IT OUT BEHIND THE SCENES.
THEN IT'S NOT ANCIENT HISTORY AT ALL...
THIS WAR IS STILL GOING ON, HUH?
IT SURE IS...
HOW DO I EXPLAIN IT, THOUGH...

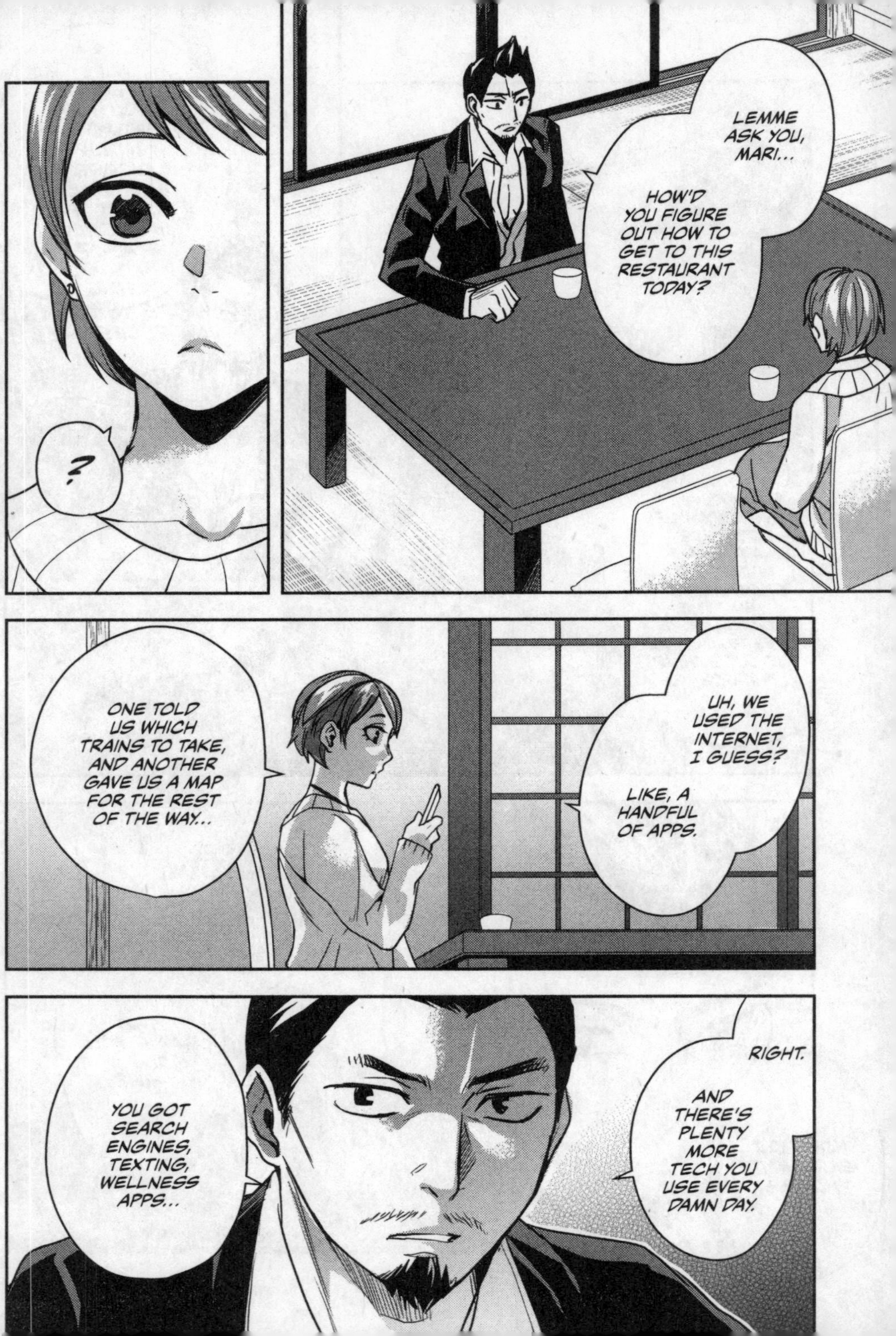
LEMME ASK YOU, MARI...
HOW'D YOU FIGURE OUT HOW TO GET TO THIS RESTAURANT TODAY?
?
UH, WE USED THE INTERNET, I GUESS?
LIKE, A HANDFUL OF APPS.
ONE TOLD US WHICH TRAINS TO TAKE, AND ANOTHER GAVE US A MAP FOR THE REST OF THE WAY...
RIGHT.
AND THERE'S PLENTY MORE TECH YOU USE EVERY DAMN DAY.
YOU GOT SEARCH ENGINES, TEXTING, WELLNESS APPS...

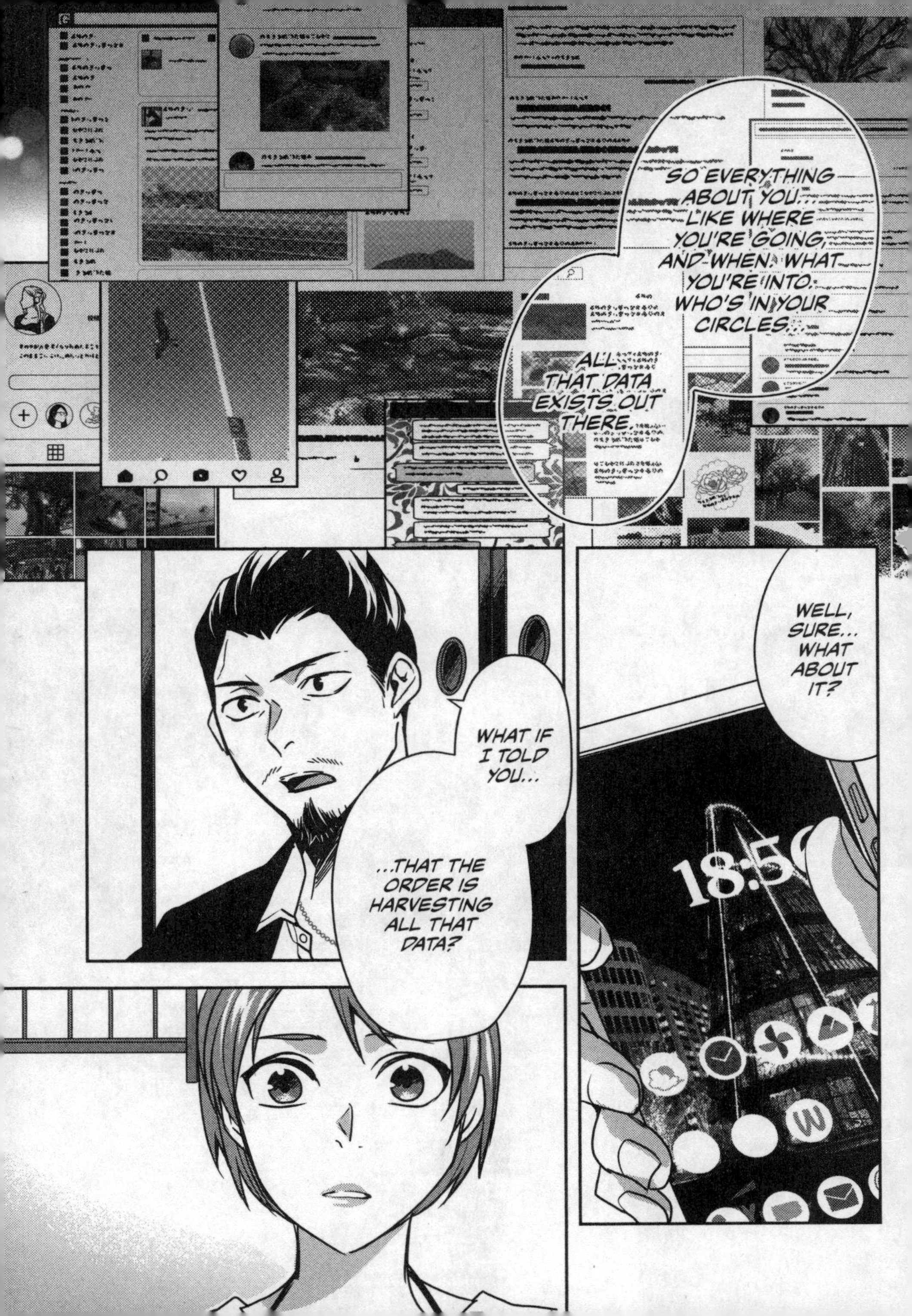
SO EVERYTHING ABOUT YOU... LIKE WHERE YOU'RE GOING, AND WHEN. WHAT YOU'RE INTO. WHO'S IN YOUR CIRCLES...
ALL THAT DATA EXISTS OUT THERE.
WELL, SURE... WHAT ABOUT IT?
WHAT IF I TOLD YOU...
...THAT THE ORDER IS HARVESTING ALL THAT DATA?

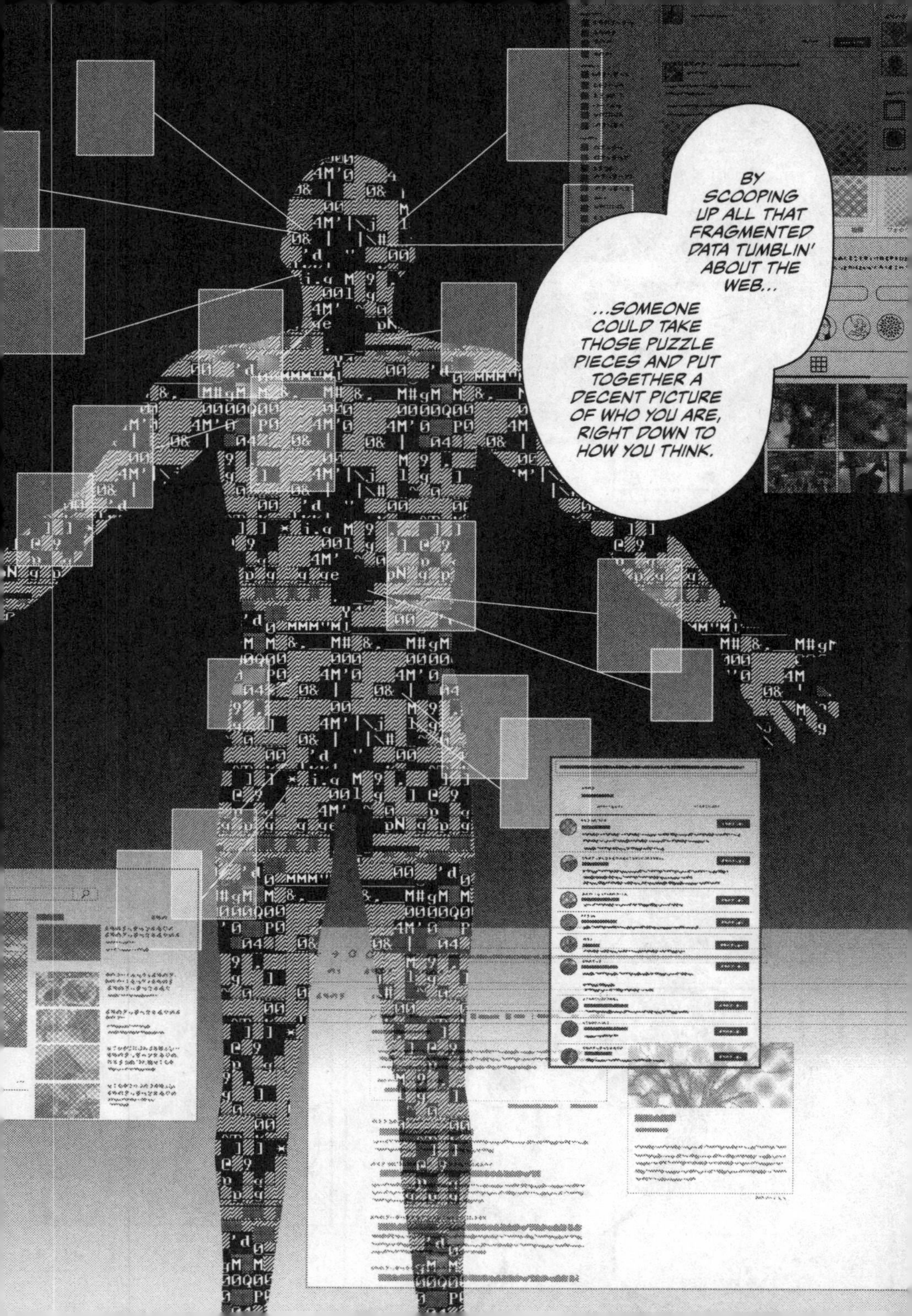
BY SCOOPING UP ALL THAT FRAGMENTED DATA TUMBLIN' ABOUT THE WEB...
...SOMEONE COULD TAKE THOSE PUZZLE PIECES AND PUT TOGETHER A DECENT PICTURE OF WHO YOU ARE, RIGHT DOWN TO HOW YOU THINK.

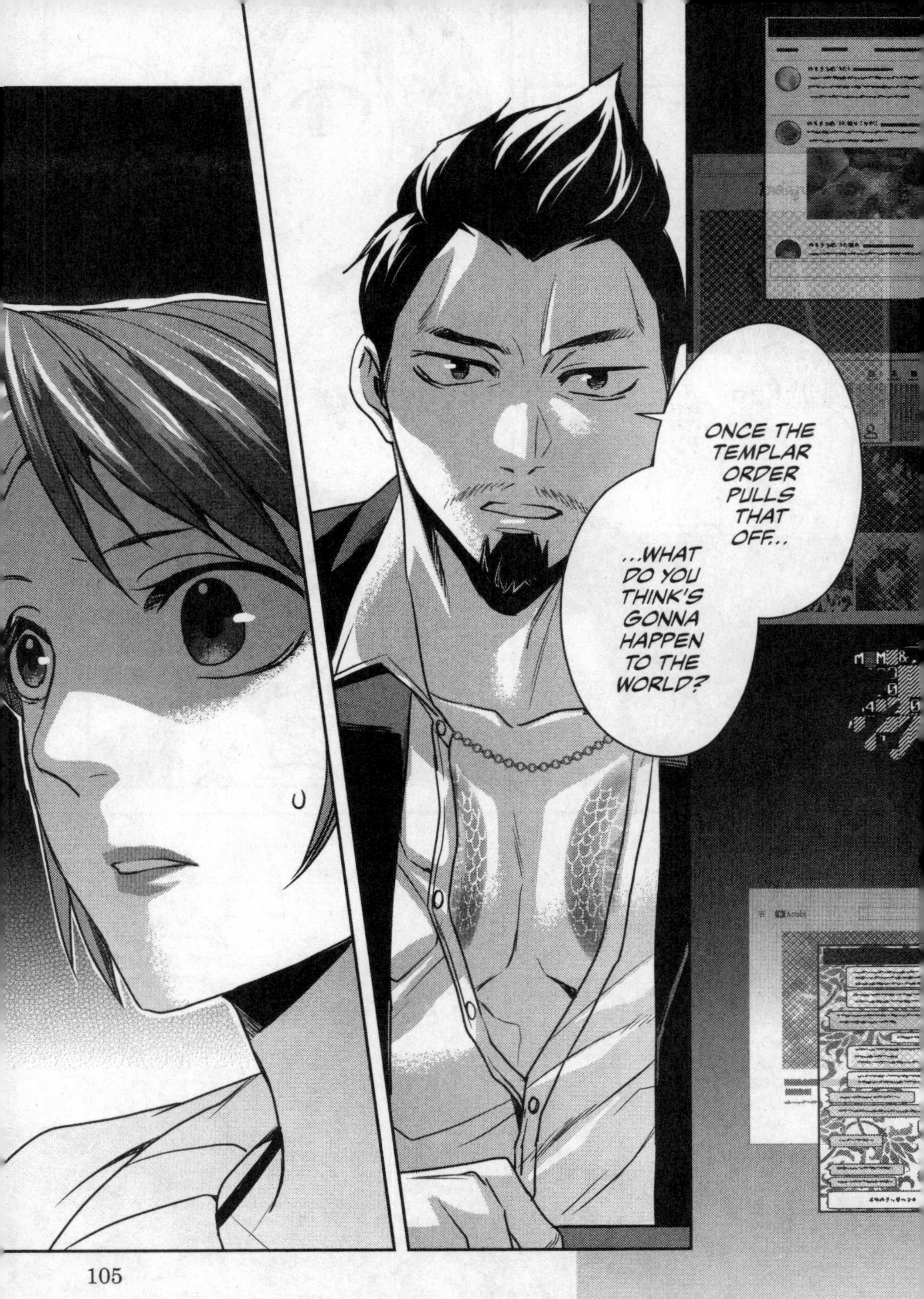
ONCE THE TEMPLAR ORDER PULLS THAT OFF...
...WHAT DO YOU THINK'S GONNA HAPPEN TO THE WORLD?

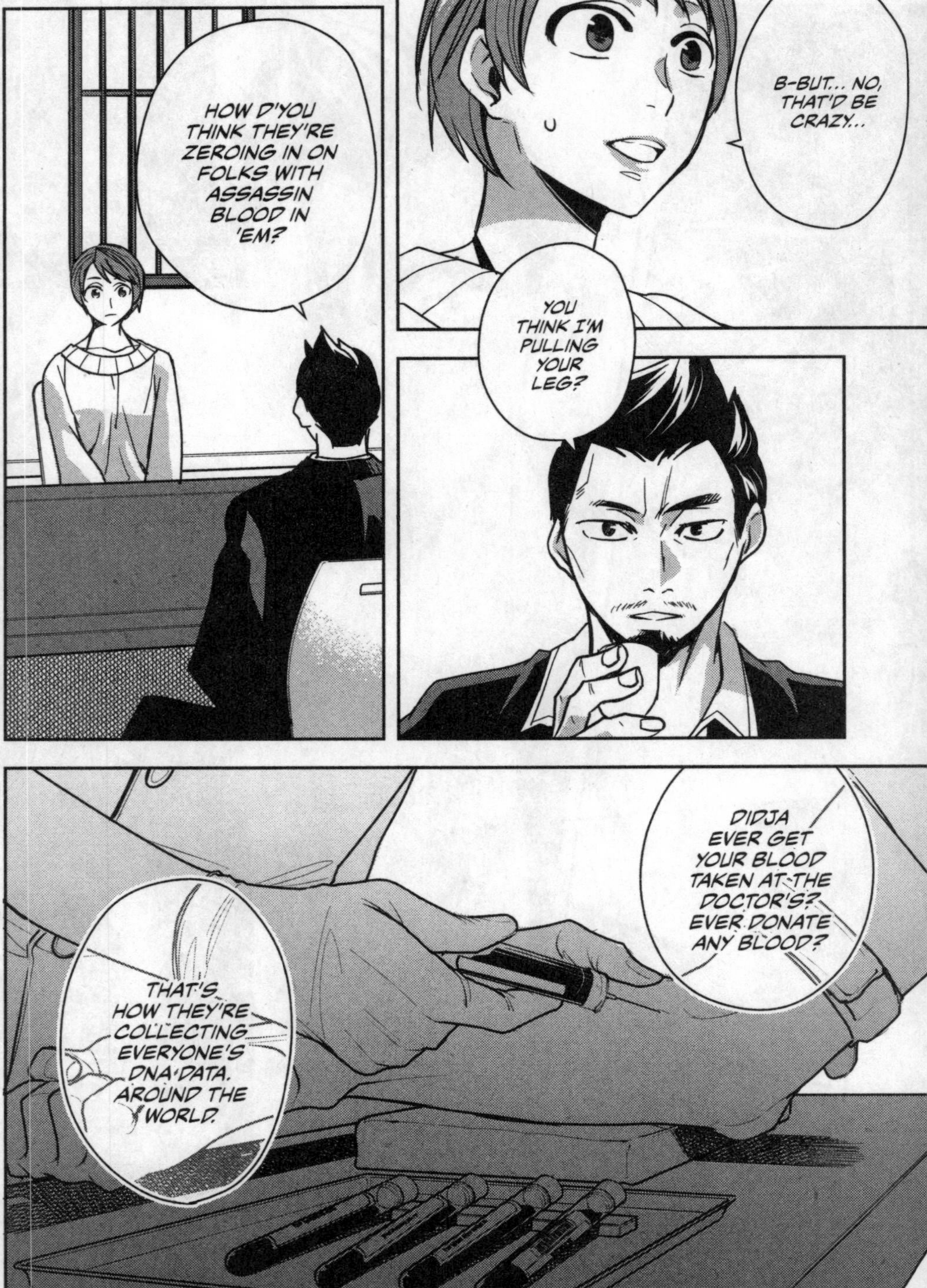
B-BUT... NO, THAT'D BE CRAZY...
YOU THINK I'M PULLING YOUR LEG?
HOW D'YOU THINK THEY'RE ZEROING IN ON FOLKS WITH ASSASSIN BLOOD IN 'EM?
DIDJA EVER GET YOUR BLOOD TAKEN AT THE DOCTOR'S? EVER DONATE ANY BLOOD?
THAT'S HOW THEY'RE COLLECTING EVERYONE'S DNA DATA, AROUND THE WORLD.

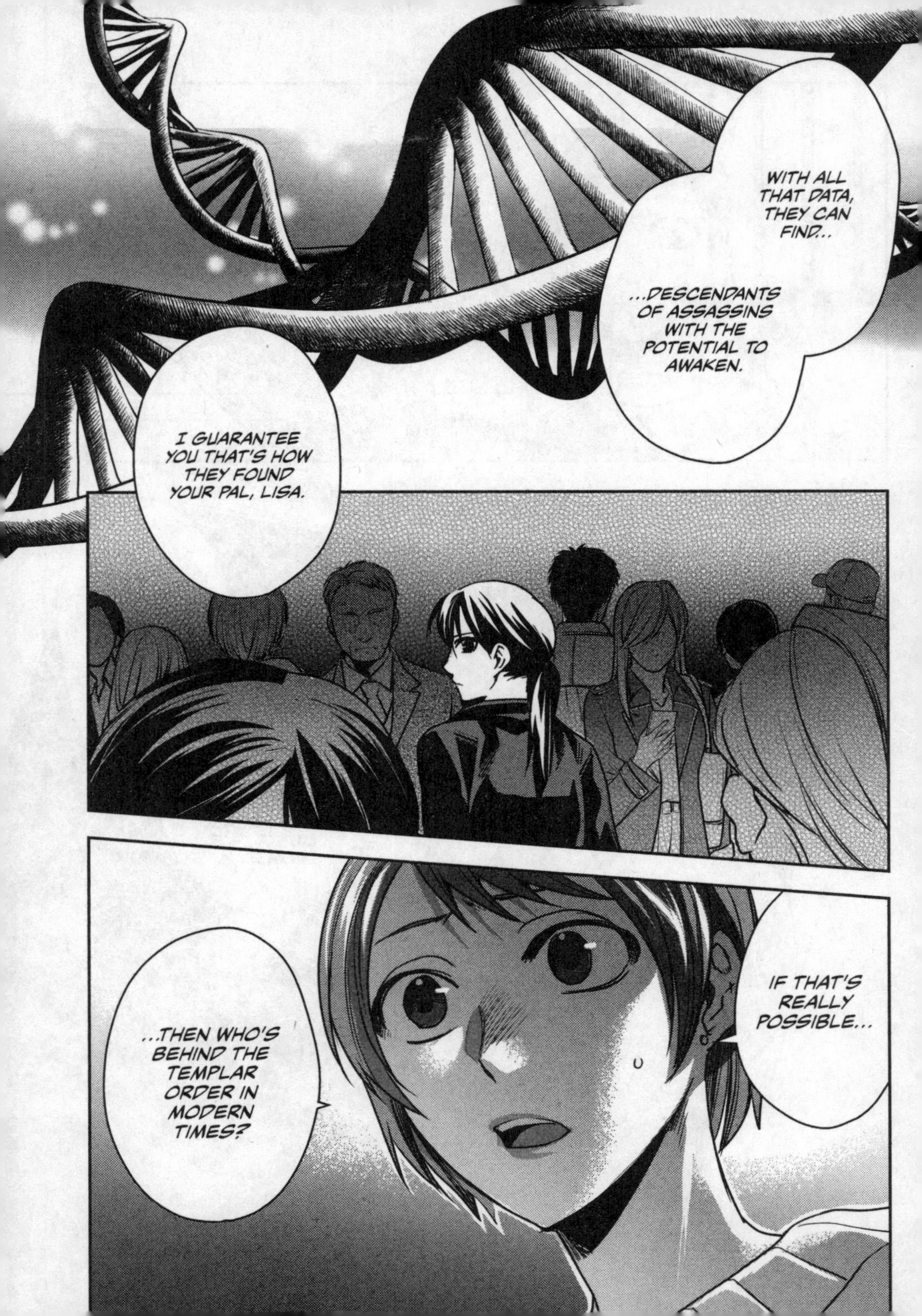
WITH ALL THAT DATA, THEY CAN FIND...
...DESCENDANTS OF ASSASSINS WITH THE POTENTIAL TO AWAKEN.
I GUARANTEE YOU THAT'S HOW THEY FOUND YOUR PAL, LISA.
IF THAT'S REALLY POSSIBLE...
...THEN WHO'S BEHIND THE TEMPLAR ORDER IN MODERN TIMES?

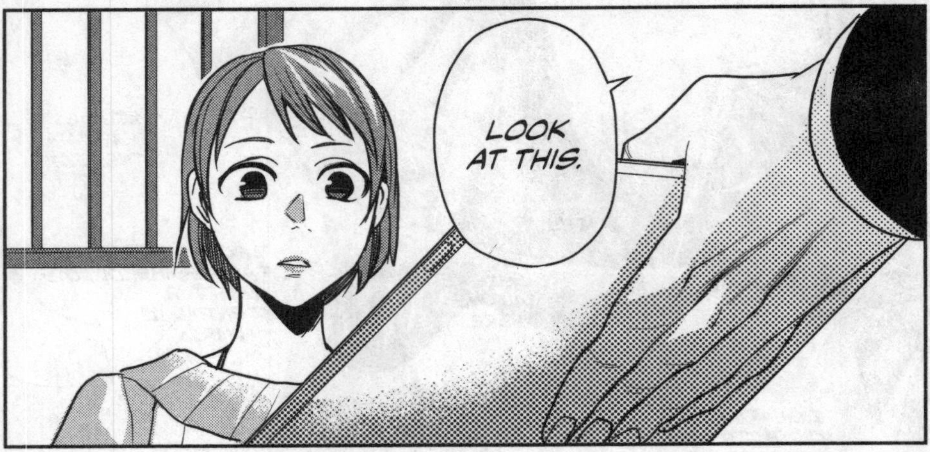
LOOK AT THIS.

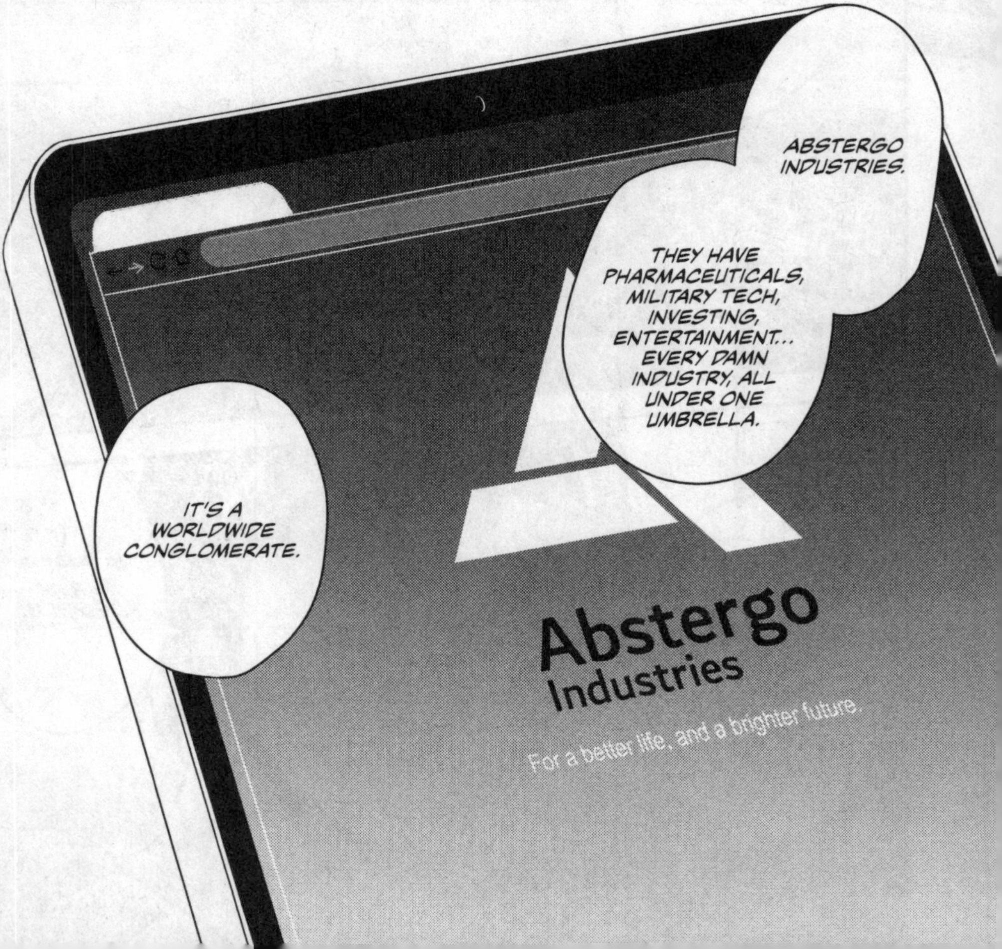
ABSTERGO INDUSTRIES.
THEY HAVE PHARMACEUTICALS, MILITARY TECH, INVESTING, ENTERTAINMENT... EVERY DAMN INDUSTRY, ALL UNDER ONE UMBRELLA.
IT'S A WORLDWIDE CONGLOMERATE.
Abstergo Industries
For a better life, and a brighter future.

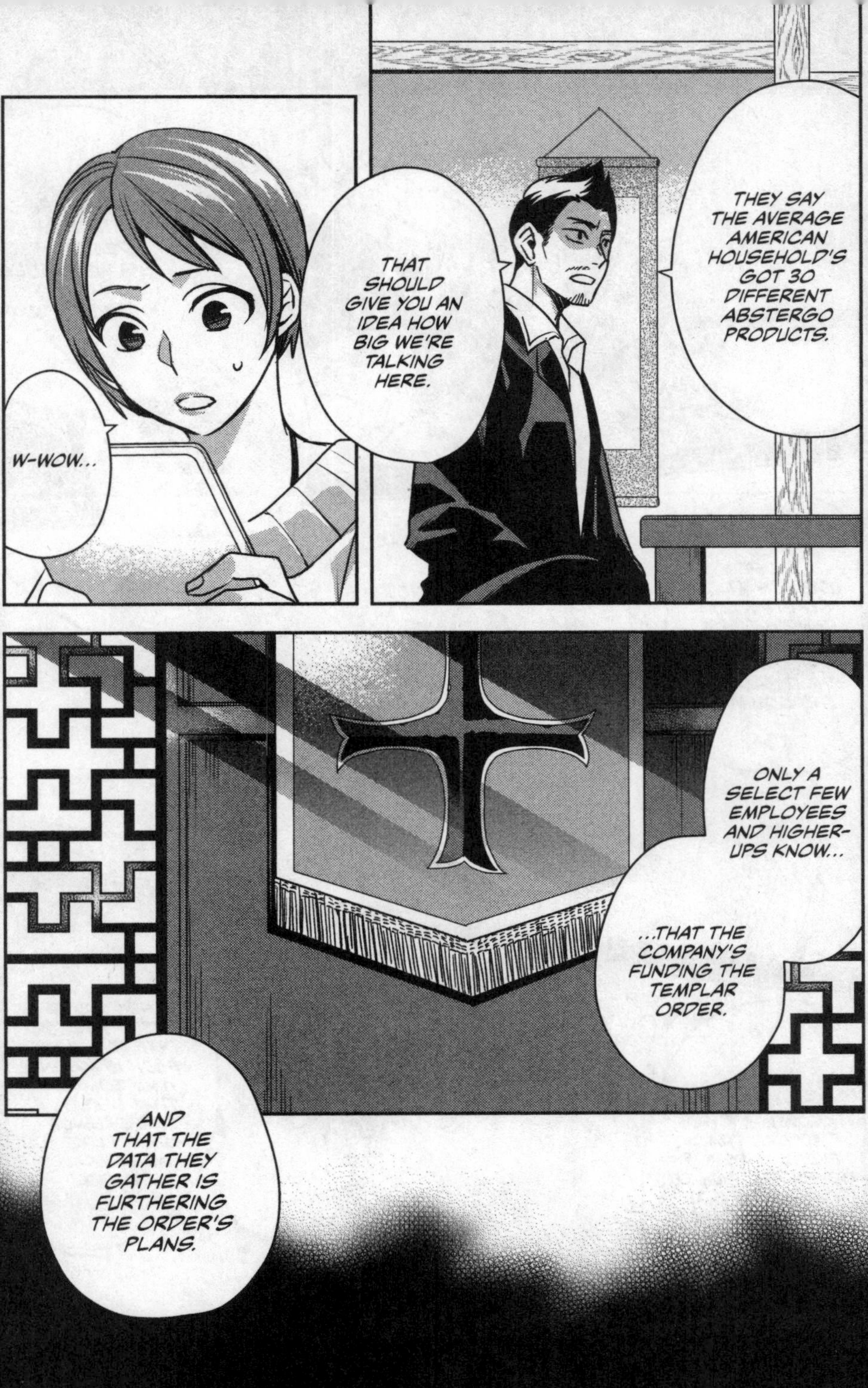
THEY SAY THE AVERAGE AMERICAN HOUSEHOLD'S GOT 30 DIFFERENT ABSTERGO PRODUCTS.
THAT SHOULD GIVE YOU AN IDEA HOW BIG WE'RE TALKING HERE.
W-WOW...
ONLY A SELECT FEW EMPLOYEES AND HIGHER-UPS KNOW...
...THAT THE COMPANY'S FUNDING THE TEMPLAR ORDER.
AND THAT THE DATA THEY GATHER IS FURTHERING THE ORDER'S PLANS.

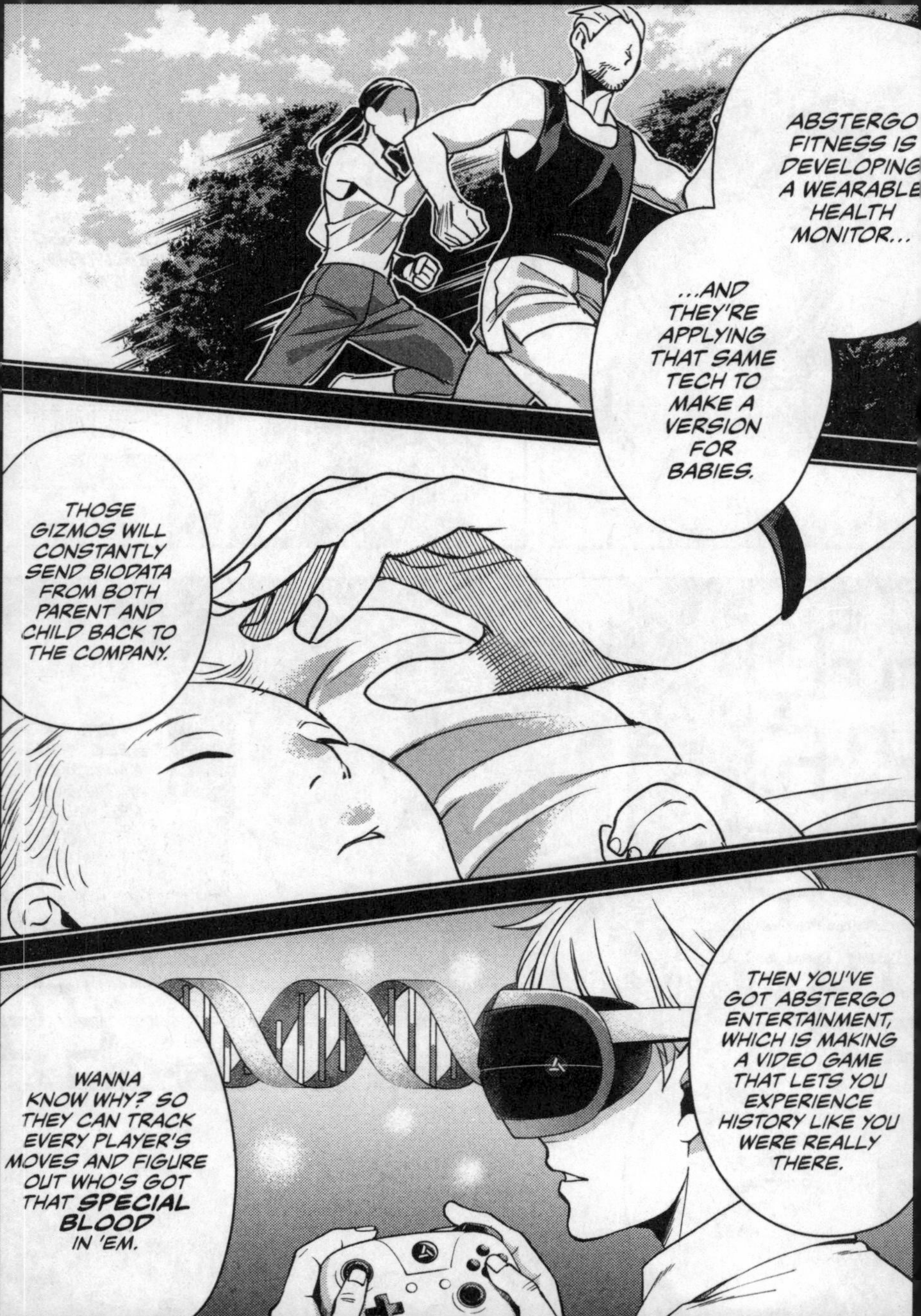
ABSTERGO FITNESS IS DEVELOPING A WEARABLE HEALTH MONITOR...
...AND THEY'RE APPLYING THAT SAME TECH TO MAKE A VERSION FOR BABIES.
THOSE GIZMOS WILL CONSTANTLY SEND BIODATA FROM BOTH PARENT AND CHILD BACK TO THE COMPANY.
THEN YOU'VE GOT ABSTERGO ENTERTAINMENT, WHICH IS MAKING A VIDEO GAME THAT LETS YOU EXPERIENCE HISTORY LIKE YOU WERE REALLY THERE.
WANNA KNOW WHY? SO THEY CAN TRACK EVERY PLAYER'S MOVES AND FIGURE OUT WHO'S GOT THAT **SPECIAL BLOOD** IN 'EM.

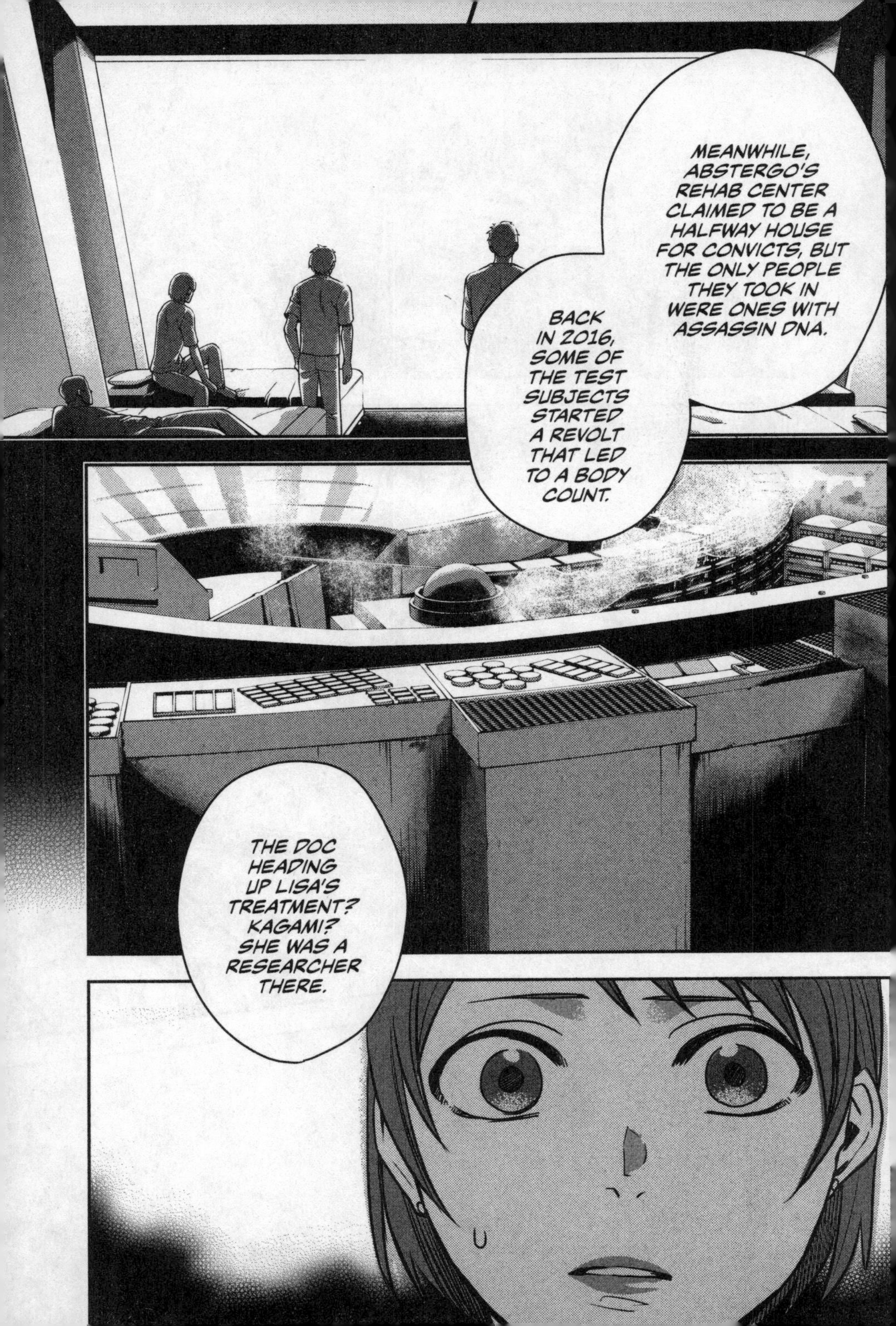
MEANWHILE, ABSTERGO'S REHAB CENTER CLAIMED TO BE A HALFWAY HOUSE FOR CONVICTS, BUT THE ONLY PEOPLE THEY TOOK IN WERE ONES WITH ASSASSIN DNA.
BACK IN 2016, SOME OF THE TEST SUBJECTS STARTED A REVOLT THAT LED TO A BODY COUNT.
THE DOC HEADING UP LISA'S TREATMENT? KAGAMI? SHE WAS A RESEARCHER THERE.

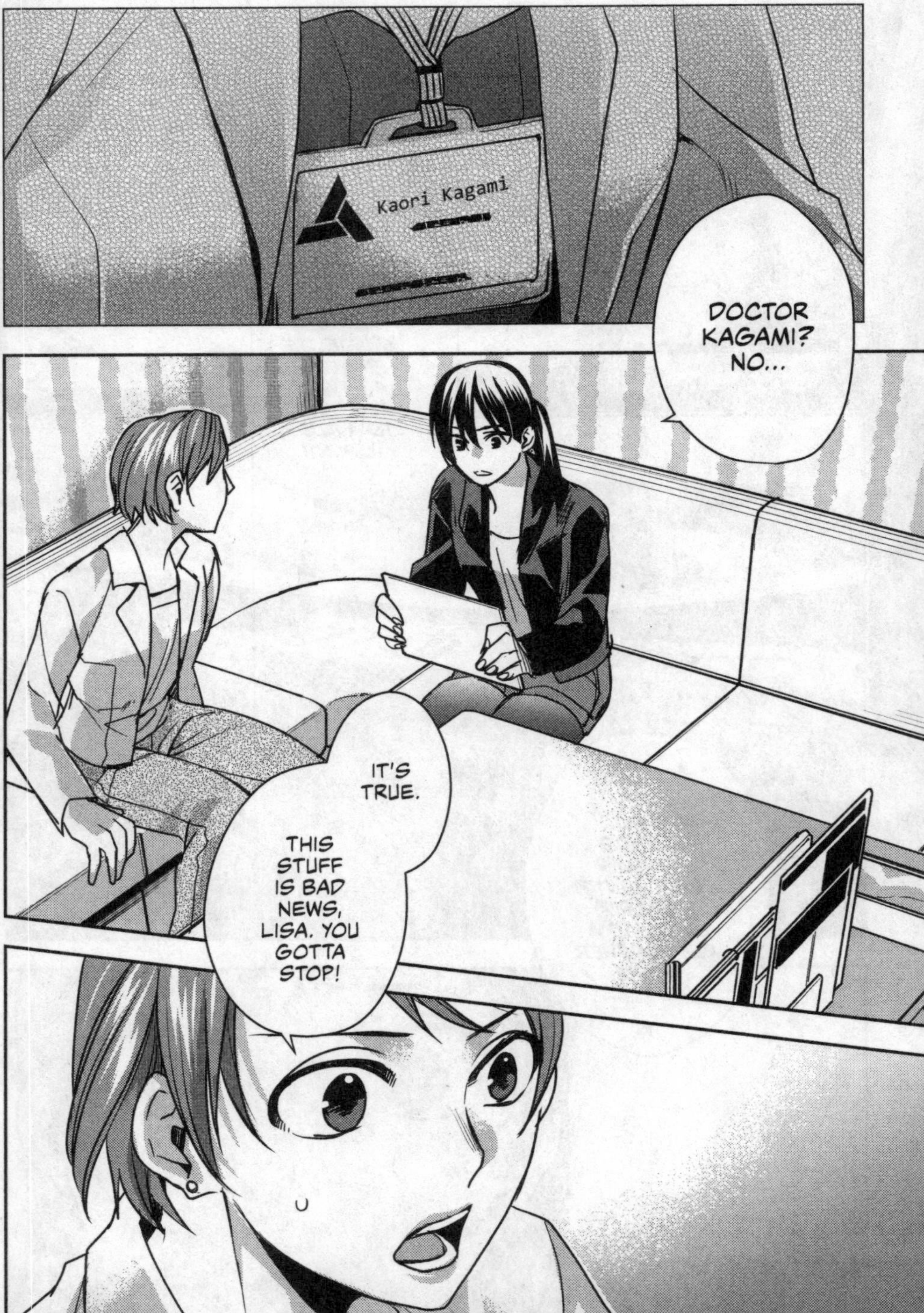
Kaori Kagami
DOCTOR KAGAMI? NO...
IT'S TRUE.
THIS STUFF IS BAD NEWS, LISA. YOU GOTTA STOP!

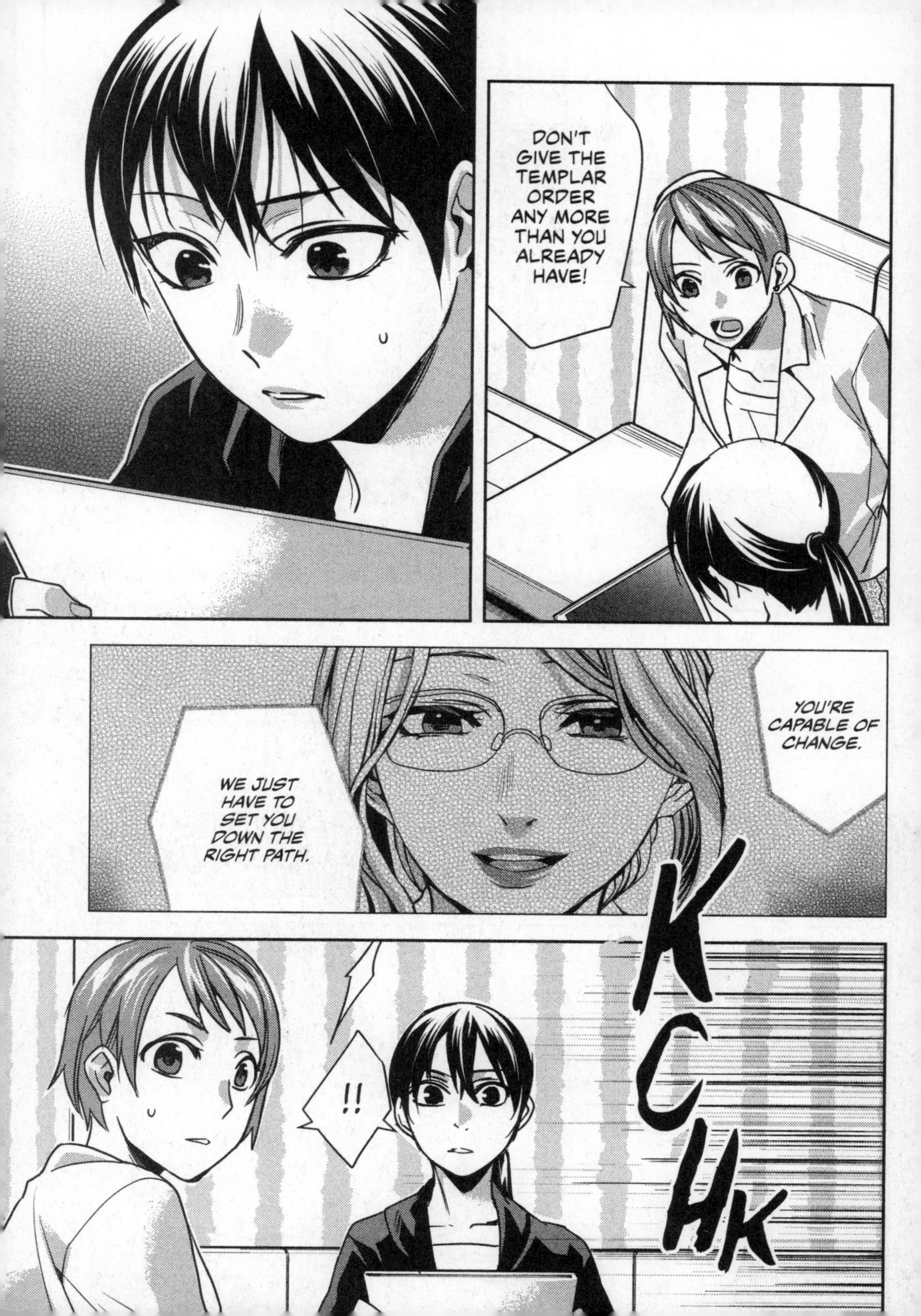
DON'T GIVE THE TEMPLAR ORDER ANY MORE THAN YOU ALREADY HAVE!
YOU'RE CAPABLE OF CHANGE.
WE JUST HAVE TO SET YOU DOWN THE RIGHT PATH.
KCHK
!!

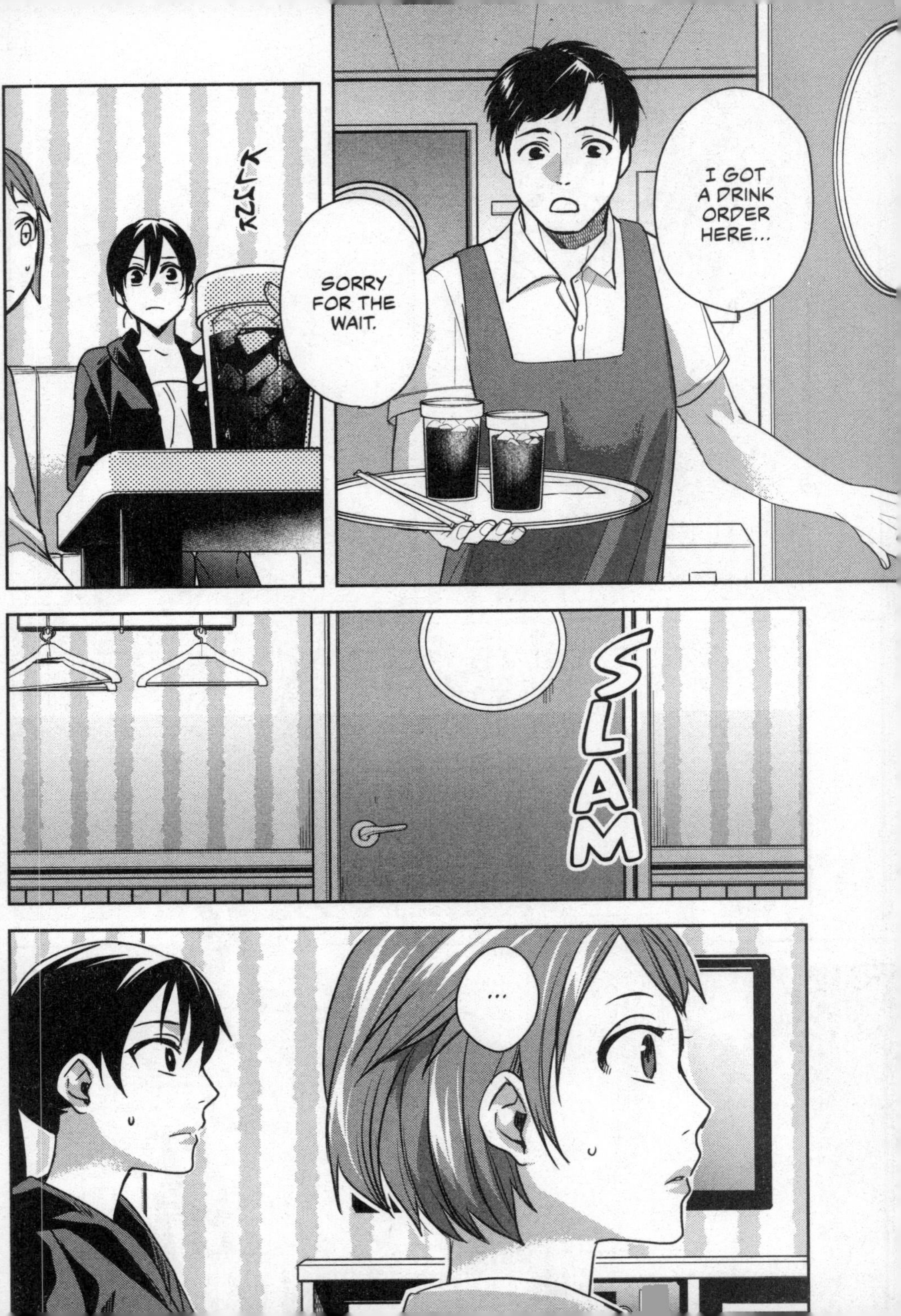
I GOT A DRINK ORDER HERE...
SORRY FOR THE WAIT.
KLUNK
SLAM
...

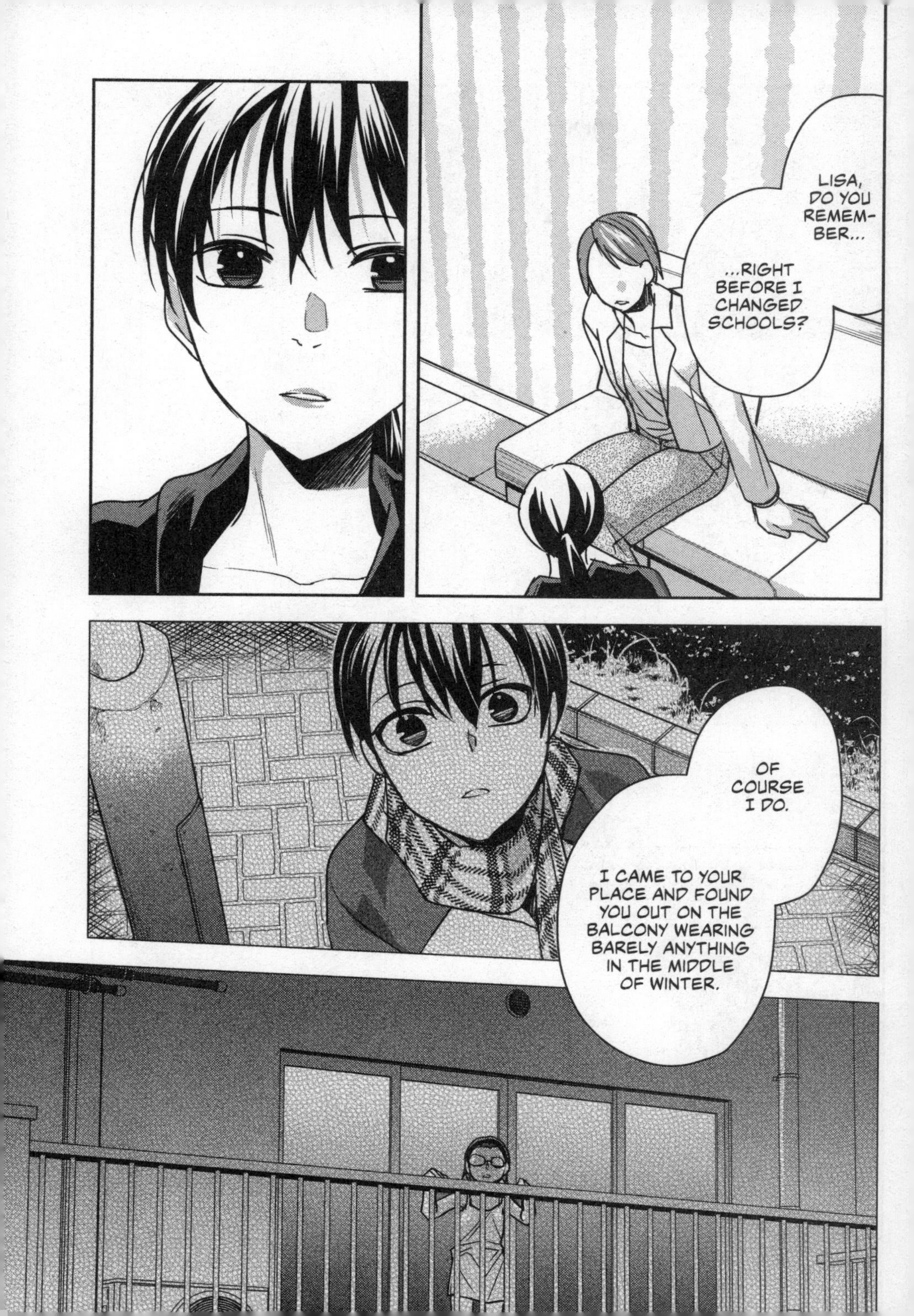
LISA, DO YOU REMEMBER...
...RIGHT BEFORE I CHANGED SCHOOLS?
OF COURSE I DO.
I CAME TO YOUR PLACE AND FOUND YOU OUT ON THE BALCONY WEARING BARELY ANYTHING IN THE MIDDLE OF WINTER.

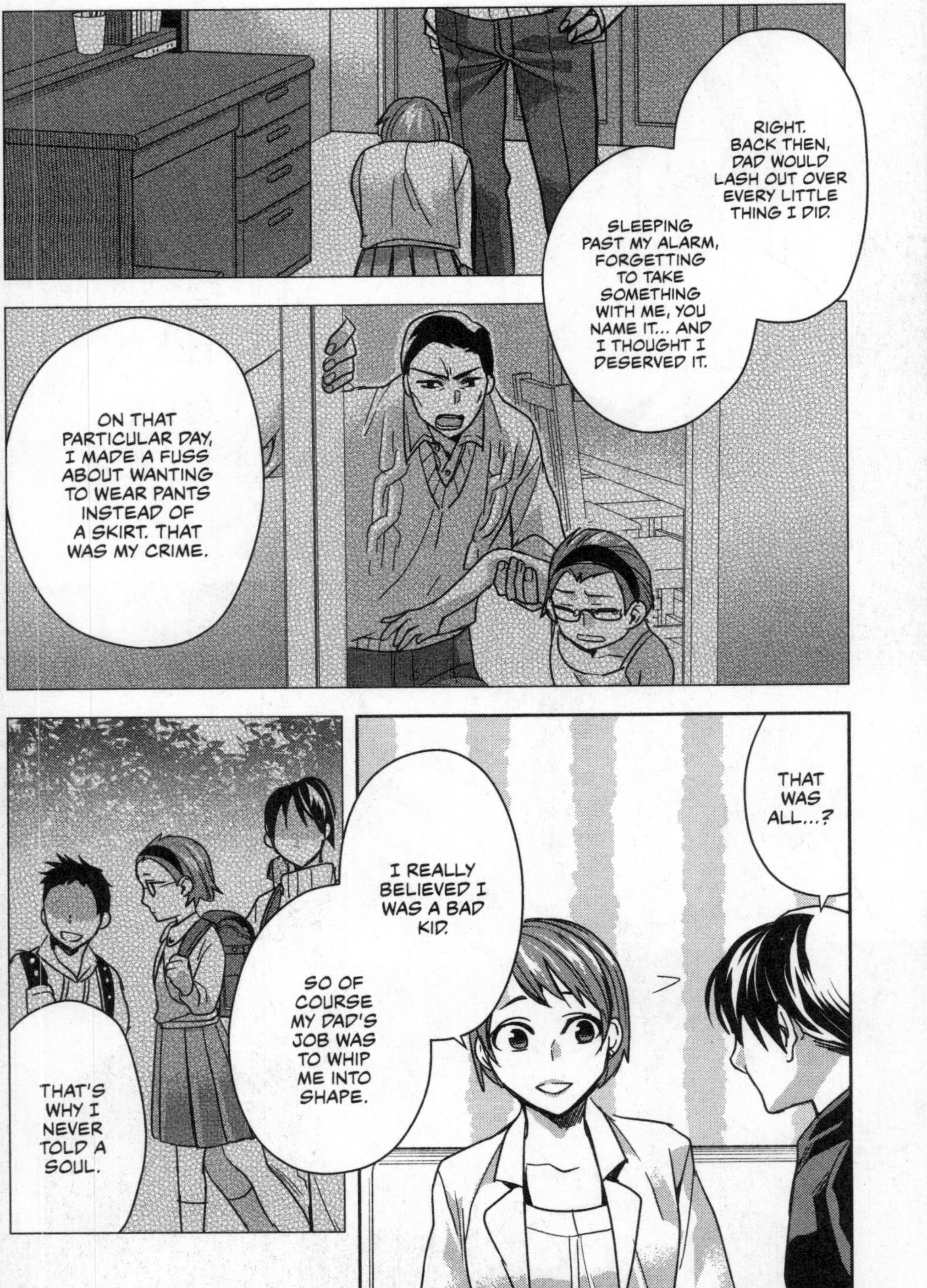
RIGHT. BACK THEN, DAD WOULD LASH OUT OVER EVERY LITTLE THING I DID.
SLEEPING PAST MY ALARM, FORGETTING TO TAKE SOMETHING WITH ME, YOU NAME IT... AND I THOUGHT I DESERVED IT.
ON THAT PARTICULAR DAY, I MADE A FUSS ABOUT WANTING TO WEAR PANTS INSTEAD OF A SKIRT. THAT WAS MY CRIME.
THAT WAS ALL...?
I REALLY BELIEVED I WAS A BAD KID.
SO OF COURSE MY DAD'S JOB WAS TO WHIP ME INTO SHAPE.
THAT'S WHY I NEVER TOLD A SOUL.

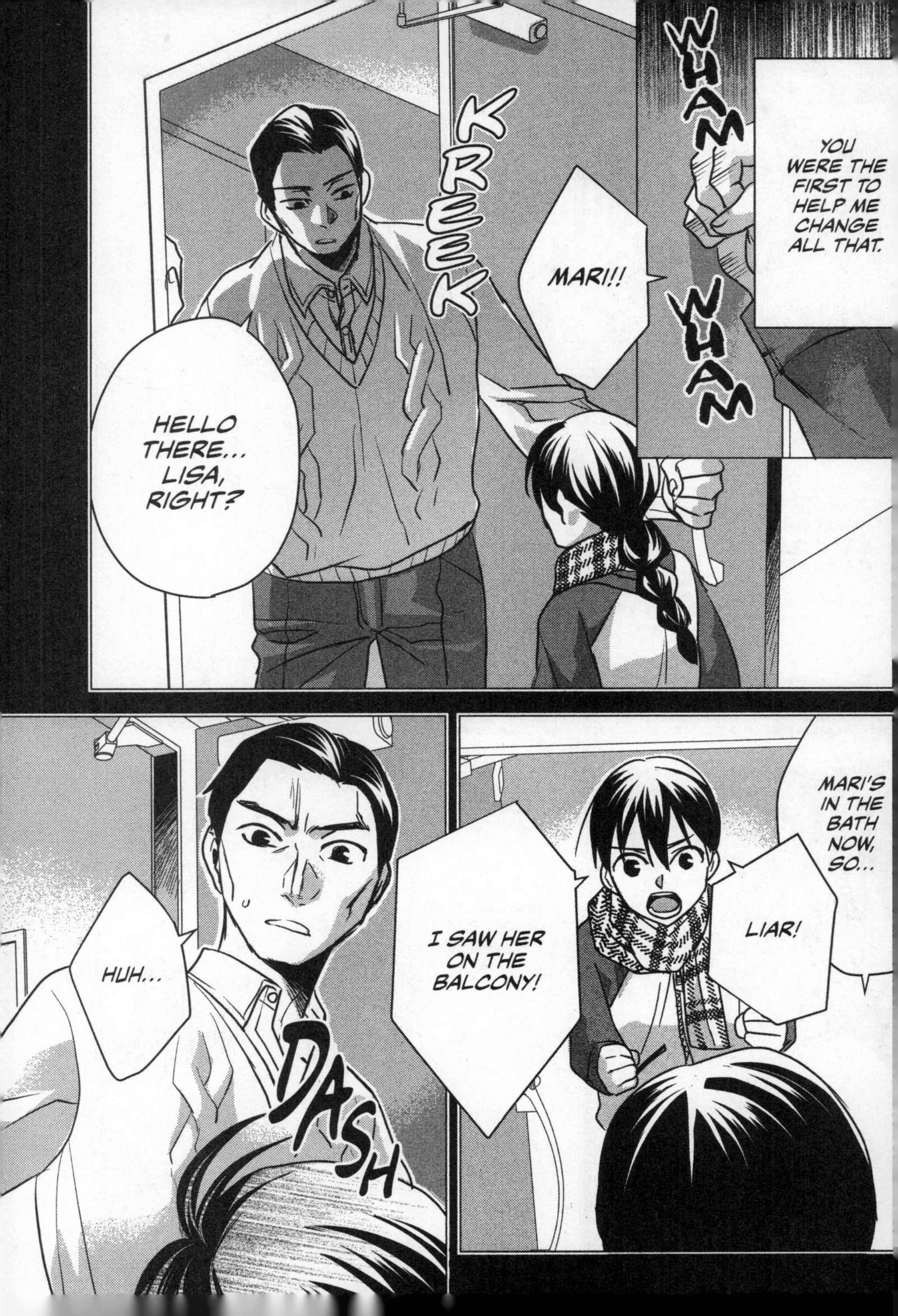
WHAM
WHAM
WHAM
YOU WERE THE FIRST TO HELP ME CHANGE ALL THAT.
KREEK
MARI!!
HELLO THERE... LISA, RIGHT?
MARI'S IN THE BATH NOW, SO...
LIAR!
I SAW HER ON THE BALCONY!
HUH...
DASH

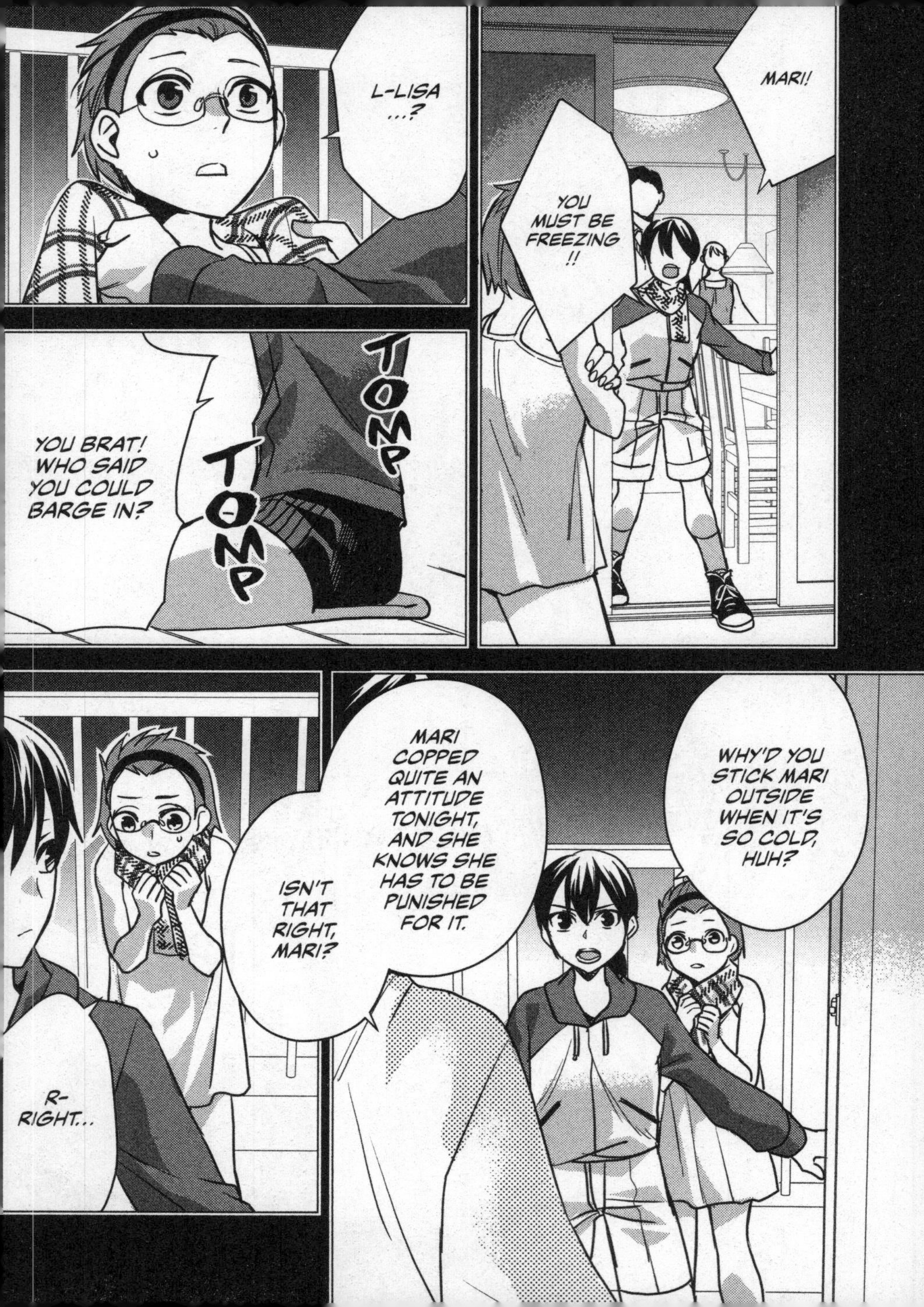
MARI!
YOU MUST BE FREEZING !!
L-LISA ...?
TOMP TOMP
YOU BRAT! WHO SAID YOU COULD BARGE IN?
WHY'D YOU STICK MARI OUTSIDE WHEN IT'S SO COLD, HUH?
MARI COPPED QUITE AN ATTITUDE TONIGHT, AND SHE KNOWS SHE HAS TO BE PUNISHED FOR IT.
ISN'T THAT RIGHT, MARI?
R- RIGHT...

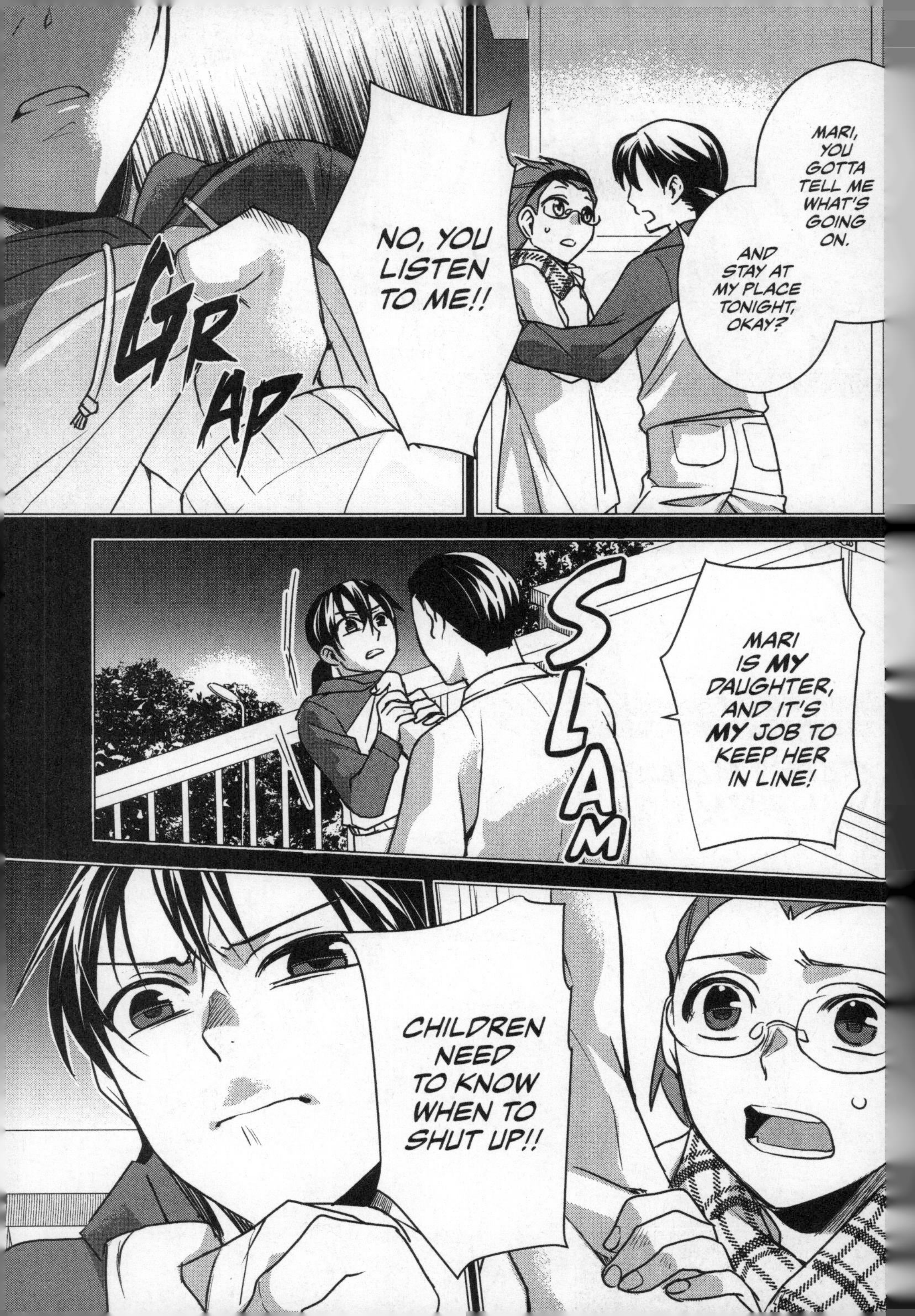
MARI, YOU GOTTA TELL ME WHAT'S GOING ON.
AND STAY AT MY PLACE TONIGHT, OKAY?
NO, YOU LISTEN TO ME!!
GRAP
MARI IS MY DAUGHTER, AND IT'S MY JOB TO KEEP HER IN LINE!
SLAM
CHILDREN NEED TO KNOW WHEN TO SHUT UP!!

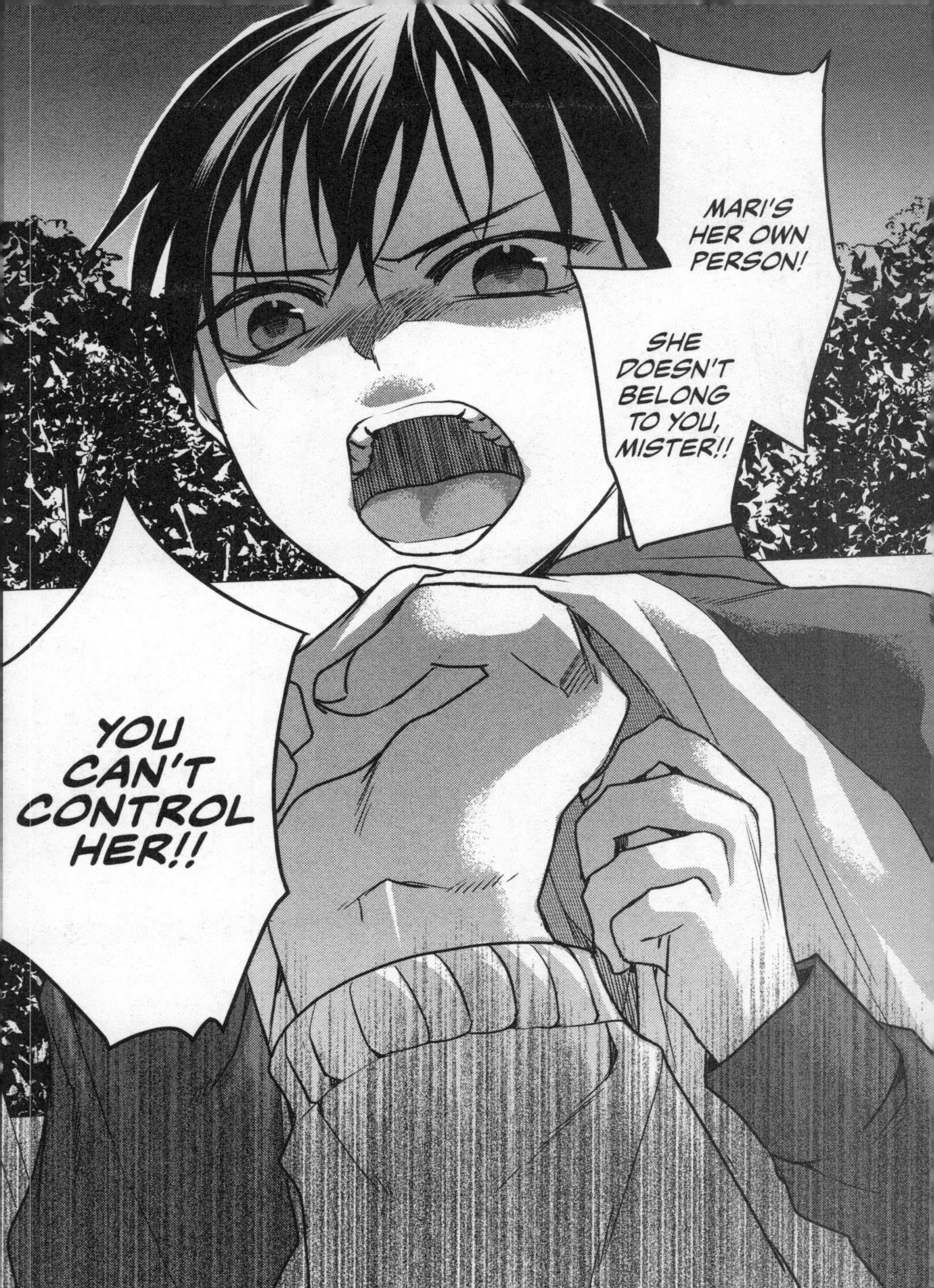
MARI'S HER OWN PERSON!
SHE DOESN'T BELONG TO YOU, MISTER!!
YOU CAN'T CONTROL HER!!

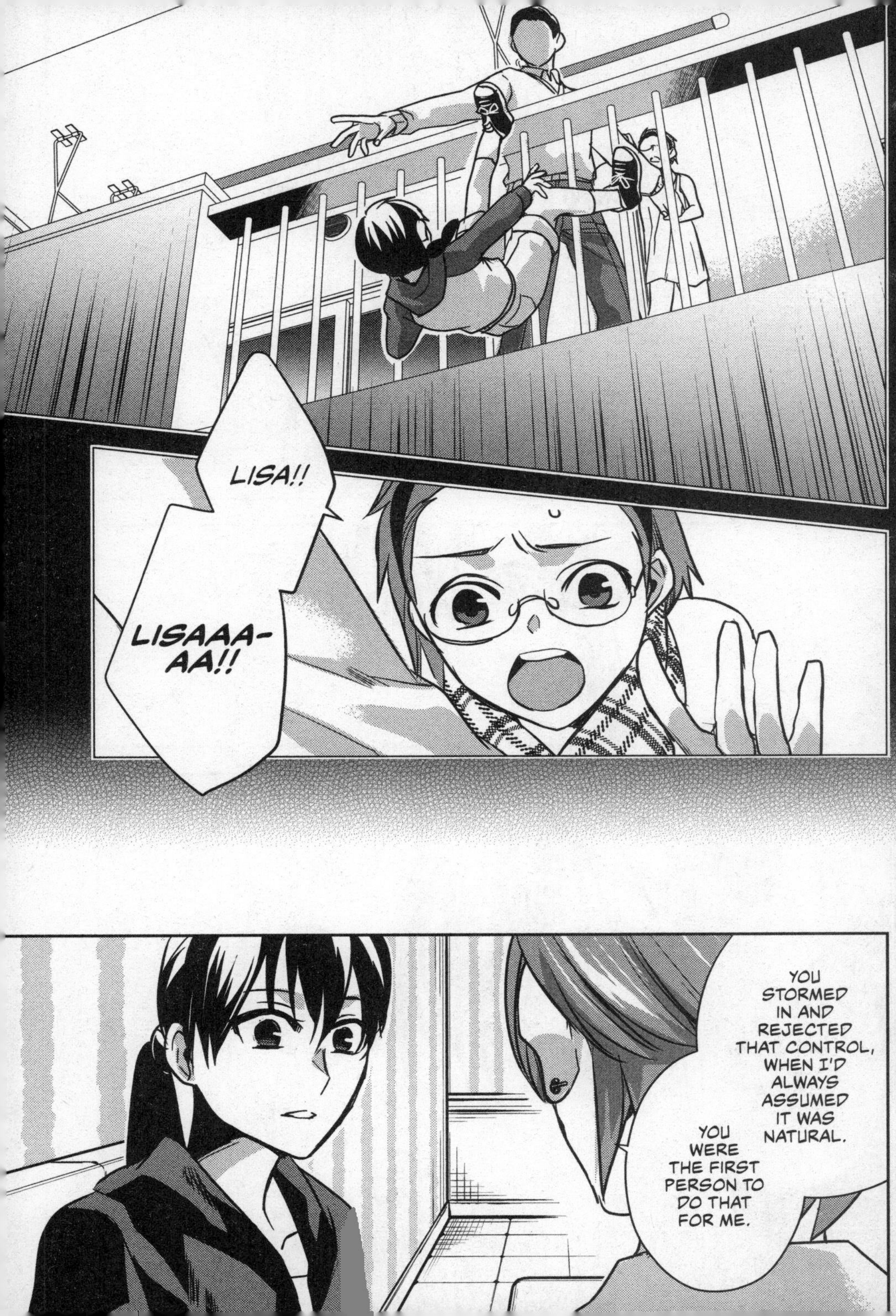
LISA!!
LISAAA-AA!!
YOU STORMED IN AND REJECTED THAT CONTROL, WHEN I'D ALWAYS ASSUMED IT WAS NATURAL.
YOU WERE THE FIRST PERSON TO DO THAT FOR ME.

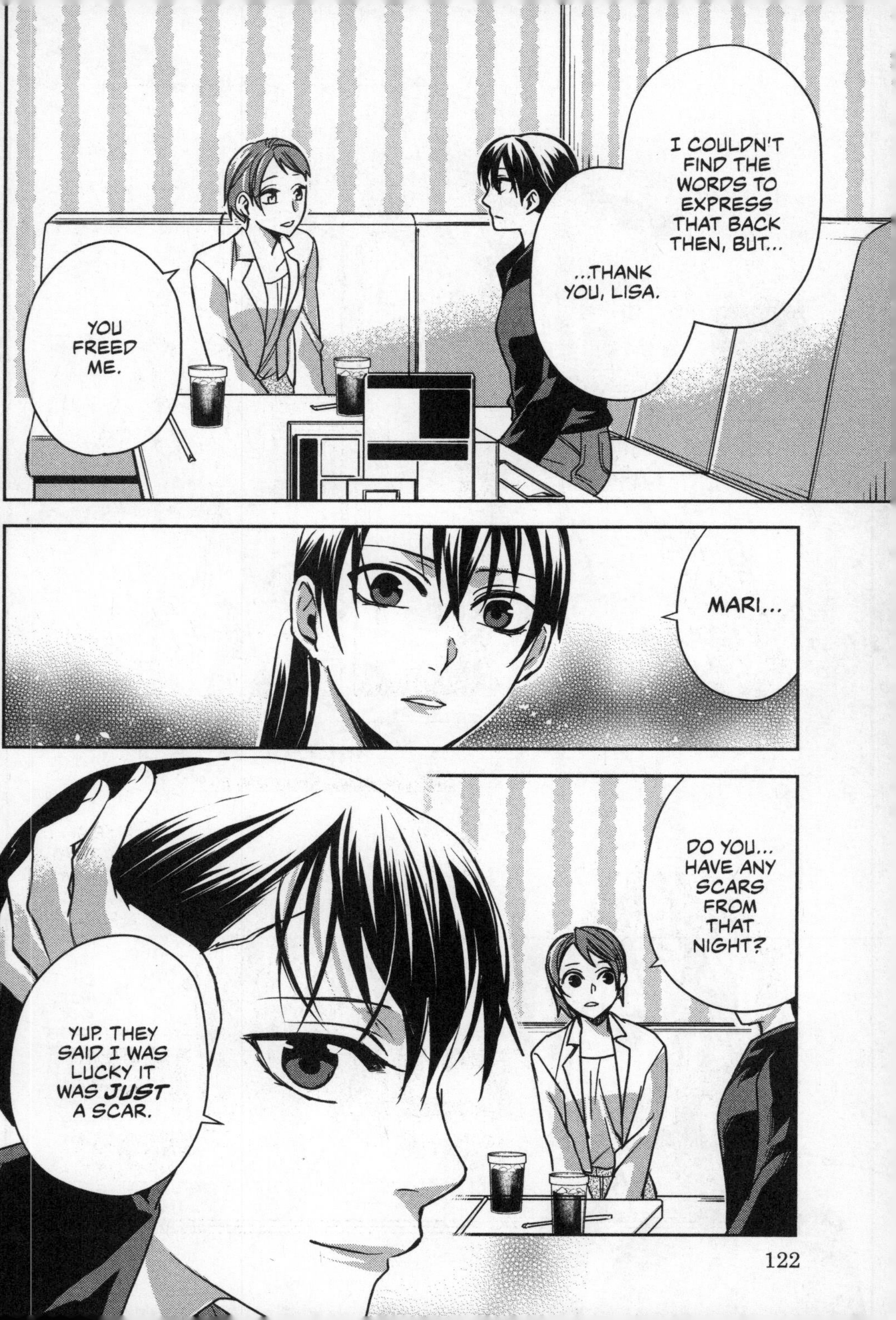
I COULDN'T FIND THE WORDS TO EXPRESS THAT BACK THEN, BUT...
...THANK YOU, LISA.
YOU FREED ME.
MARI...
DO YOU... HAVE ANY SCARS FROM THAT NIGHT?
YUP. THEY SAID I WAS LUCKY IT WAS *JUST* A SCAR.

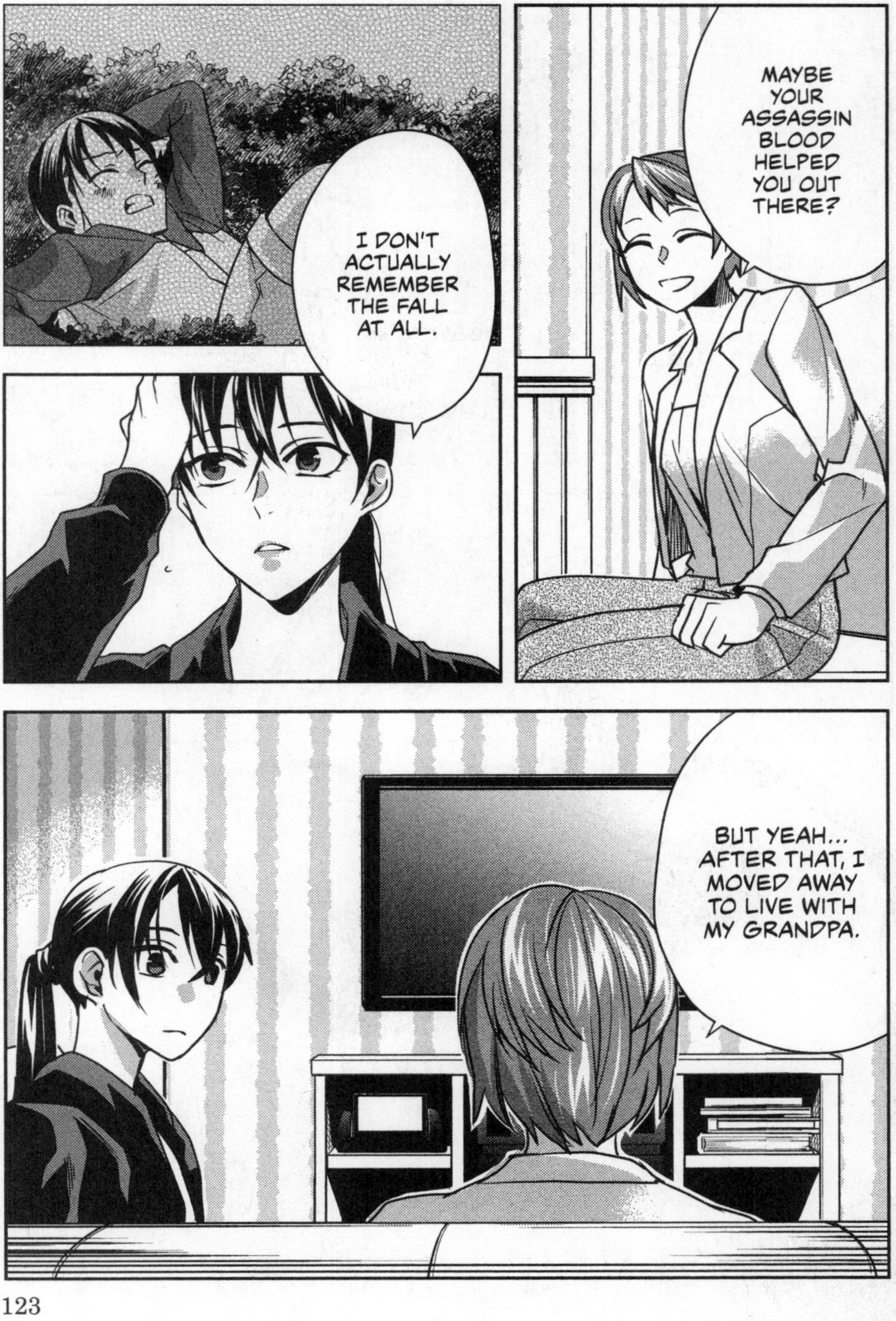
MAYBE YOUR ASSASSIN BLOOD HELPED YOU OUT THERE?
I DON'T ACTUALLY REMEMBER THE FALL AT ALL.
BUT YEAH... AFTER THAT, I MOVED AWAY TO LIVE WITH MY GRANDPA.

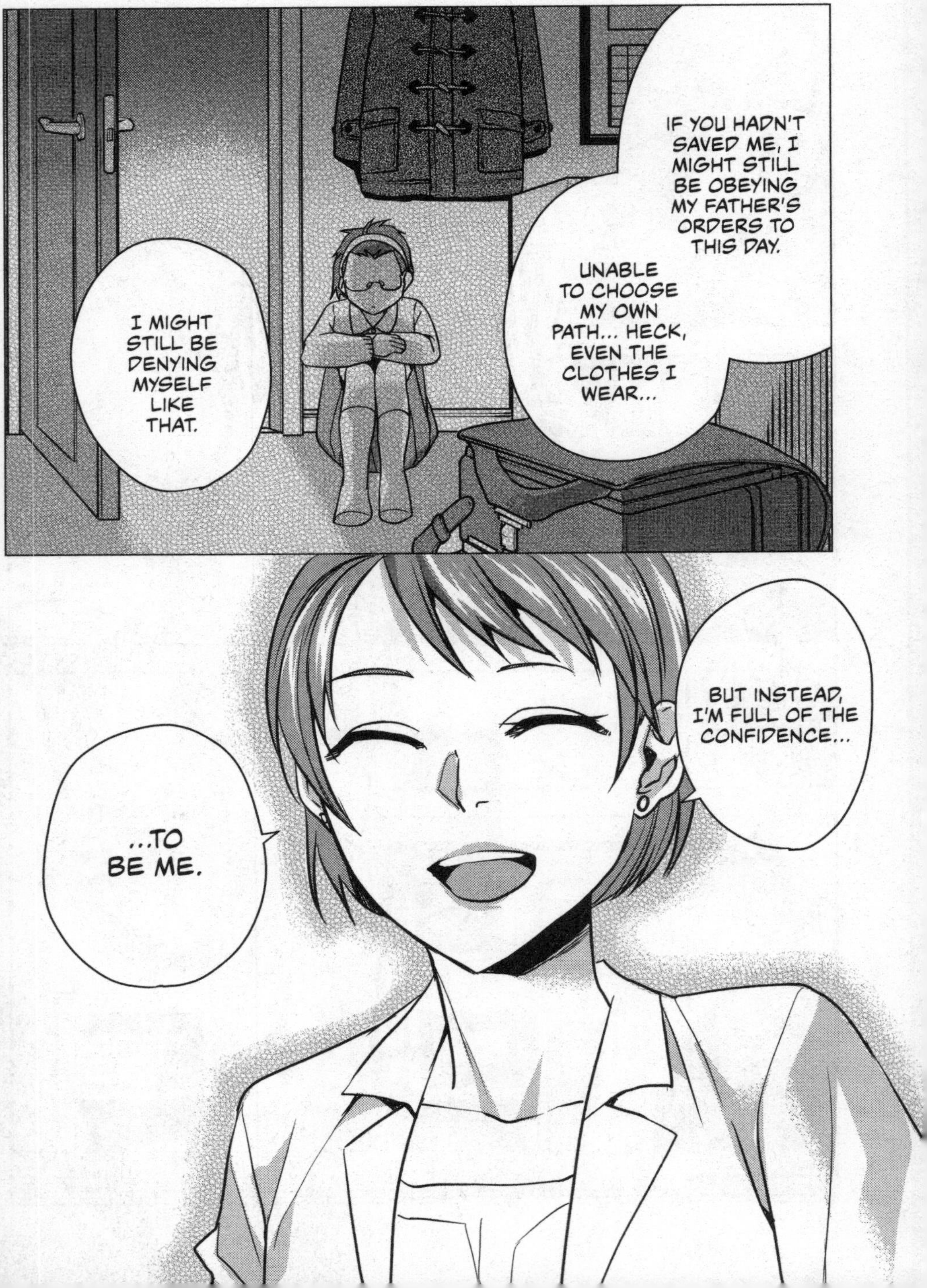
IF YOU HADN'T SAVED ME, I MIGHT STILL BE OBEYING MY FATHER'S ORDERS TO THIS DAY.
UNABLE TO CHOOSE MY OWN PATH... HECK, EVEN THE CLOTHES I WEAR...
I MIGHT STILL BE DENYING MYSELF LIKE THAT.
BUT INSTEAD, I'M FULL OF THE CONFIDENCE...
...TO BE ME.

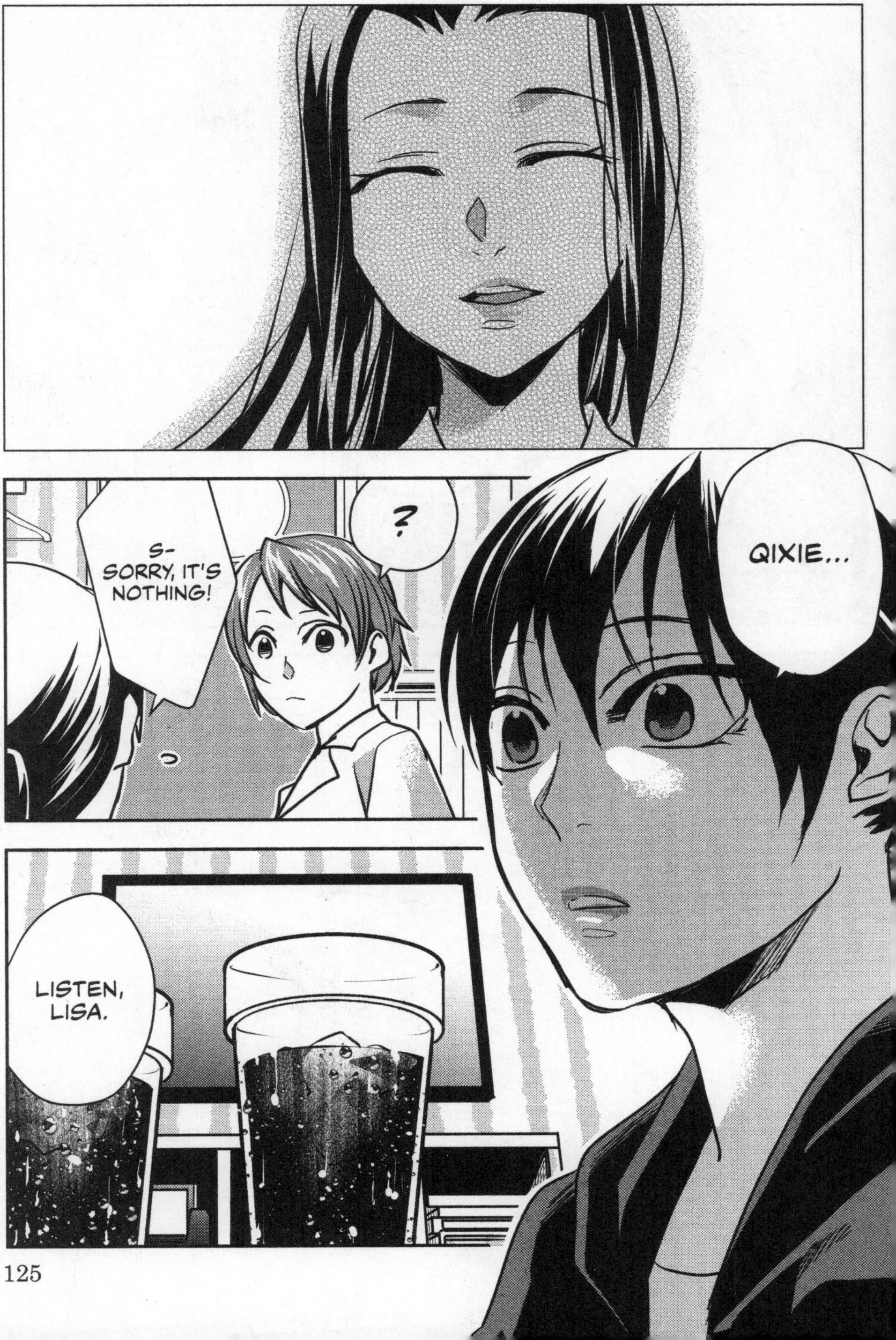
QIXIE...
?
S-SORRY, IT'S NOTHING!
LISTEN, LISA.

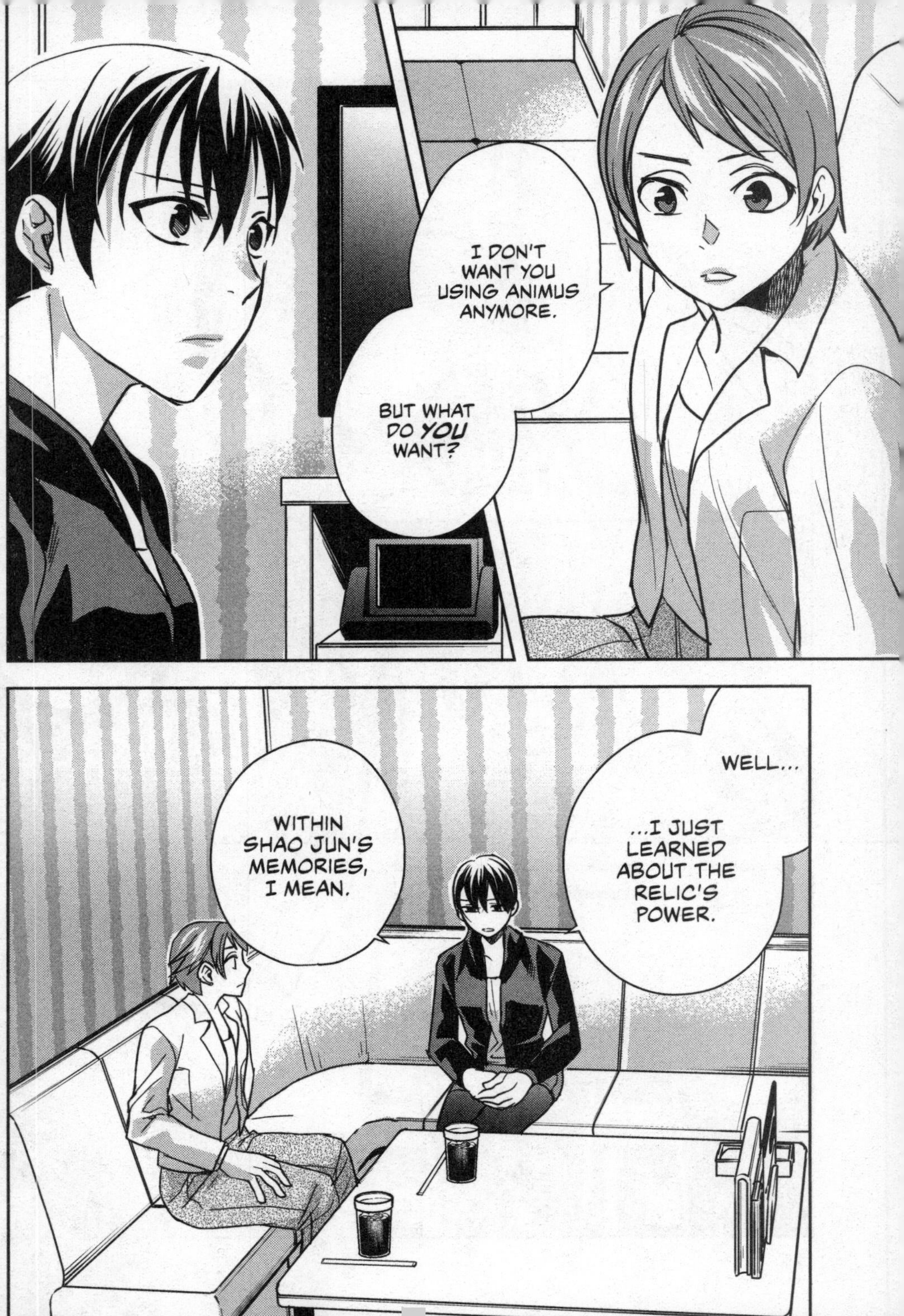
I DON'T WANT YOU USING ANIMUS ANYMORE.
BUT WHAT DO *YOU* WANT?
WELL...
...I JUST LEARNED ABOUT THE RELIC'S POWER.
WITHIN SHAO JUN'S MEMORIES, I MEAN.

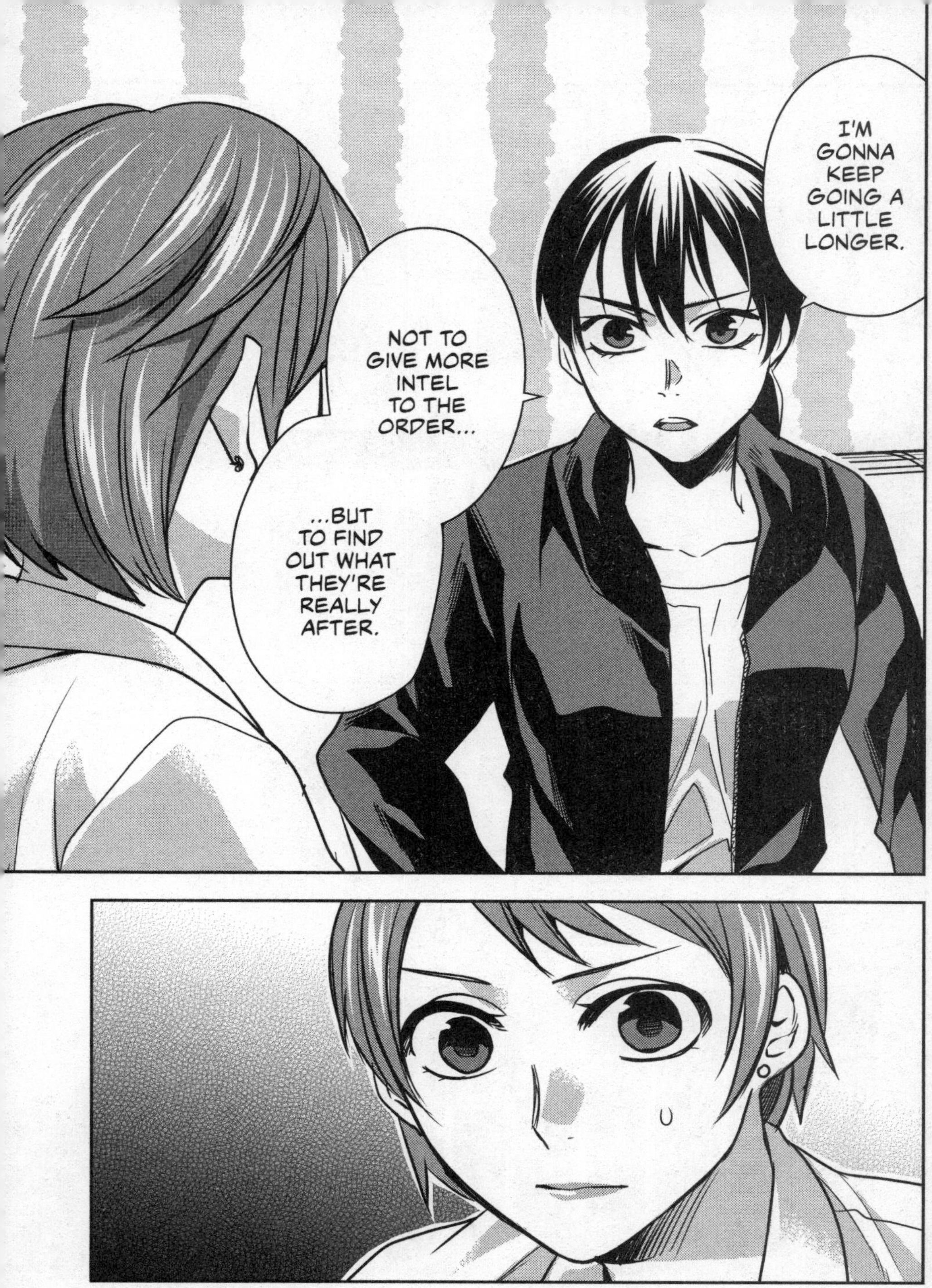
I'M GONNA KEEP GOING A LITTLE LONGER.
NOT TO GIVE MORE INTEL TO THE ORDER...
...BUT TO FIND OUT WHAT THEY'RE REALLY AFTER.

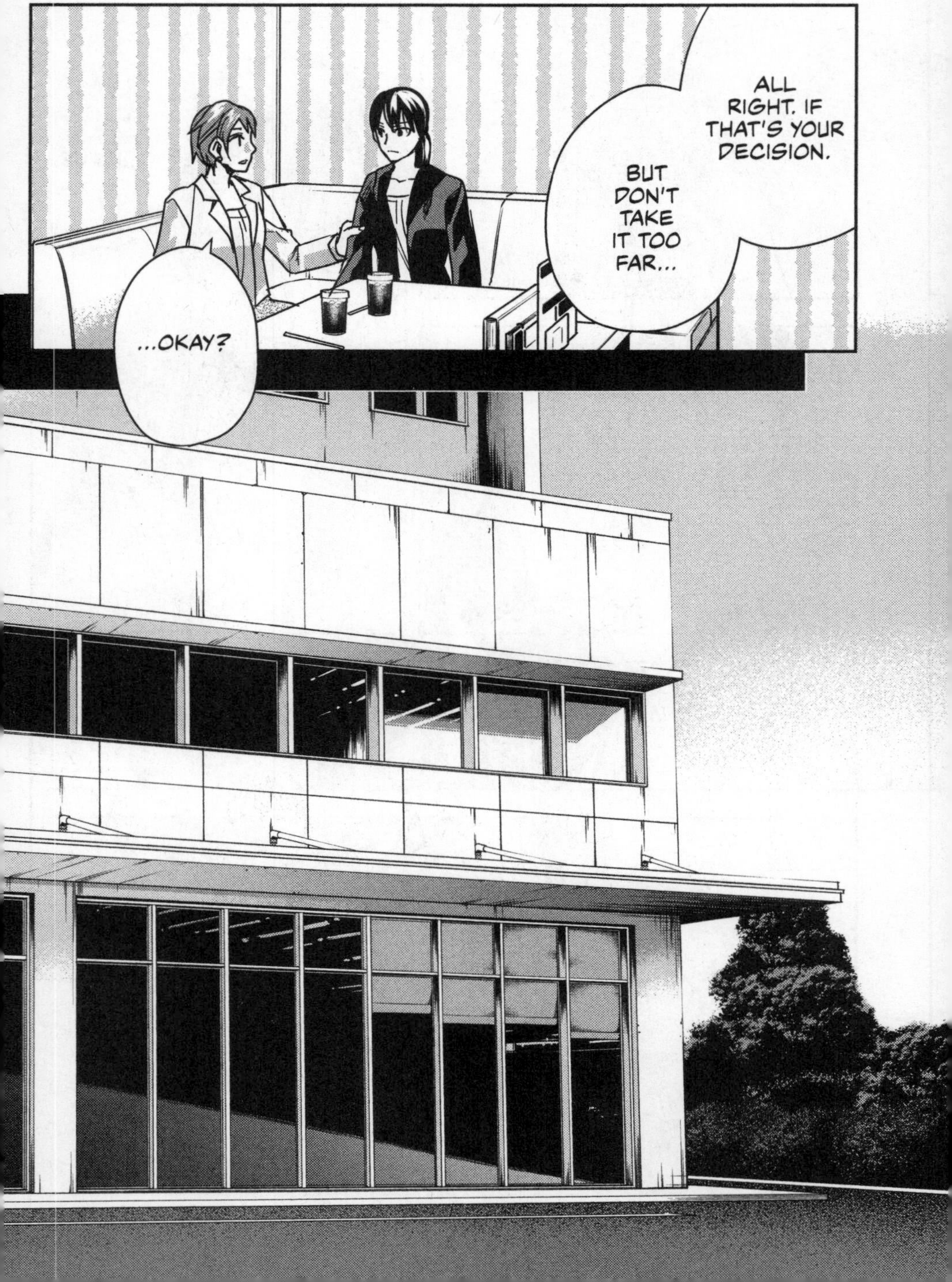
ALL RIGHT. IF THAT'S YOUR DECISION.
BUT DON'T TAKE IT TOO FAR...
...OKAY?

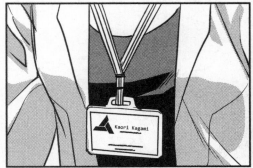

READY TO BEGIN, LISA?

YES.

I CAN'T TRUST HER ANYMORE.

ALL THAT DR. KAGAMI WANTS IS THE RELIC.

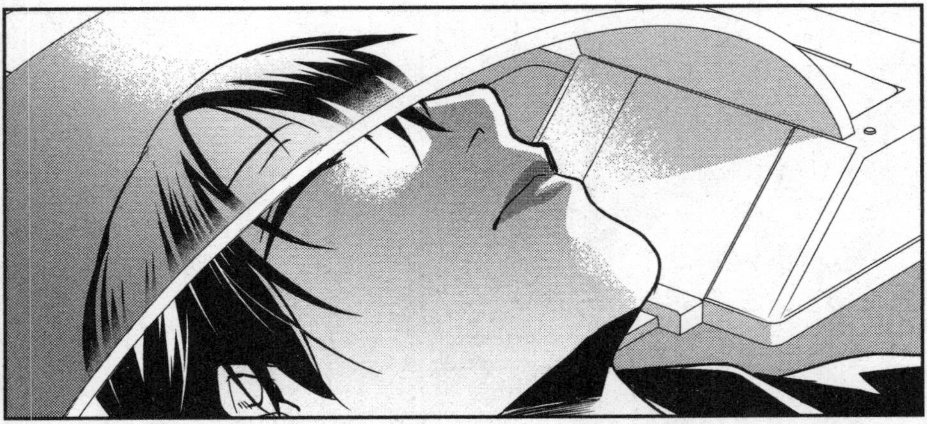

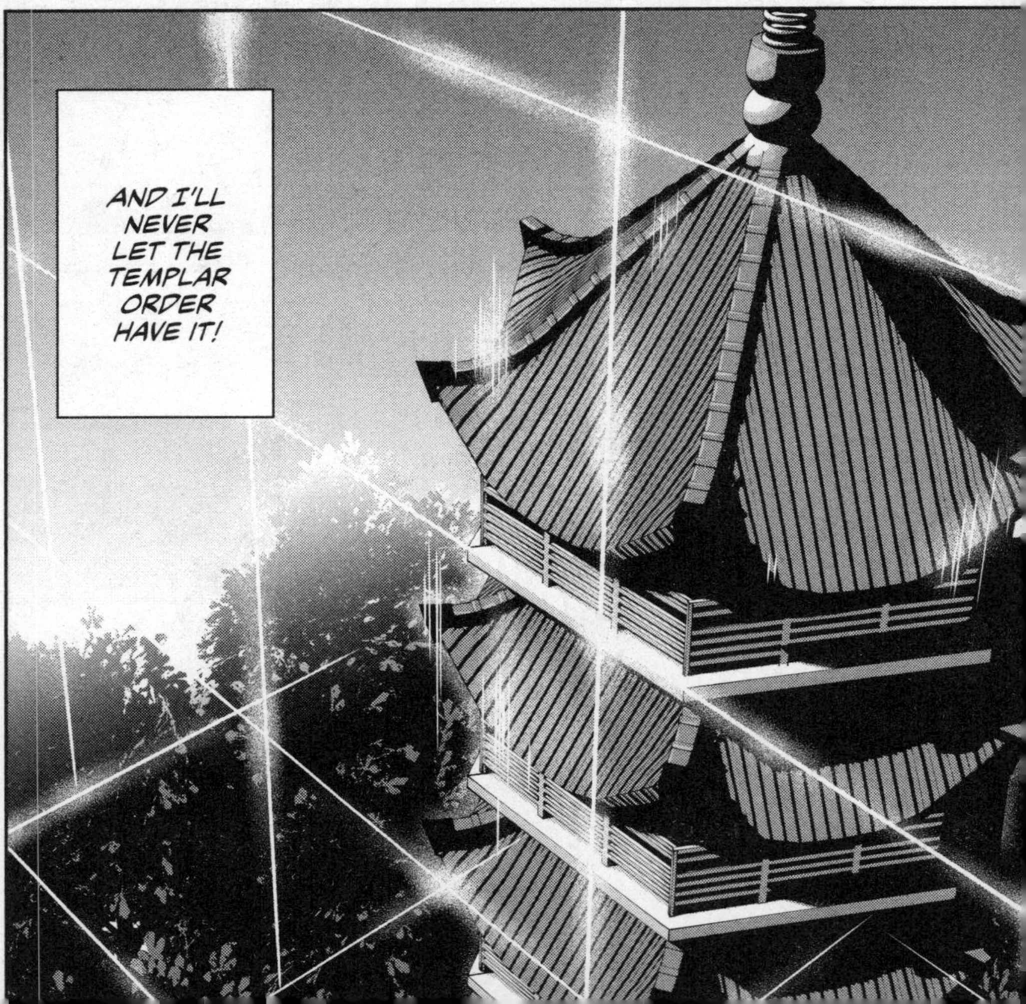
AND I'LL NEVER LET THE TEMPLAR ORDER HAVE IT!

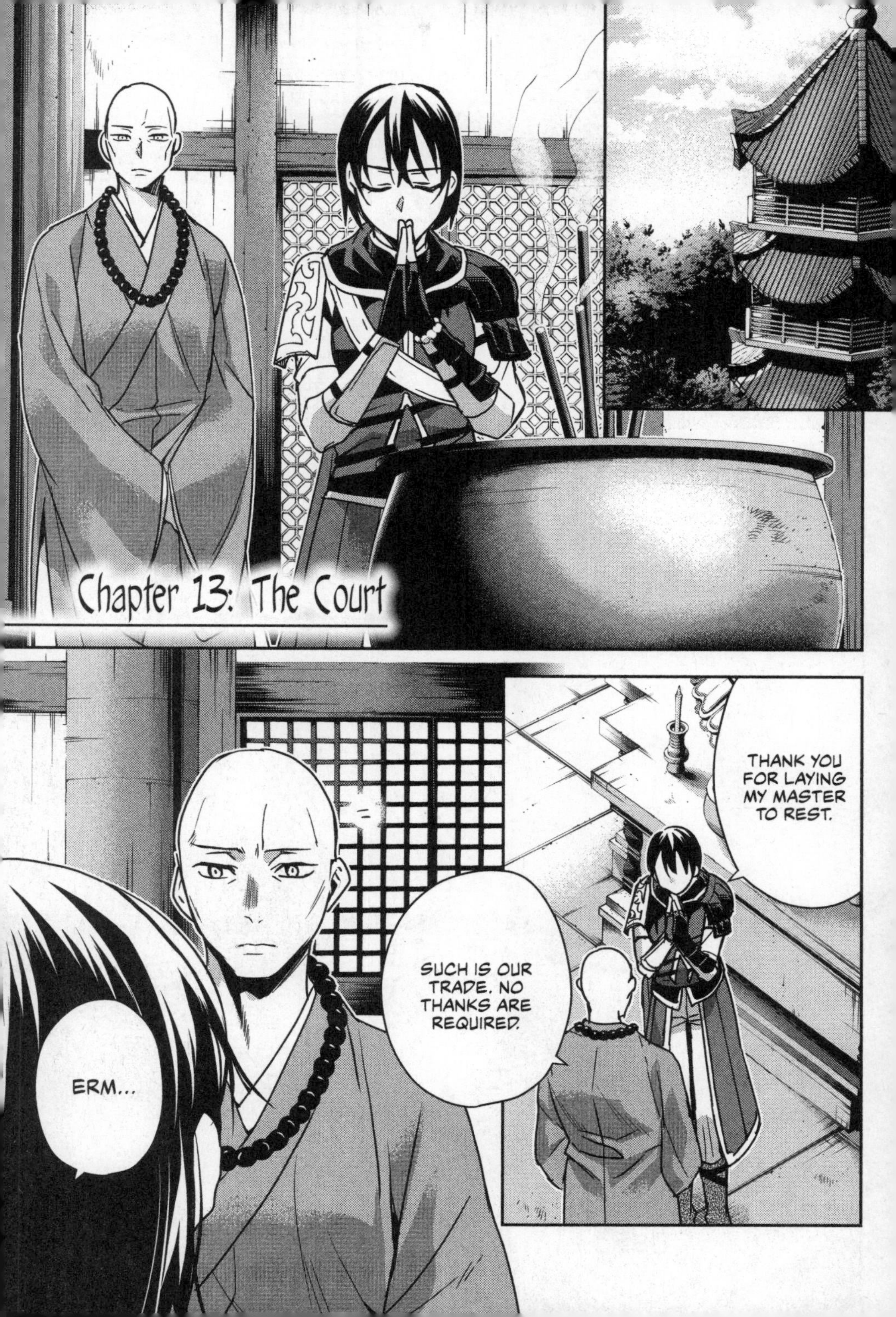
Chapter 13: The Court
THANK YOU FOR LAYING MY MASTER TO REST.
SUCH IS OUR TRADE. NO THANKS ARE REQUIRED.
ERM...

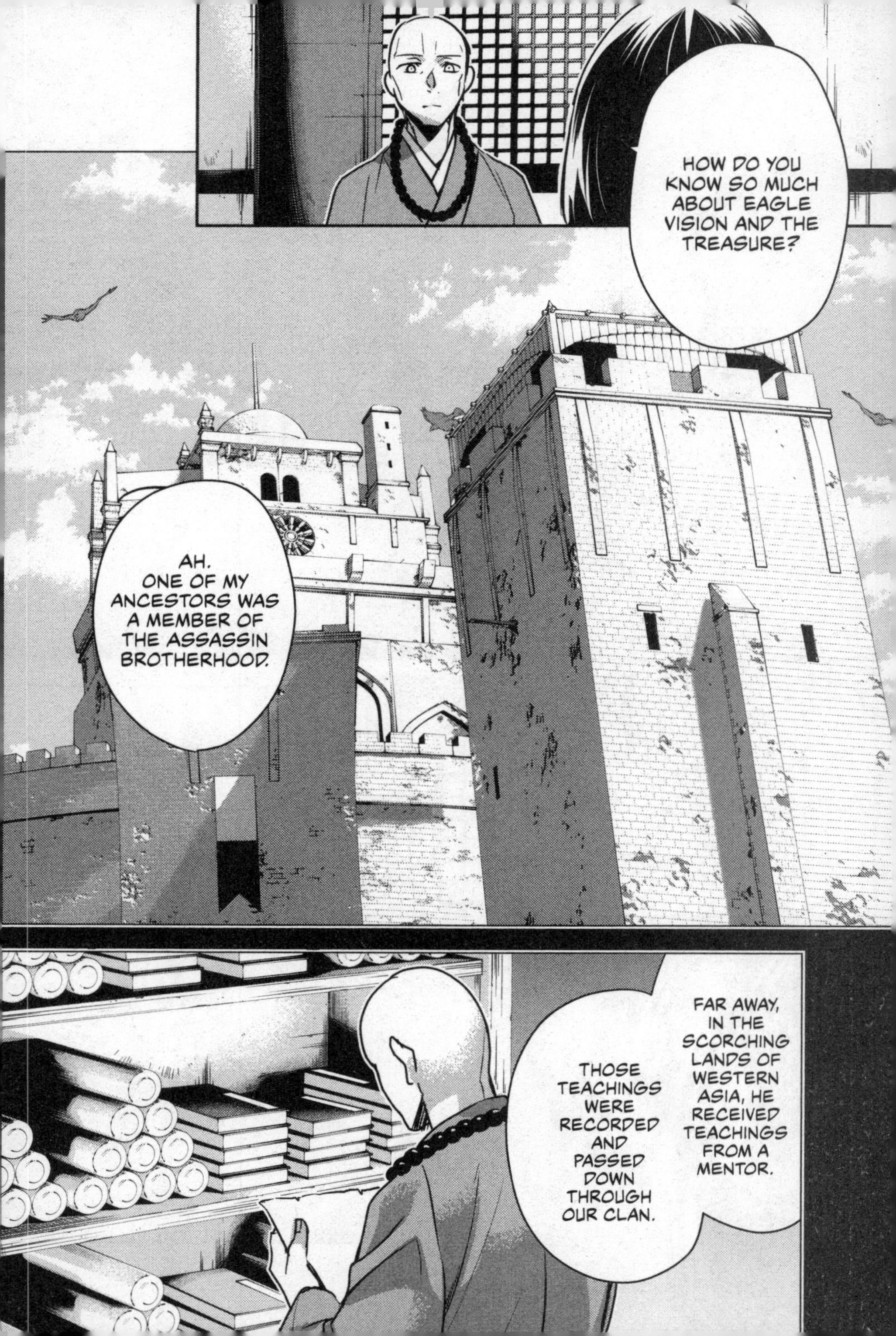

HOW DO YOU KNOW SO MUCH ABOUT EAGLE VISION AND THE TREASURE?
AH. ONE OF MY ANCESTORS WAS A MEMBER OF THE ASSASSIN BROTHERHOOD.
FAR AWAY, IN THE SCORCHING LANDS OF WESTERN ASIA, HE RECEIVED TEACHINGS FROM A MENTOR.
THOSE TEACHINGS WERE RECORDED AND PASSED DOWN THROUGH OUR CLAN.

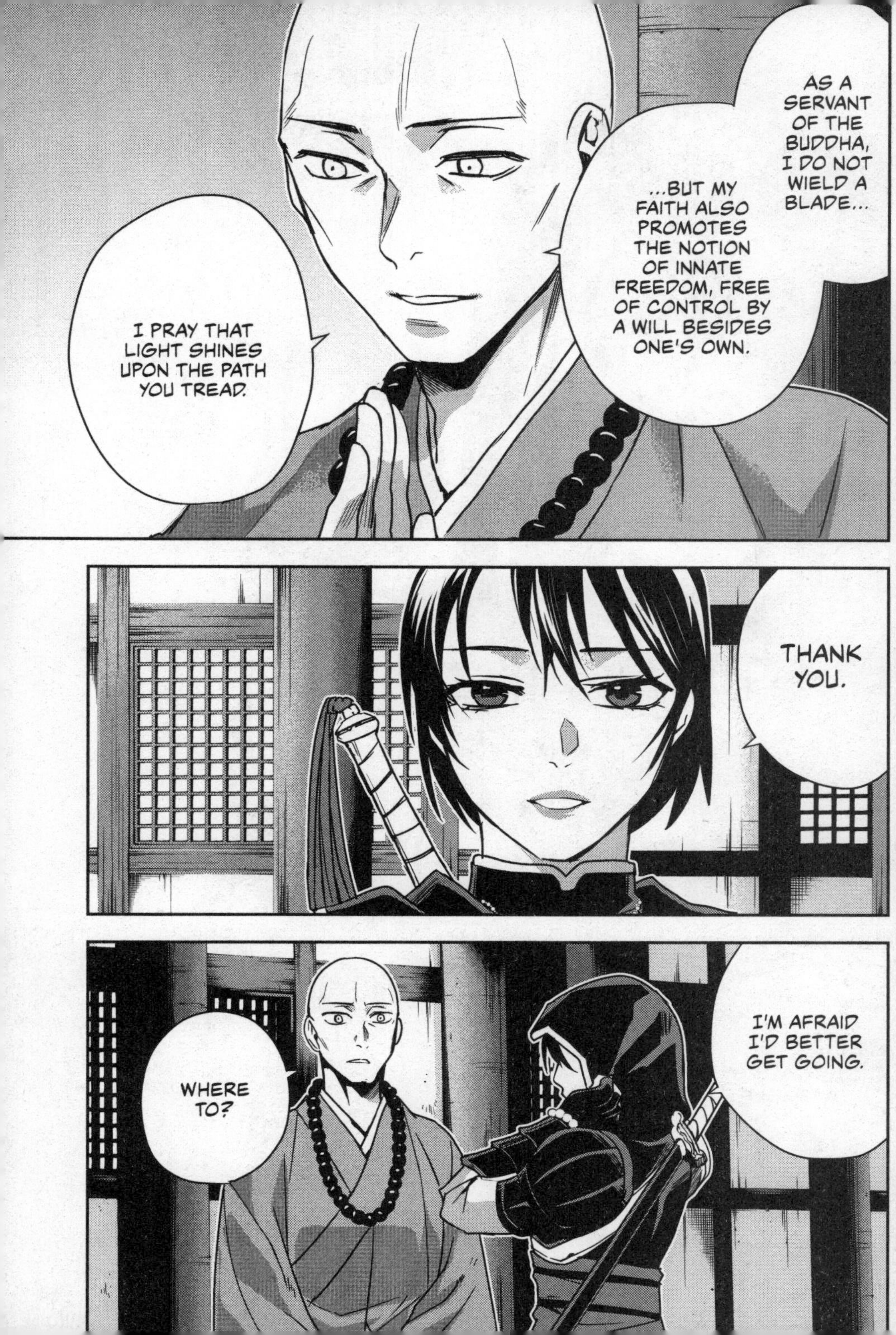
AS A SERVANT OF THE BUDDHA, I DO NOT WIELD A BLADE...
...BUT MY FAITH ALSO PROMOTES THE NOTION OF INNATE FREEDOM, FREE OF CONTROL BY A WILL BESIDES ONE'S OWN.
I PRAY THAT LIGHT SHINES UPON THE PATH YOU TREAD.
THANK YOU.
I'M AFRAID I'D BETTER GET GOING.
WHERE TO?

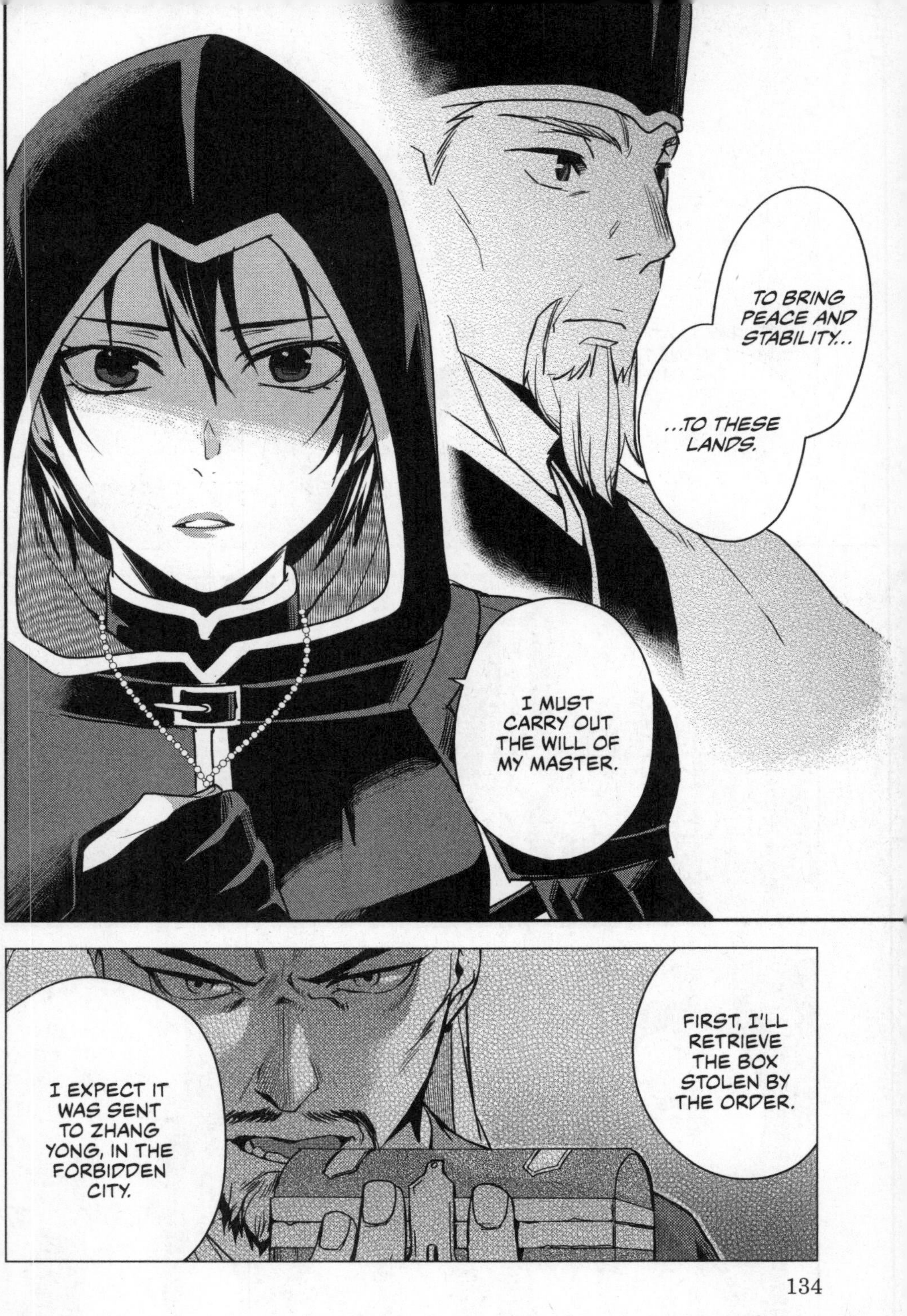
TO BRING PEACE AND STABILITY...
...TO THESE LANDS.
I MUST CARRY OUT THE WILL OF MY MASTER.
FIRST, I'LL RETRIEVE THE BOX STOLEN BY THE ORDER.
I EXPECT IT WAS SENT TO ZHANG YONG, IN THE FORBIDDEN CITY.

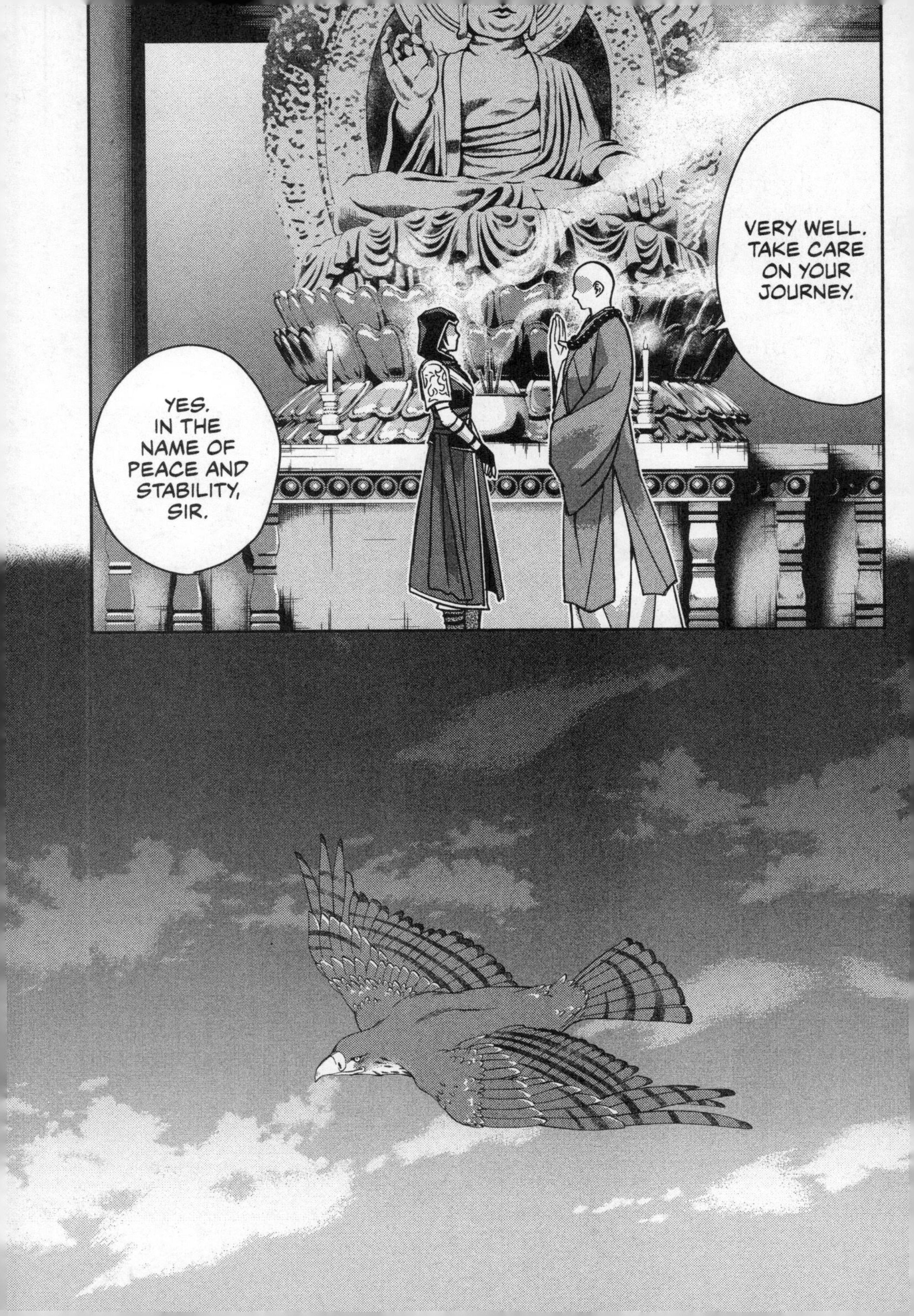
VERY WELL. TAKE CARE ON YOUR JOURNEY.
YES. IN THE NAME OF PEACE AND STABILITY, SIR.

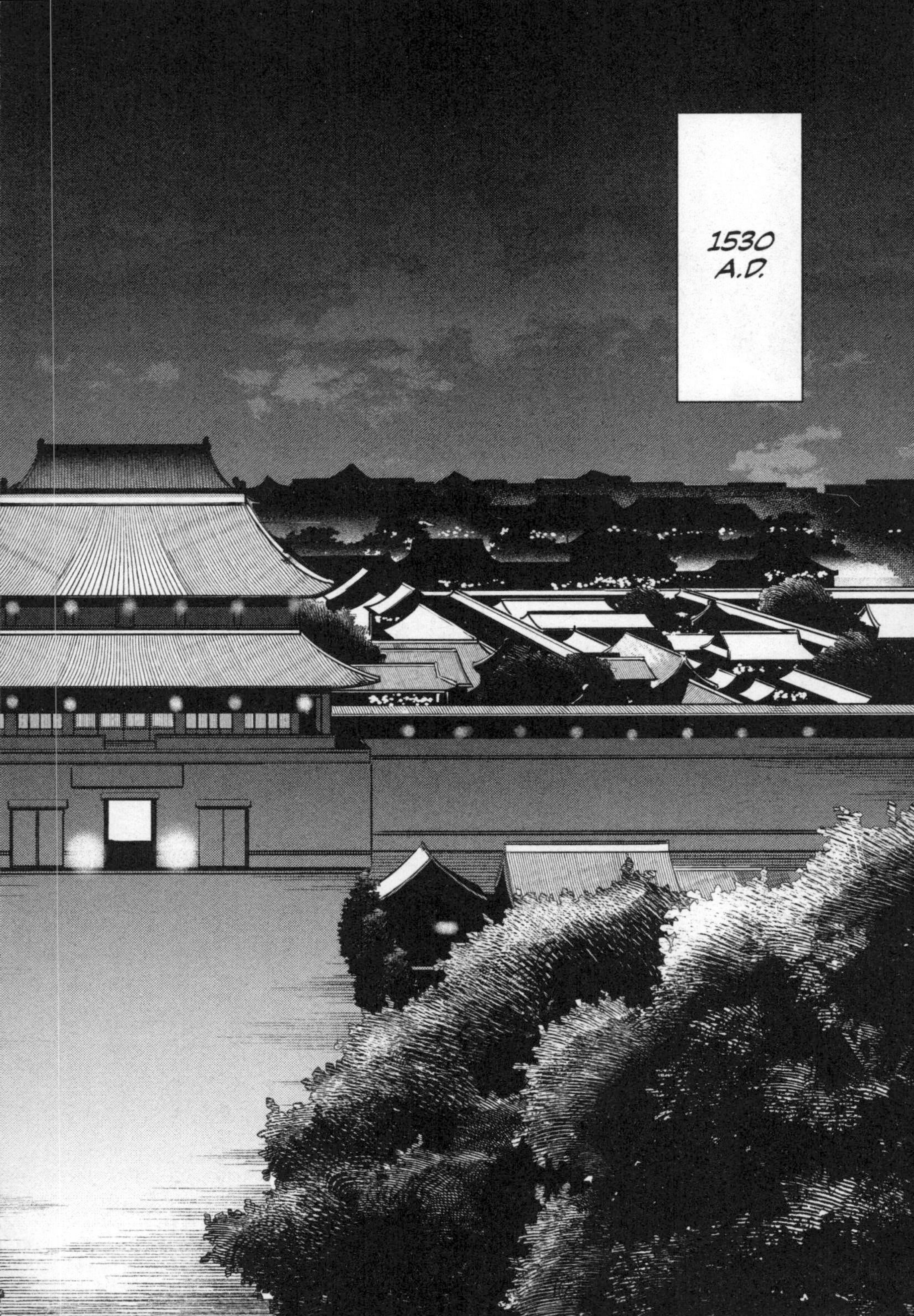
1530 A.D.

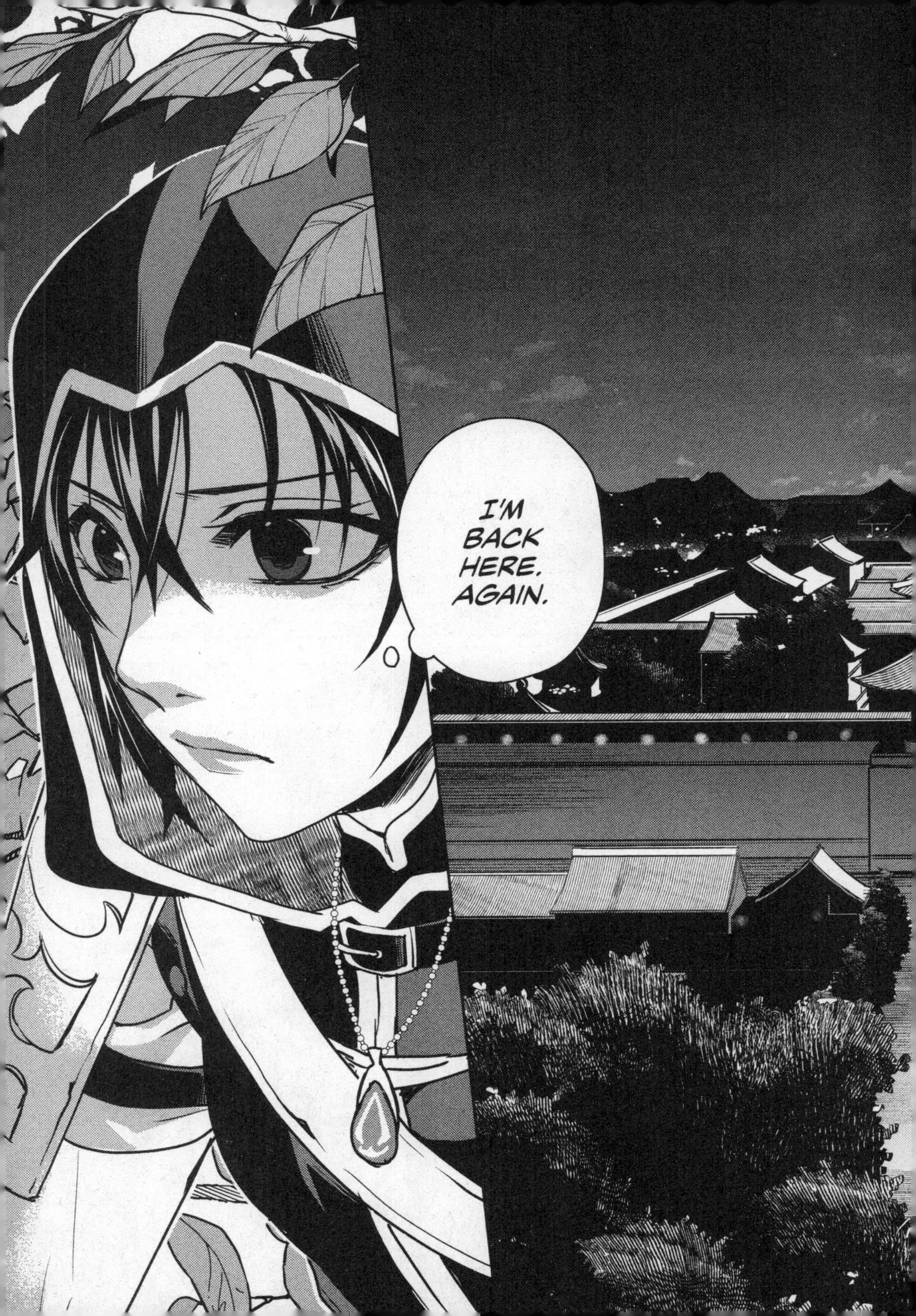
I'M BACK HERE. AGAIN.

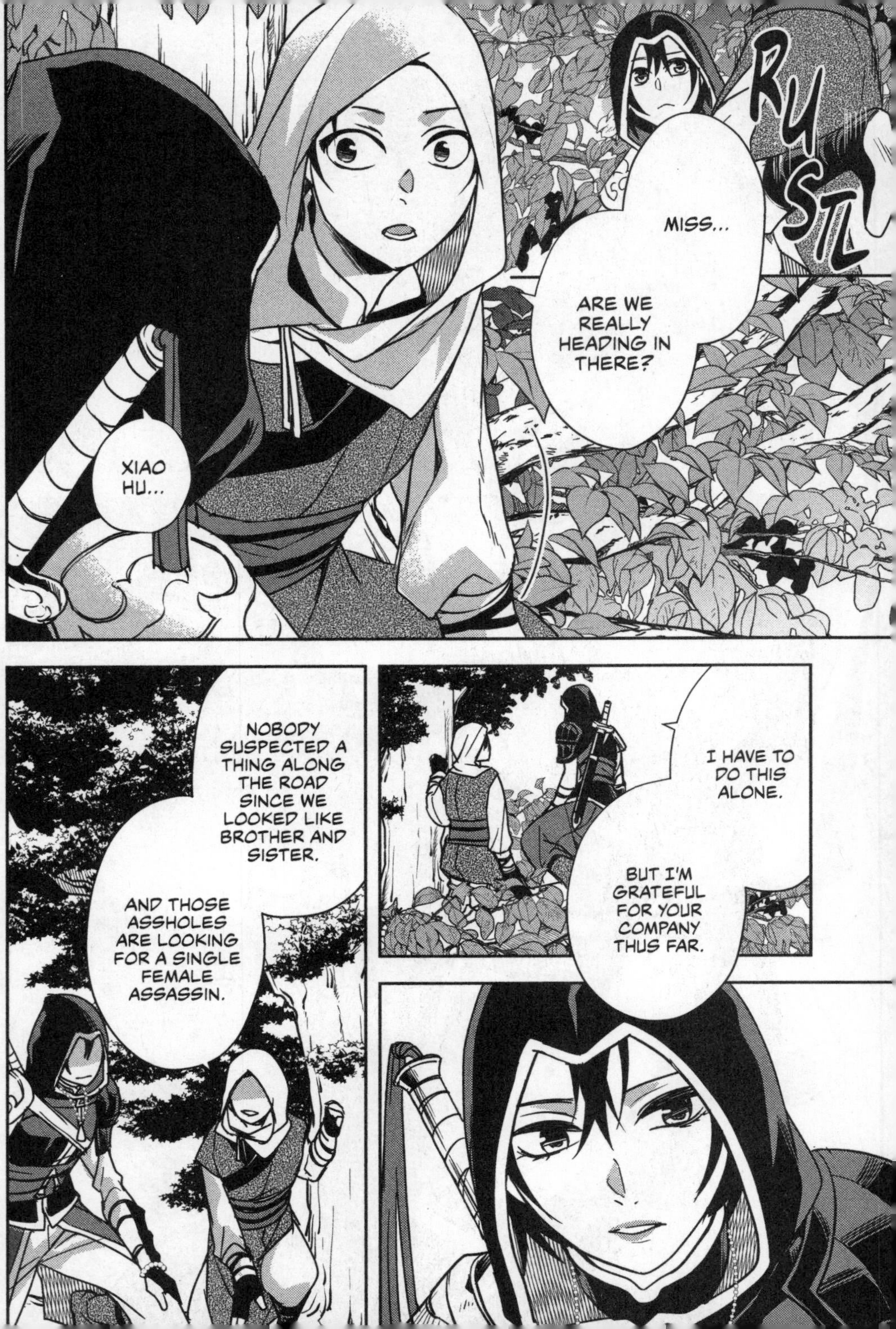
RUSTL
MISS...
ARE WE REALLY HEADING IN THERE?
XIAO HU...
I HAVE TO DO THIS ALONE.
BUT I'M GRATEFUL FOR YOUR COMPANY THUS FAR.
NOBODY SUSPECTED A THING ALONG THE ROAD SINCE WE LOOKED LIKE BROTHER AND SISTER.
AND THOSE ASSHOLES ARE LOOKING FOR A SINGLE FEMALE ASSASSIN.

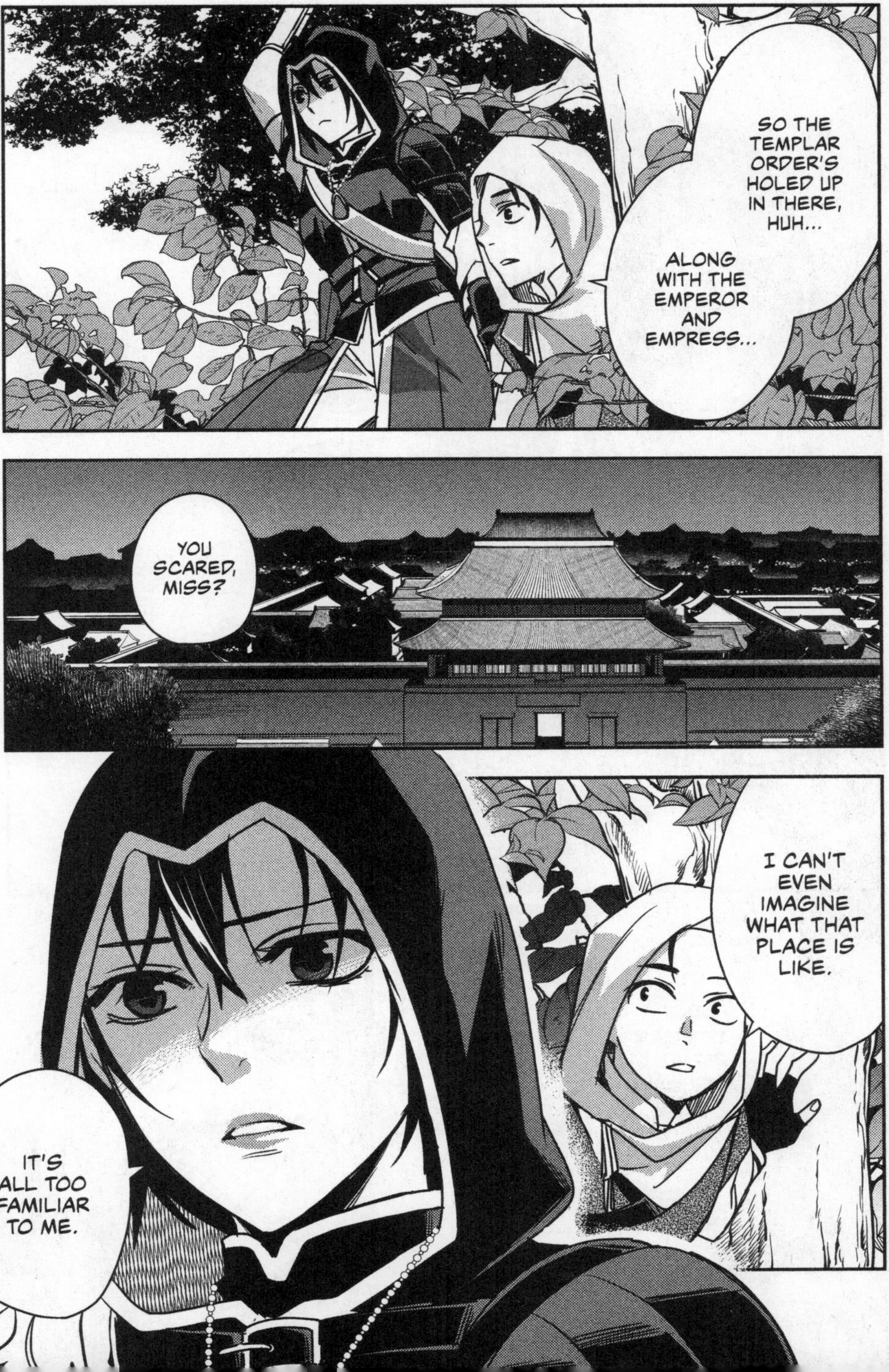
SO THE TEMPLAR ORDER'S HOLED UP IN THERE, HUH...
ALONG WITH THE EMPEROR AND EMPRESS...
YOU SCARED, MISS?
I CAN'T EVEN IMAGINE WHAT THAT PLACE IS LIKE.
IT'S ALL TOO FAMILIAR TO ME.

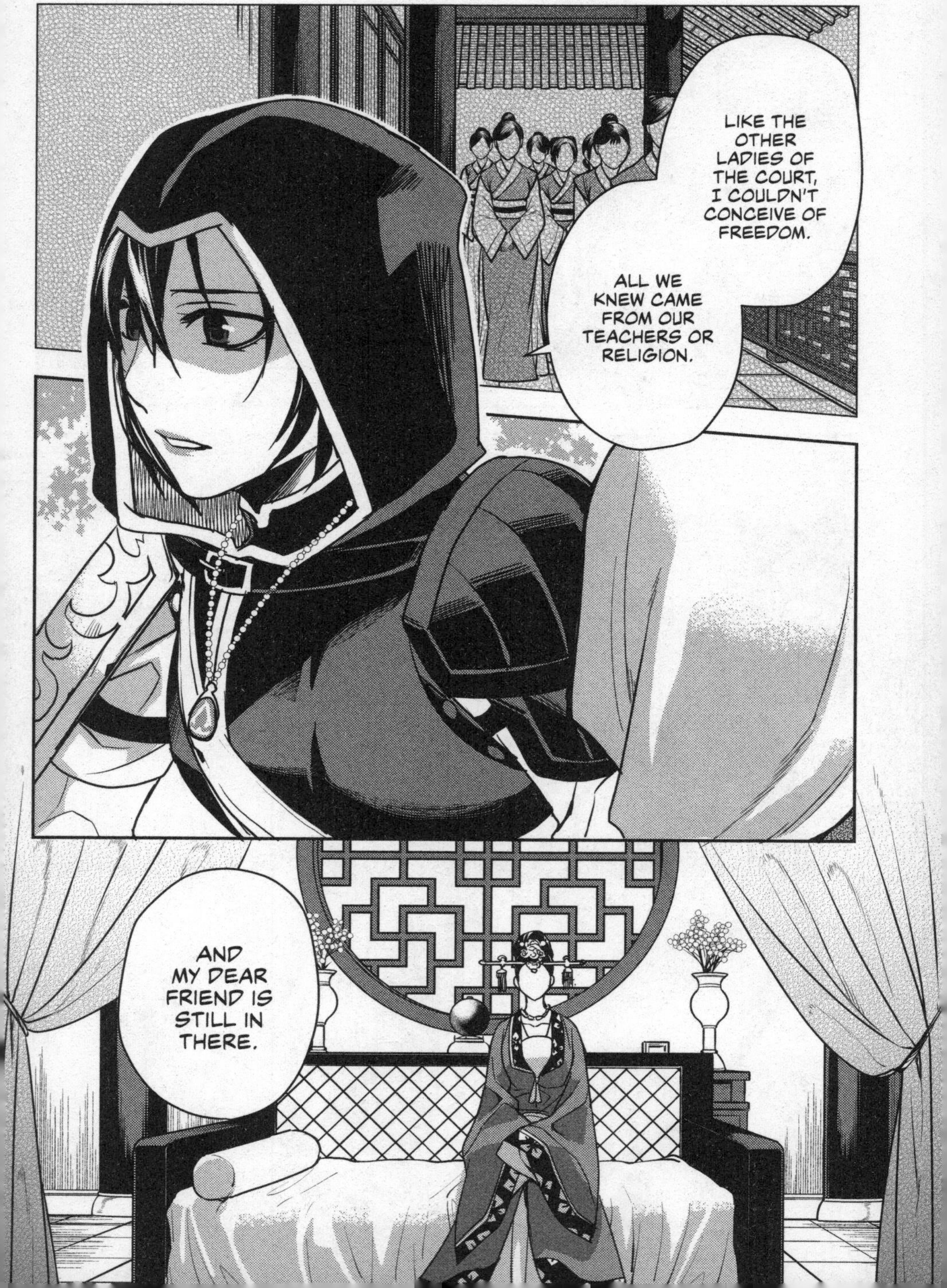
LIKE THE OTHER LADIES OF THE COURT, I COULDN'T CONCEIVE OF FREEDOM.
ALL WE KNEW CAME FROM OUR TEACHERS OR RELIGION.
AND MY DEAR FRIEND IS STILL IN THERE.

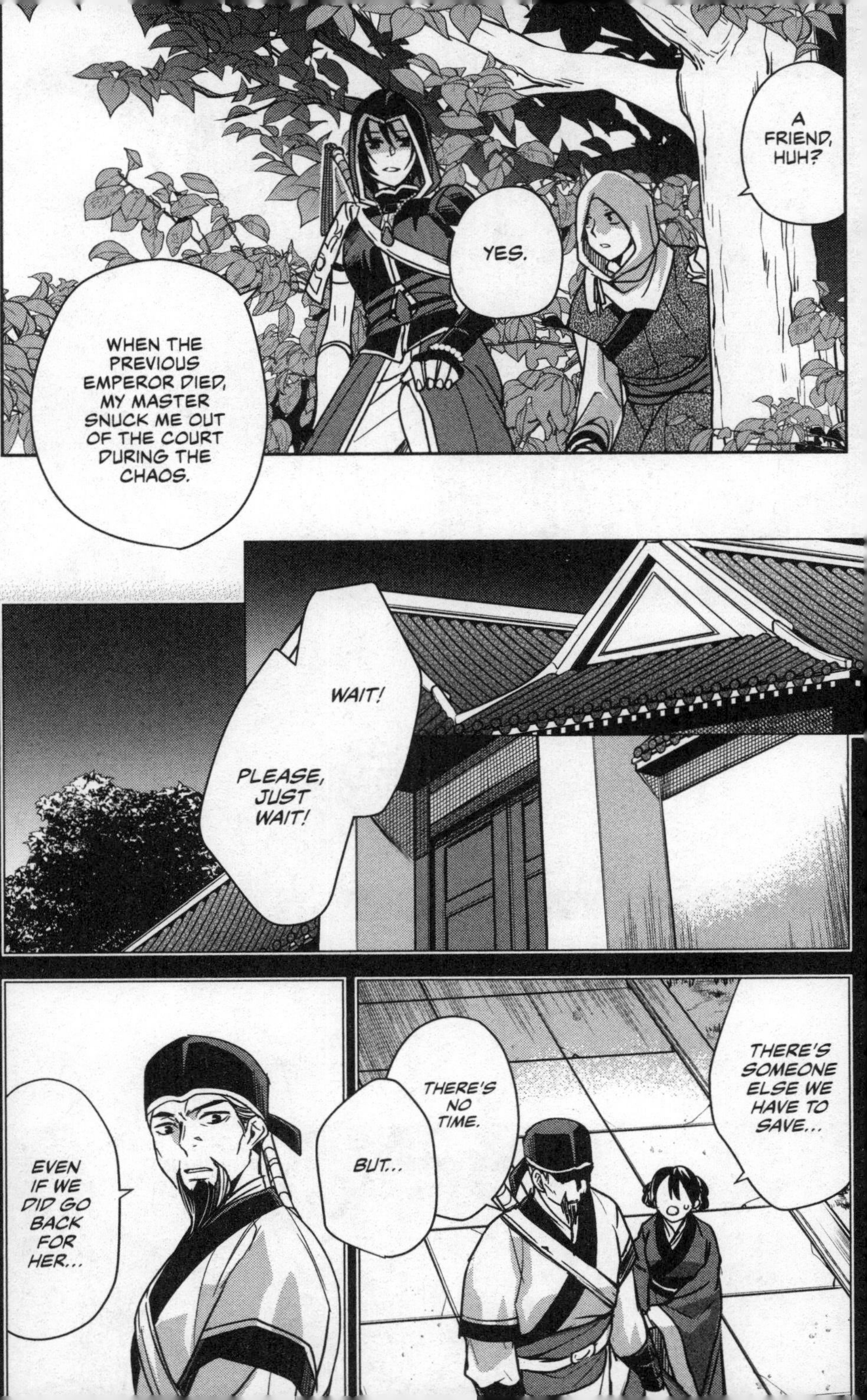
A FRIEND, HUH?
YES.
WHEN THE PREVIOUS EMPEROR DIED, MY MASTER SNUCK ME OUT OF THE COURT DURING THE CHAOS.
WAIT!
PLEASE, JUST WAIT!
THERE'S SOMEONE ELSE WE HAVE TO SAVE...
THERE'S NO TIME.
BUT...
EVEN IF WE DID GO BACK FOR HER...

I CAN'T...

COULD SHE RUN AS WELL AS YOU?

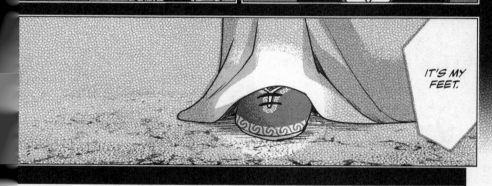

IT'S MY FEET.

ALL THIS TIME, I'VE REGRETTED LEAVING HER BEHIND.

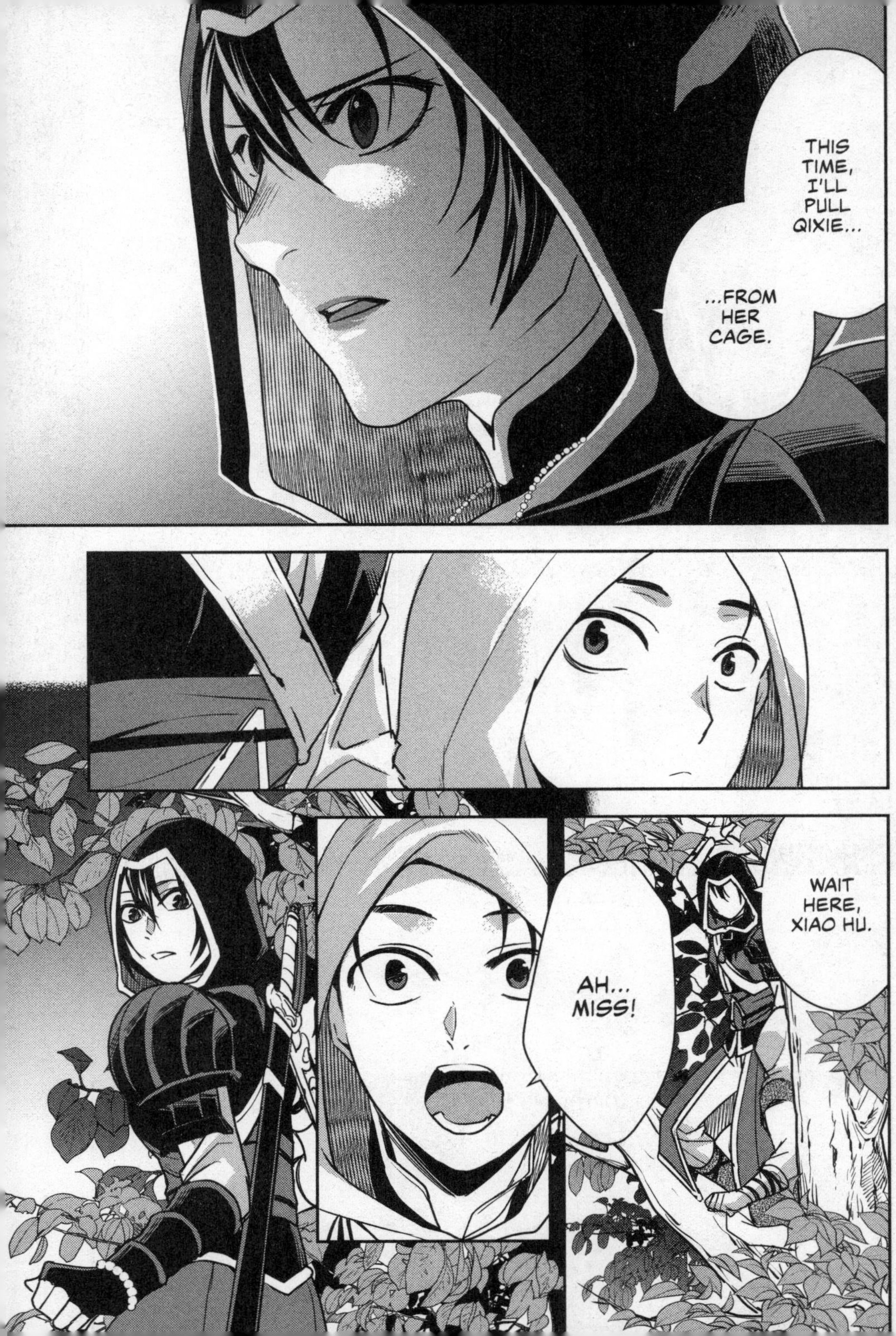
THIS TIME, I'LL PULL QIXIE...
...FROM HER CAGE.
WAIT HERE, XIAO HU.
AH... MISS!

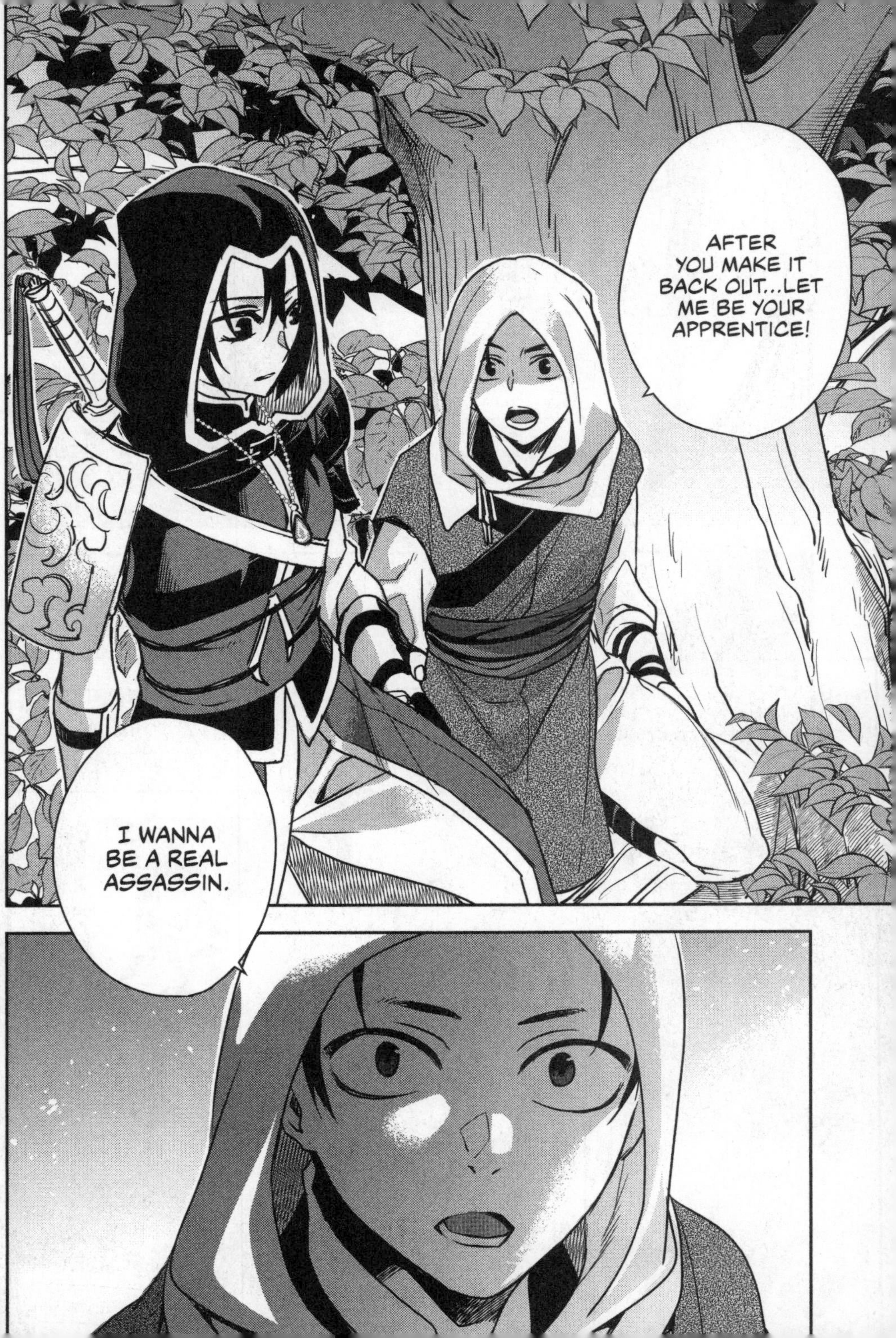
AFTER YOU MAKE IT BACK OUT...LET ME BE YOUR APPRENTICE!
I WANNA BE A REAL ASSASSIN.

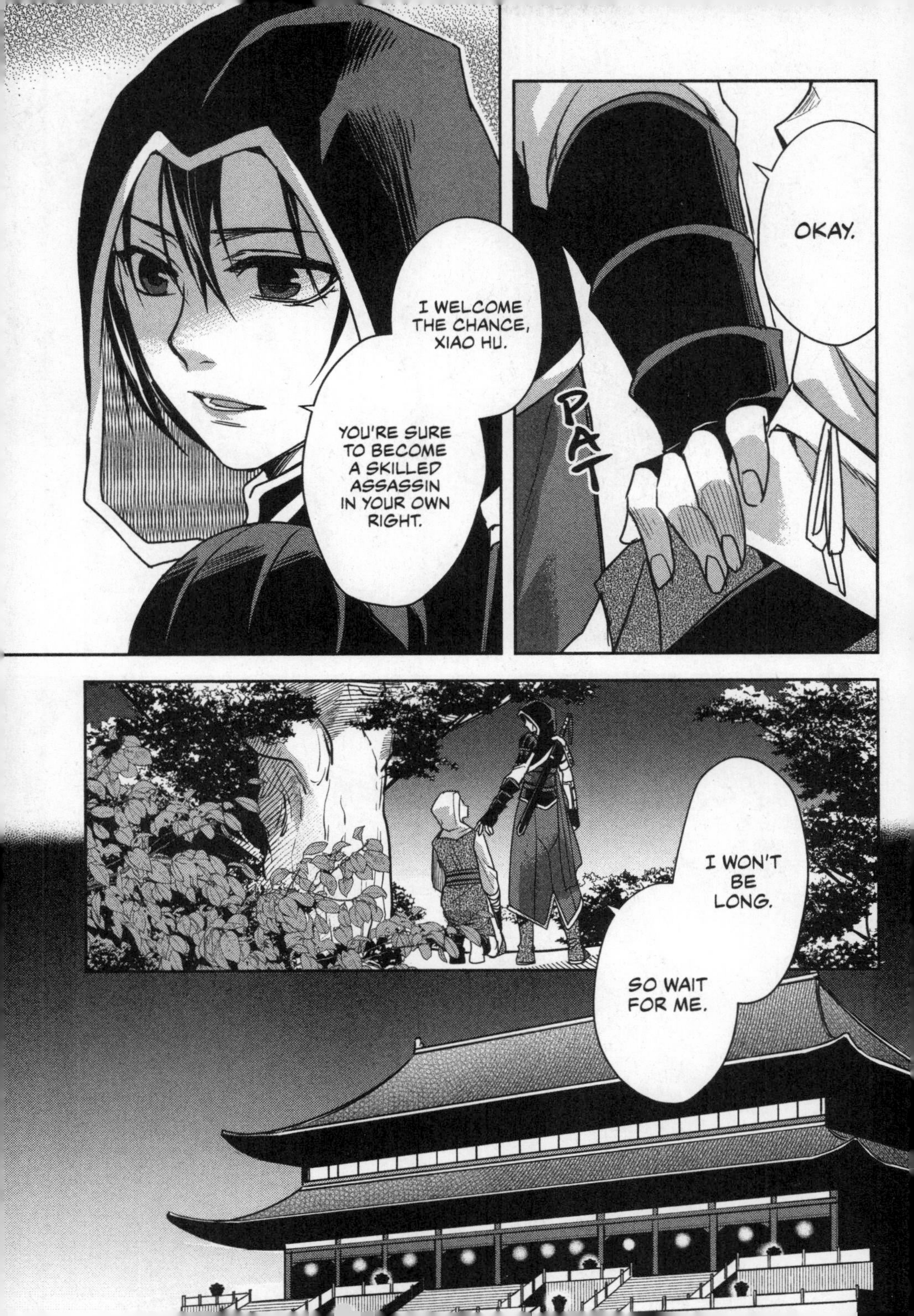
OKAY.
PAT
I WELCOME THE CHANCE, XIAO HU.
YOU'RE SURE TO BECOME A SKILLED ASSASSIN IN YOUR OWN RIGHT.
I WON'T BE LONG.
SO WAIT FOR ME.

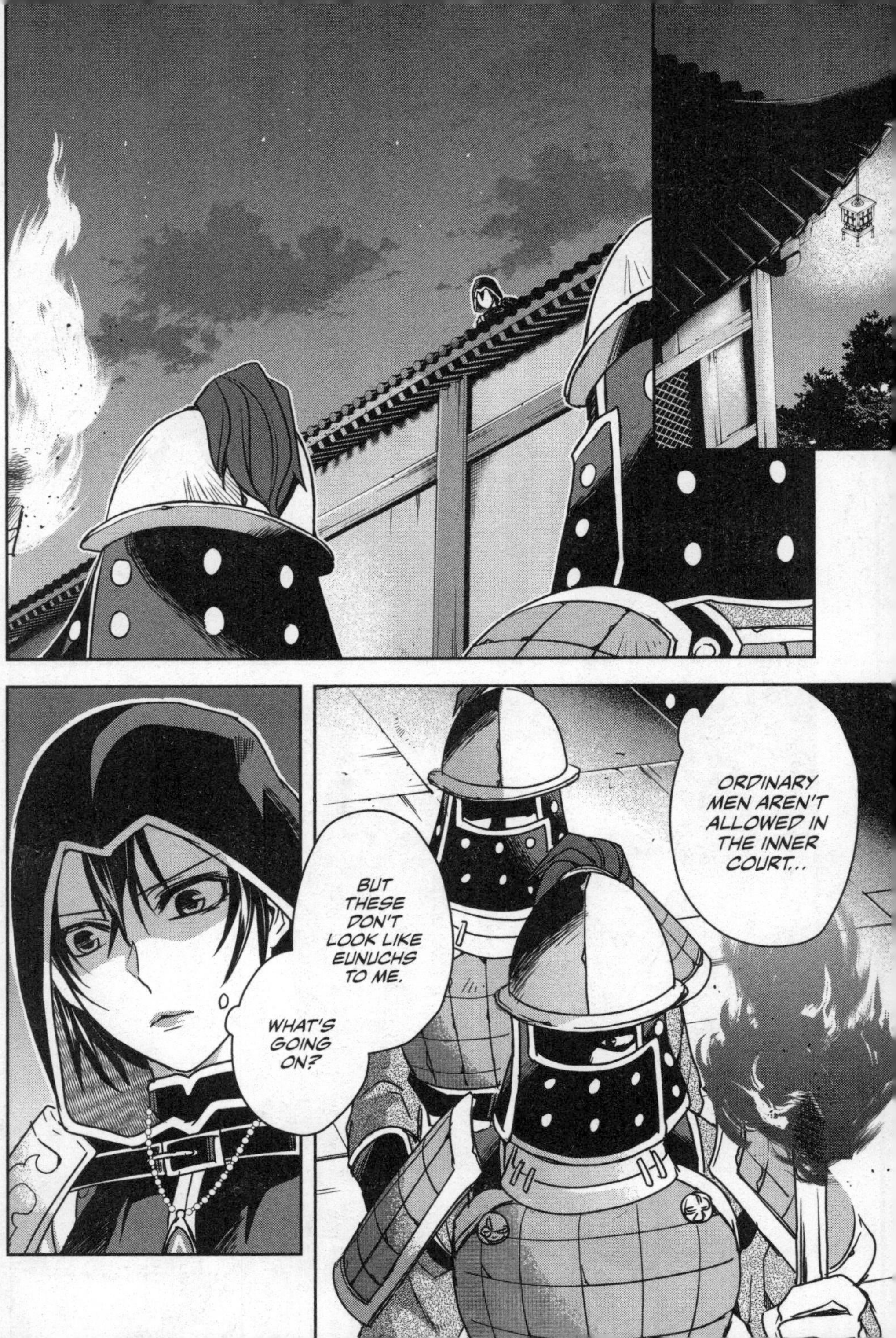
ORDINARY MEN AREN'T ALLOWED IN THE INNER COURT...
BUT THESE DON'T LOOK LIKE EUNUCHS TO ME.
WHAT'S GOING ON?

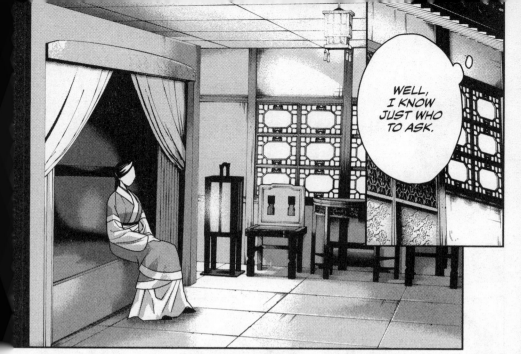

WELL,
I KNOW
JUST WHO
TO ASK.

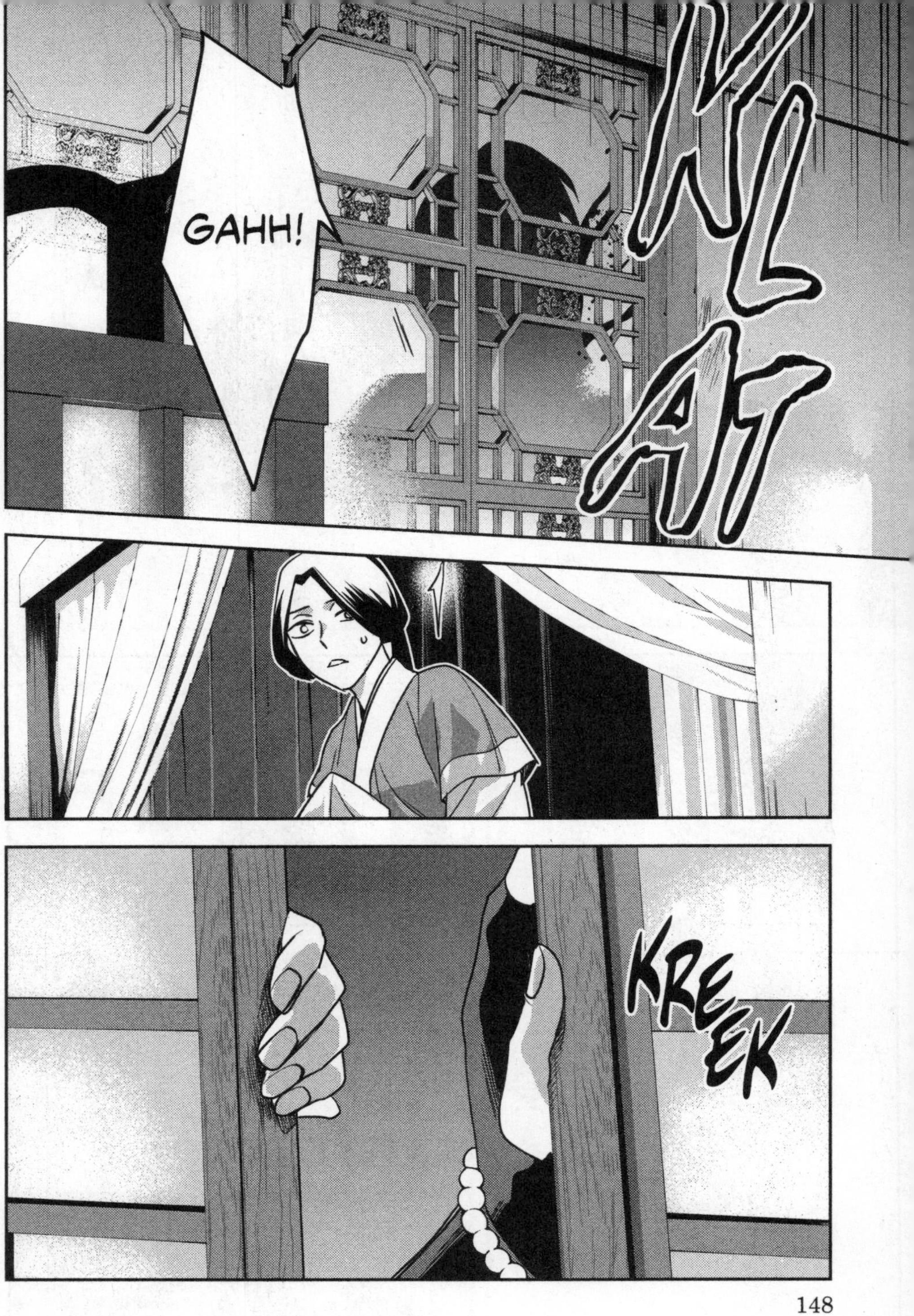
GAHH!
KREEEK

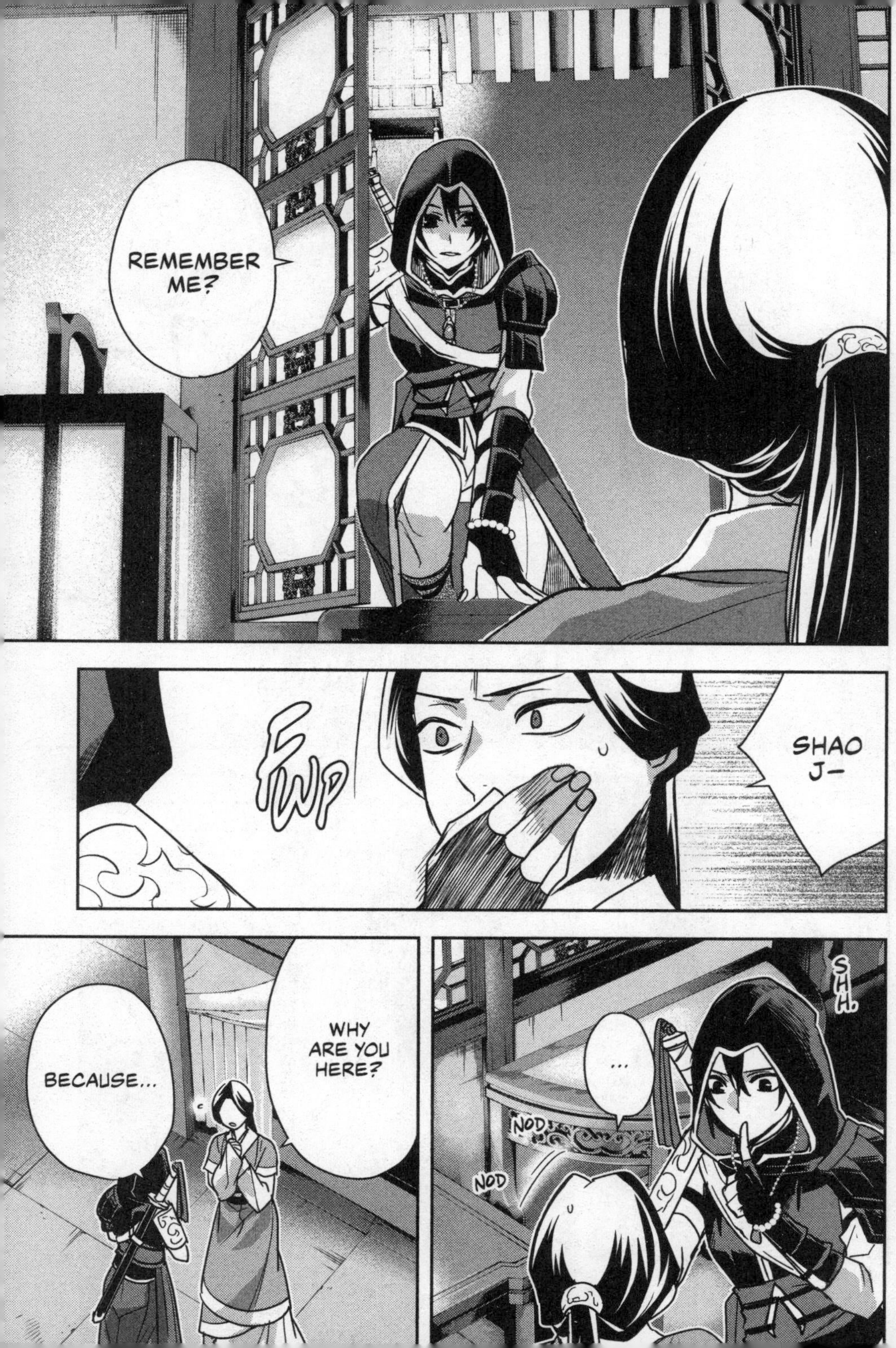
REMEMBER ME?
SHAO J—
FWP
SHH.
...
NOD
NOD
WHY ARE YOU HERE?
BECAUSE...

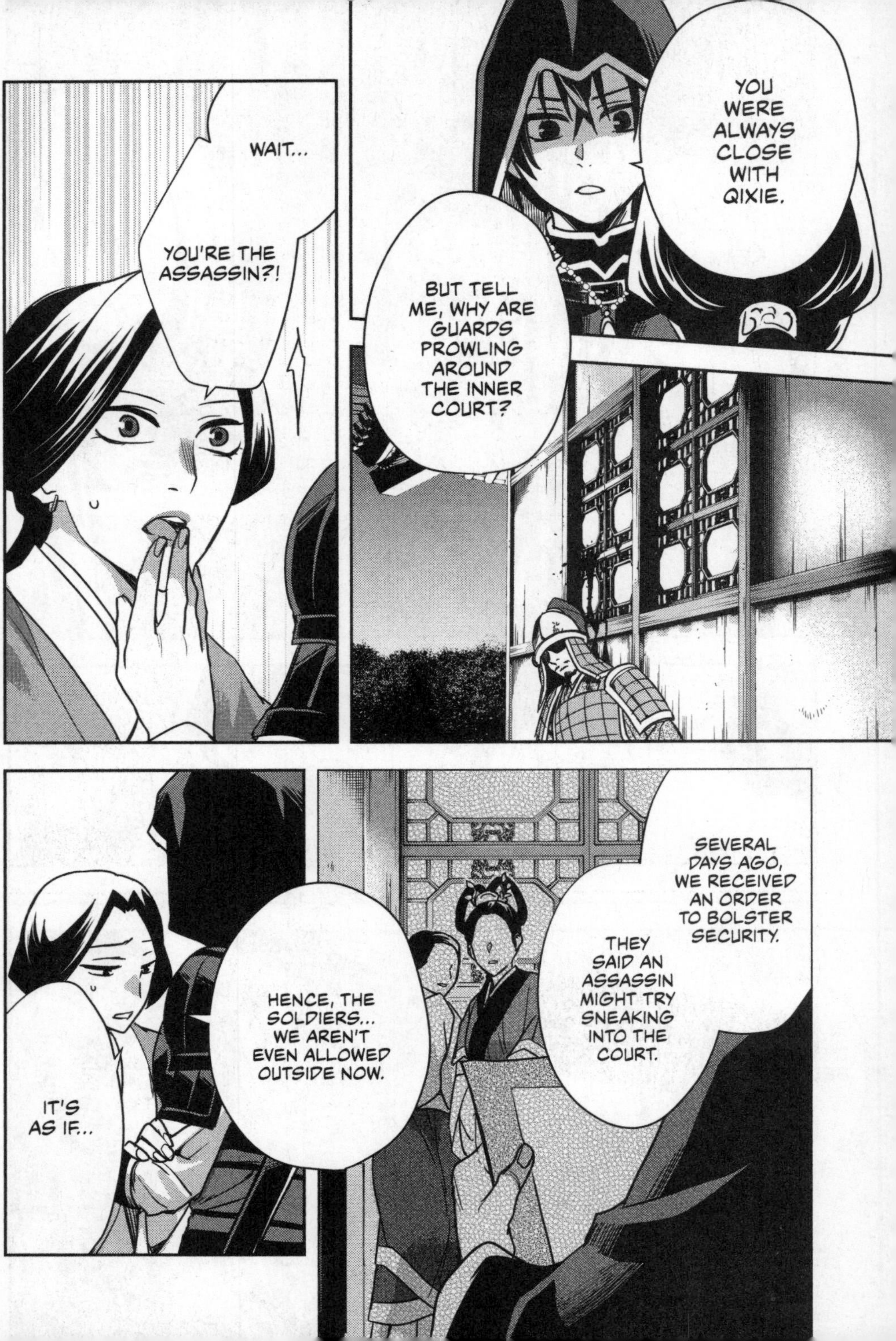
YOU WERE ALWAYS CLOSE WITH QIXIE.
BUT TELL ME, WHY ARE GUARDS PROWLING AROUND THE INNER COURT?
WAIT...
YOU'RE THE ASSASSIN?!
SEVERAL DAYS AGO, WE RECEIVED AN ORDER TO BOLSTER SECURITY.
THEY SAID AN ASSASSIN MIGHT TRY SNEAKING INTO THE COURT.
HENCE, THE SOLDIERS... WE AREN'T EVEN ALLOWED OUTSIDE NOW.
IT'S AS IF...

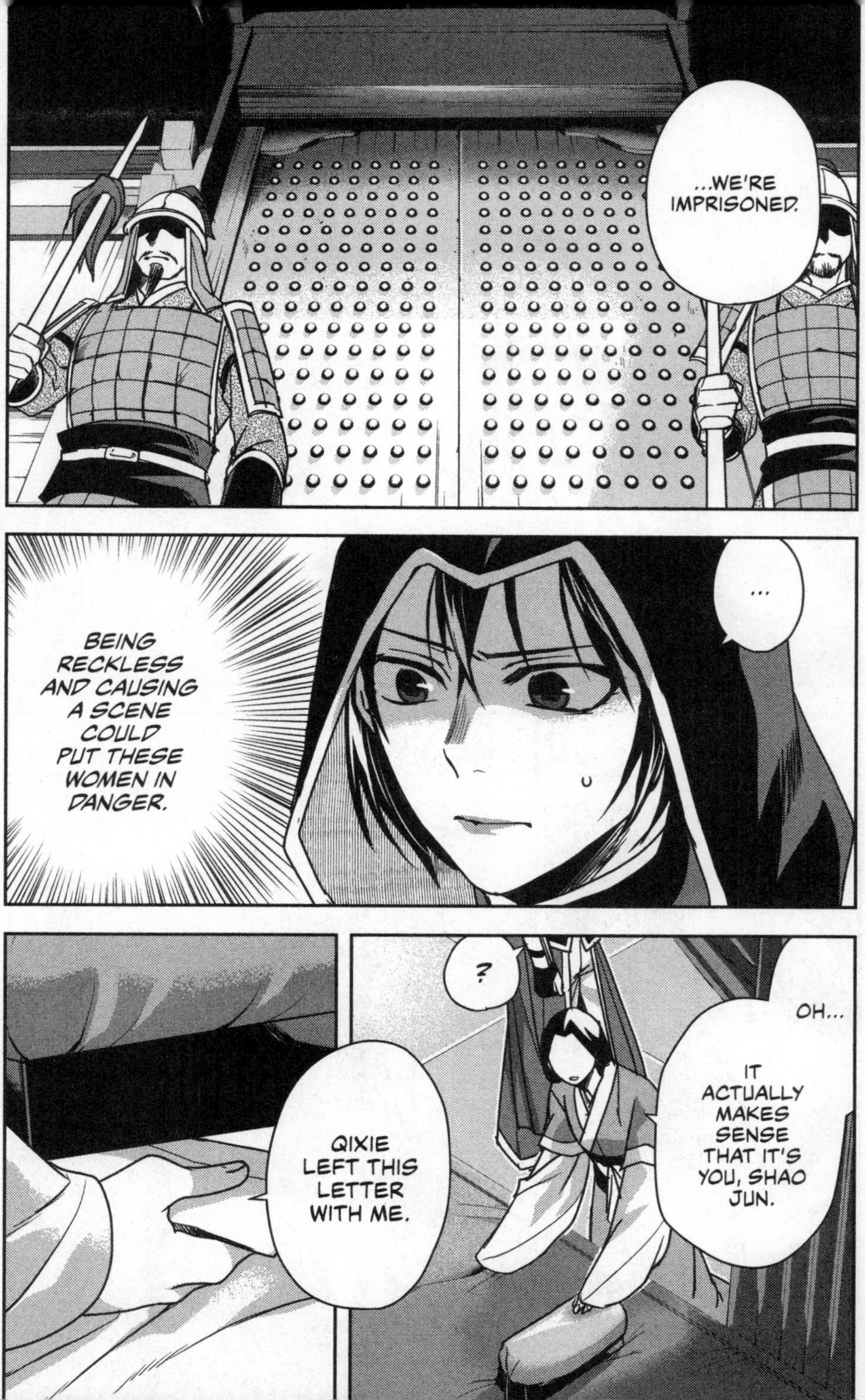
...WE'RE IMPRISONED.
...
BEING RECKLESS AND CAUSING A SCENE COULD PUT THESE WOMEN IN DANGER.
?
OH...
IT ACTUALLY MAKES SENSE THAT IT'S YOU, SHAO JUN.
QIXIE LEFT THIS LETTER WITH ME.

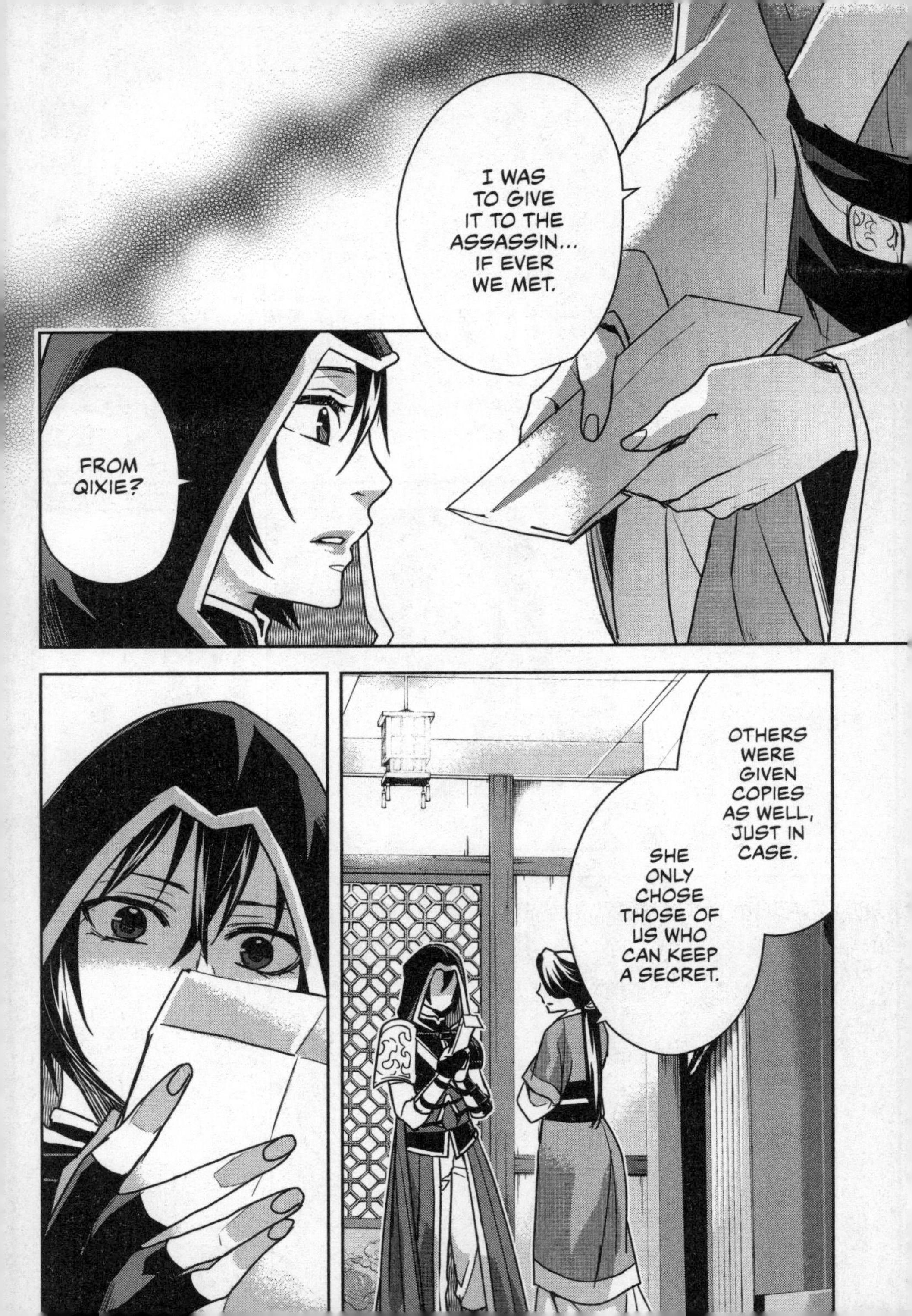
I WAS TO GIVE IT TO THE ASSASSIN... IF EVER WE MET.
FROM QIXIE?
OTHERS WERE GIVEN COPIES AS WELL, JUST IN CASE.
SHE ONLY CHOSE THOSE OF US WHO CAN KEEP A SECRET.

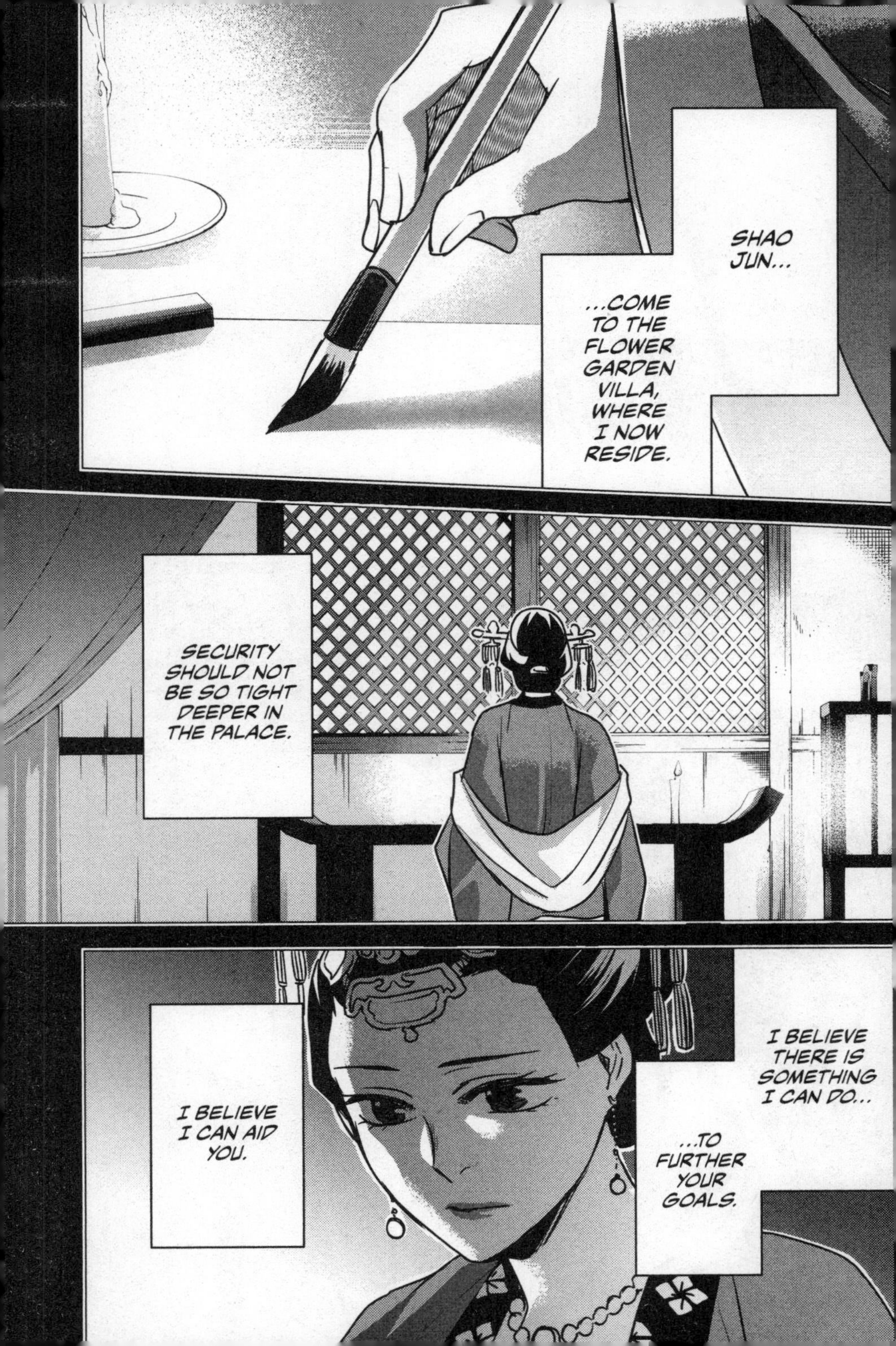
SHAO JUN...
...COME TO THE FLOWER GARDEN VILLA, WHERE I NOW RESIDE.
SECURITY SHOULD NOT BE SO TIGHT DEEPER IN THE PALACE.
I BELIEVE THERE IS SOMETHING I CAN DO...
...TO FURTHER YOUR GOALS.
I BELIEVE I CAN AID YOU.

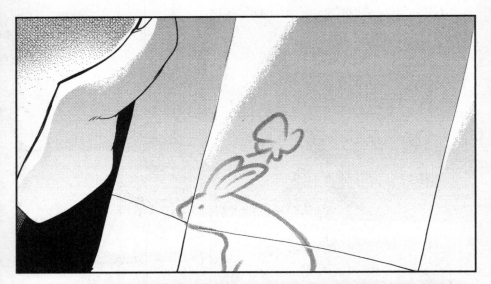

YOU AND I ARE LIKE A RABBIT AND A BUTTERFLY.

QIXIE...

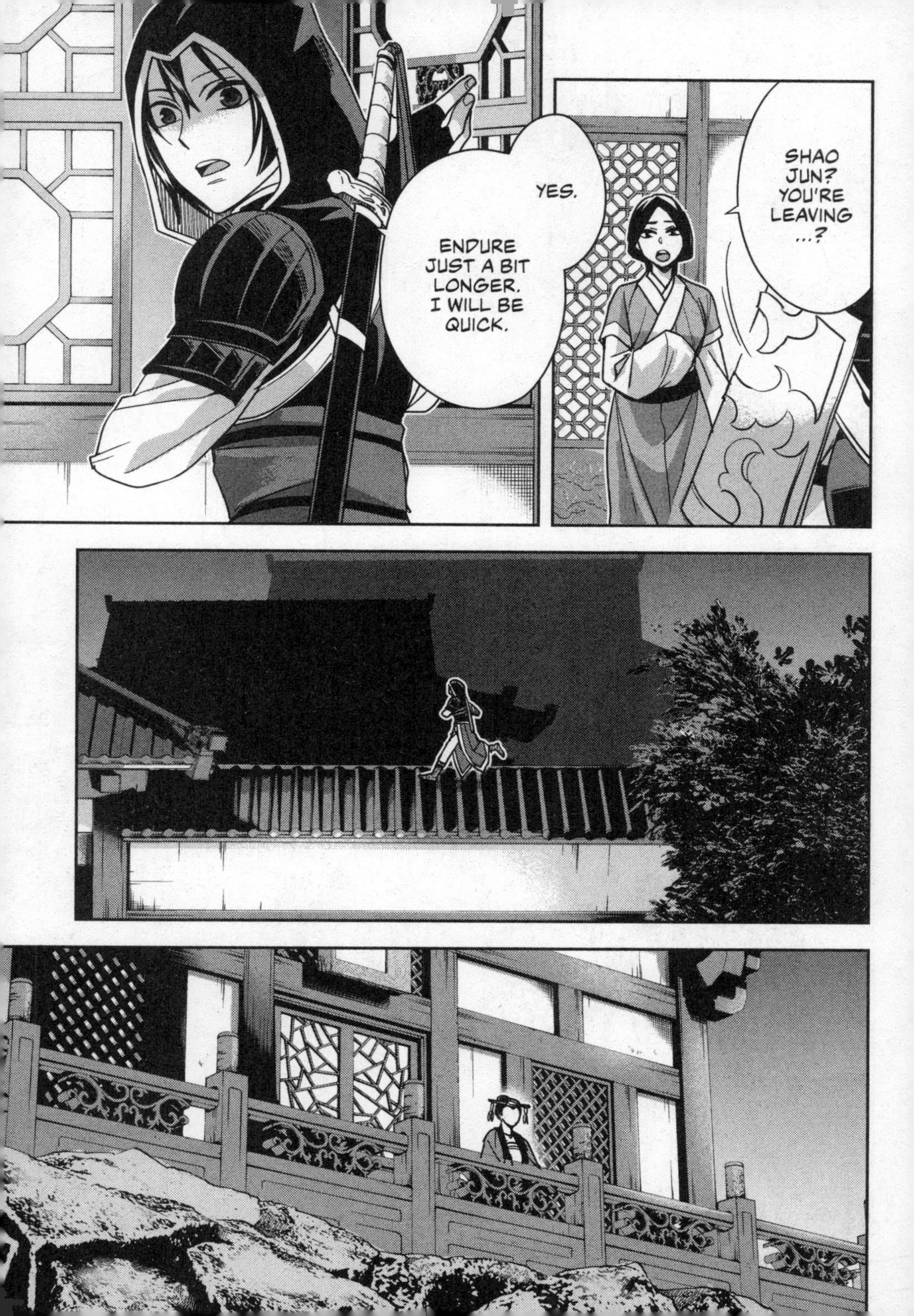
SHAO JUN? YOU'RE LEAVING ...?
YES.
ENDURE JUST A BIT LONGER. I WILL BE QUICK.

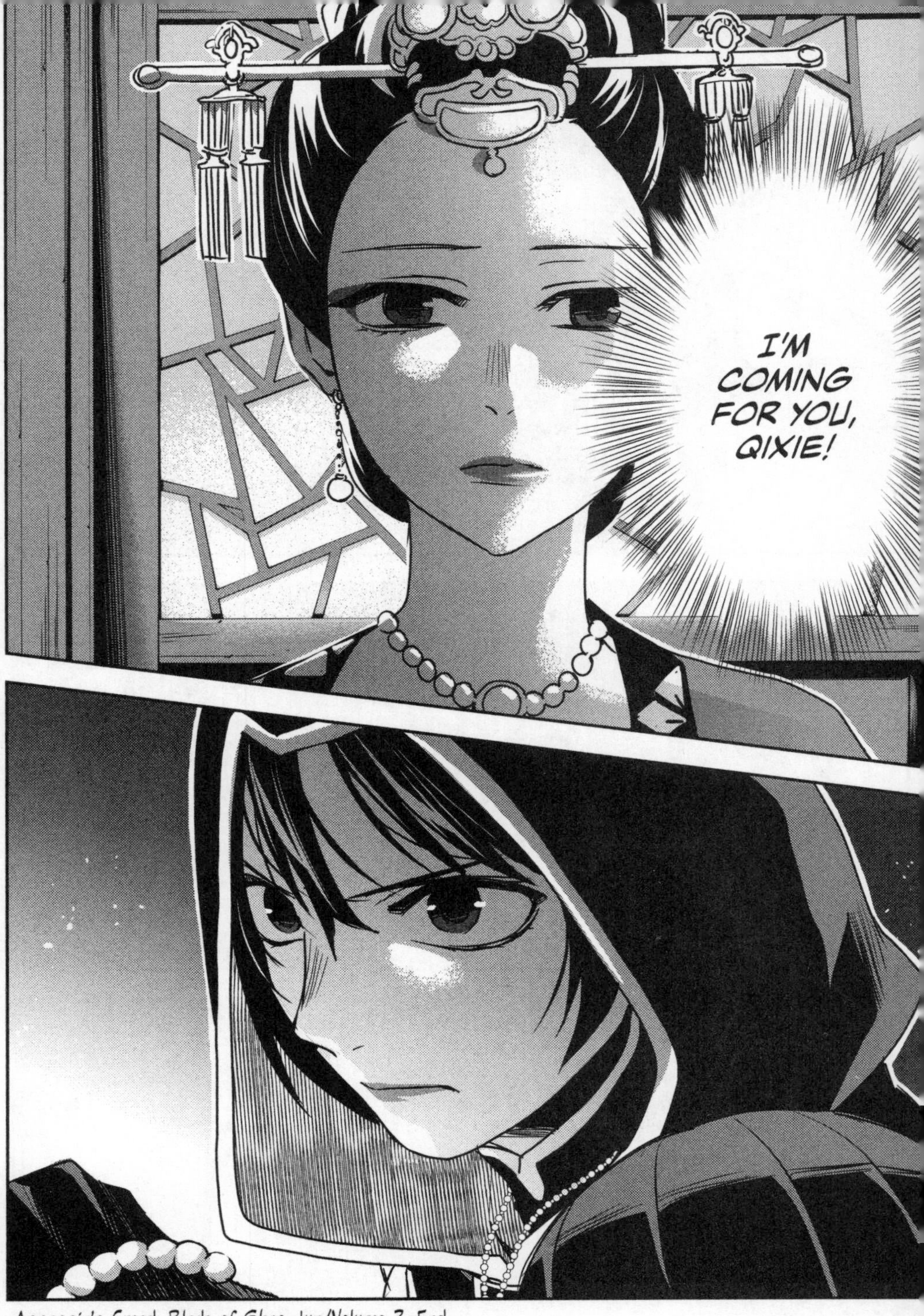
I'M COMING FOR YOU, QIXIE!

Assassin's Creed: Blade of Shao Jun/Volume 3-End

ASSASSIN'S CREED

BLADE OF SHAO JUN

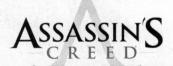

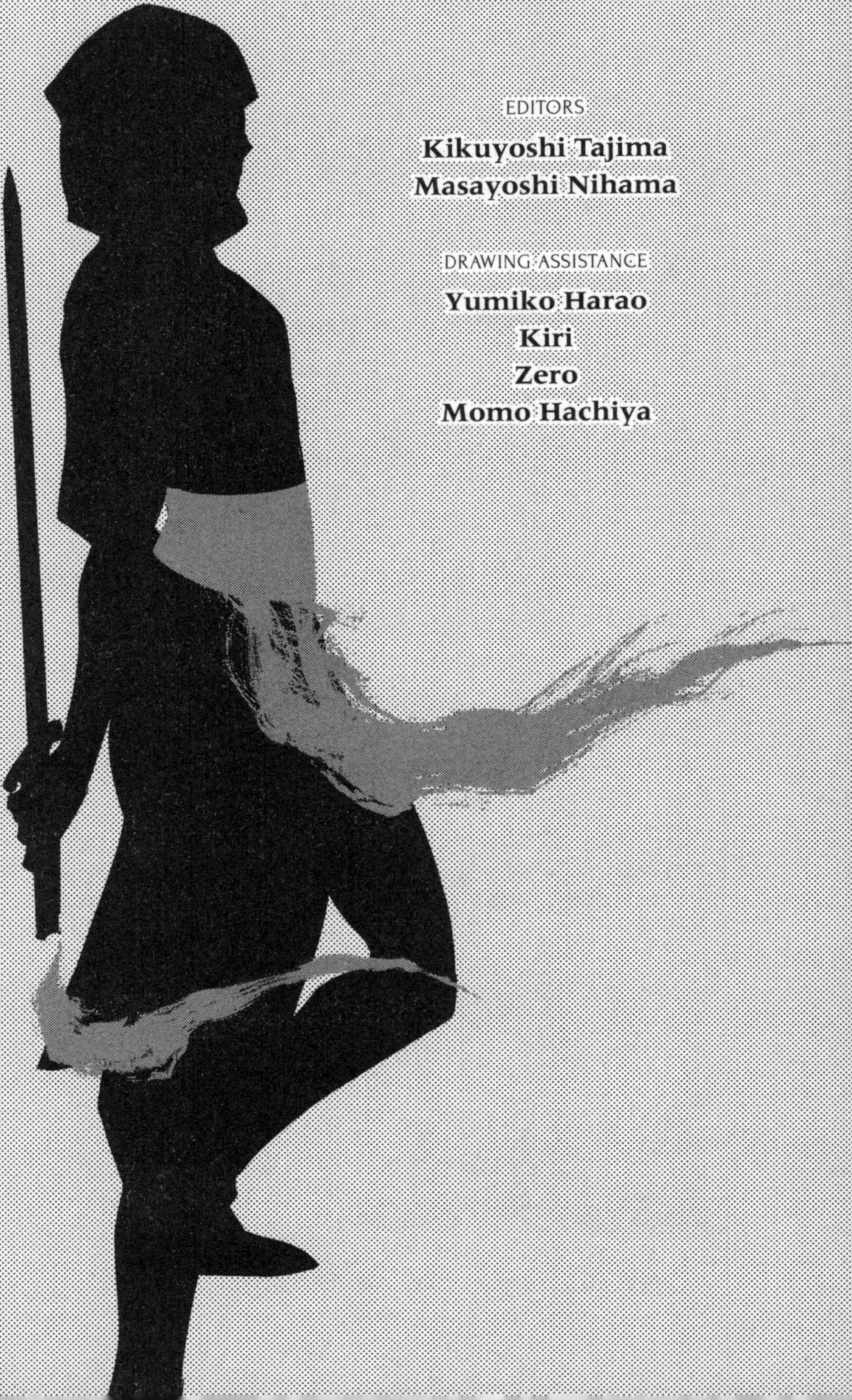

EDITORS

Kikuyoshi Tajima

Masayoshi Nihama

DRAWING ASSISTANCE

Yumiko Harao

Kiri

Zero

Momo Hachiya